THE "I" IN INEZ

INSPIRED BY LOVE . . . THE LONG WAY HOME

TERESA MACALPINE

Teresa MacAlpine

THE "I" IN INEZ

ISBN 978-0-578-28932-8 paperback

Book Design: Clarity Designworks

For "Rosie's" other loves:
Lynda, Dave, Christine, Paul, Emery, Boone
—and yes,
Steve and Randy.

Contents

Family Ancestry

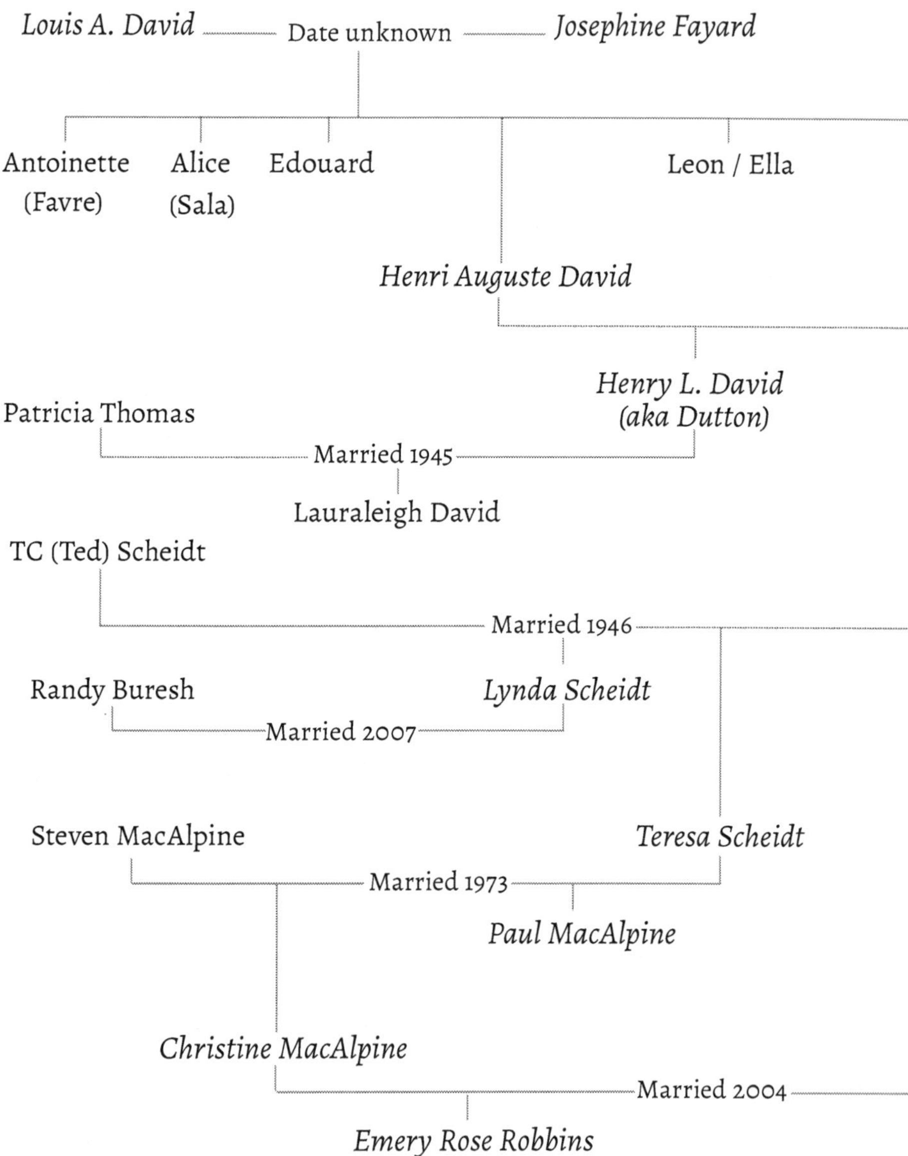

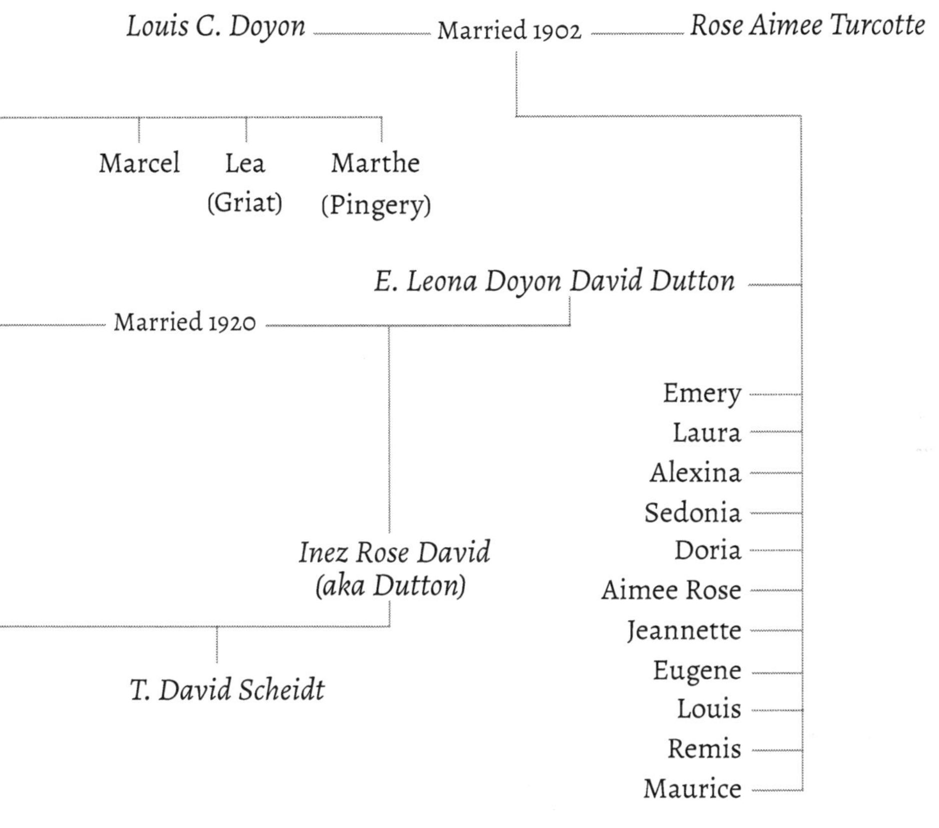

John Robbins

Boone P. Robbins

Names in italics indicate the direct lineage of Inez Rose David

~

The Wedding Celebration

The special date of August 7th, 1920, happened over a century ago as of this writing. It was the wedding of Emelia Leona Doyon to Henri Auguste David, who would become the parents of my mother, Inez. The circumstances of the marriage ignited my desire to tell the family "rememberings." The spirit of their storytelling gave heart and wings to my imagination.

—Teresa Scheidt MacAlpine

Henri David soaked his sore feet in a creek near the Montana-Canada border. Whiffs of oasis greenery held a distinct and pleasant contrast to the dry, seared plains. The soothing hum of water, insects, and birds ministered to his tired body.

New brogue wingtips rested on the bank next to him, a clear reminder that his wedding celebration had already lasted several days. Sharp-looking dress shoes were the man's indulgence, but chronic aching feet proved to be his physical weakness—along with frail, damaged lungs.

He sighed and said to himself, "Such handsome shoes. Too bad I didn't have time to break them in."

Even with attractive shoes, Henri would never win any beauty contest. His complexion was sallow and his ears too big. Narrow, stooped shoulders and wide hips gave his body the shape of a bass fiddle. He chuckled to himself, *Yet, here I am, a sickly old bachelor now married to a girl like Leona.*

Nevertheless, the perfect setting could not stop invading thoughts, darker and more irritating than ill-fitting shoes. Henri frowned. *That two-faced S.O.B. father of Leona's, acting brokenhearted over her marriage.*

Violent behavior and out-of-control temper often defined Leona's father. He mistreated his animals—and then started to punish Leona with a blacksnake whip until she passed out. Rumors whispered her life was in danger if she stayed in that home.

Despite the abuse she'd suffered, Leona sported a fun-loving, strong spirit, a *joie de vivre*. Charmed by her playfulness, Henri liked that they shared a French background. When his family commented on the brutal whippings, he decided to marry Leona—before her father killed her.

Yet, he wrestled with his feelings. *No one should be treated like that. But is this a mistake? Will I stay healthy enough to take care of this girl?*

Henri threw a twig into the water. He contemplated his new wife, twelve years his junior. She was downright thin and scrawny and wore spectacles to correct her nearsightedness. Blessed with thick, wavy, chestnut-colored hair and delicate hands, Leona was confident, energetic, and a quick learner. *She's a spunky little thing. She makes me feel alive. . . . Although, we have our differences.*

Both Leona and Henri's families had immigrated to the Montana drylands to homestead. Leona came as a ten-year-old child from the French-Canadian area of Québec. The oldest in a large family, Leona soon functioned as her father's farmhand. Neighbors worried she was overworked.

Henri left his home at the base of the French Alps as a teenager to journey to America. In truth, he was not a farmer, but a homestead offered him the chance to own land. Farm work was an adjustment for someone like Henri. The dust aggravated his lung condition.

Besides, he hated to get dirty. If he had his druthers, he would dress up daily in a fine three-piece suit with a starched white dress shirt. His outfit would include a snappy, colorful tie and a nice-looking pair of comfortable dress shoes.

A voice behind Henri aroused him from his daydreaming. "So, there you are, my married brother—the knight in shining armor."

"*Moi*? Surely you are mistaken." Henri's eyes danced with laughter at the notion.

Marcel placed his hand on his brother's shoulder and said in a hushed voice, "Henri, you know you saved Leona's life, don't you? . . . No doubt about it. *Tu as sauvé sa vie*."

Henri shrugged. Both brothers stared mute into the rippling creek.

Marcel took a deep breath. "Well, as *Meilleur Homme*—your Best Man, I was sent to look for you. How are your poor feet?"

"*Comme neuf*—As good as new," Henri said with a smile. He pulled out a handkerchief, dried his feet, and put on his socks and shoes. In the background, he could hear fiddles being tuned.

"The dancing and festivities are about to begin again," said Henri. He rose from his perch and slapped his brother on the back. "Let's go find Leona, she promised to save me a piece of that delicious plum pie."

Part One

The Family
1900–1917

The Start of Inez's Journaling

"With my family 'nipping at my heels' and insisting that I put down on paper what they call my 'interesting life,' I find myself settled in my easy chair wondering where to begin. I am not a writer. I don't know how to put a story together. Someday, when someone tries to decipher my writing here, I shudder to think what a hard task they will have to make 'hide or hair' out of this scribbling.

"I guess in all respects, I do have a somewhat strange, yet interesting tale to tell; perhaps one not many can attest to. My parents were foreign born. My own father was from France, my mother from Canada.

"My father, Henri Auguste David was born about 1891 in a village outside the city of Grenoble, France: called Varacieux in the Département De L'Isère République Françoise. He was schooled at the Académie de Grenoble until June 19, 1903, at the age of 12, when he received his Certificat D'Etude Primaires. From all indications, he had no further formal schooling. Although, he could read and write English, as well as French.

" . . . He and my grandparents, Louis and Josephine David (née Fayard) and six of their younger children came to the United States. The oldest daughter, Antoinette, stayed in France. She was married or hoped to be married soon. My Uncle Edouard was the oldest son and from then on, I believe the order went: Alice, my father Henri, Léon, Marcel, Lea and Marthe.

"The family journeyed first to Saskatchewan and then settled in the northern Montana prairie, near the intersecting borders of Saskatchewan, North Dakota and upper Montana. There they farmed mostly dryland wheat, along with other grains."

~

The Arrival

Henri leaned on the rails of the *SS Parisian* as the ship docked at the inland Port of Québec. It was May 11, 1907. Jumbled yells from the dock workers, screeching machinery, and grinding gears confronted him. Rain, a factor in the bon voyage send-off in France, now greeted the steamship in Canada. Henri adjusted his brown tweed newsboy cap and knitted muffler. The weather, wet and unseasonably cool for May, could not dampen his spirits. He smiled. The smell of fish, wet wood, and a salty breeze suggested the aroma of an adventure.

The vastness of the inland harbor gave Henri the impression of still being out on the open seas. The Old Québec City with its fortified perimeter and romantic European-French charm, welcomed him. Off in the distance through the misty rain, he could see the large cantilever Québec Bridge under construction. One end supported a projected arm while the other end spanned the St. Lawrence River. Three months later, the arm would break off, triggering the world's worst bridge construction disaster.

To receive steerage passage from Europe to Canada, Henri, his mother and younger brother declared themselves as farmers and his sister, a domestic. The other three siblings, ages nine, seven, and four, did not declare occupations. The father and older brother were elsewhere.

Tall and thin with an observant, caring demeanor, Henri appeared older than his sixteen years. During the transatlantic trip, he was given the task of guiding and protecting his mother and siblings. Though he was a middle child with untested leadership abilities, his family depended on him.

As the ship neared its destination, Henri took advantage of his brief time alone on deck. He reflected, *Do I have what I need for the family to clear the Canadian customs? Mon Dieu! I hope I am up to the task. Thankfully, Uncle Regis is here to help.*

~

The David Family Genealogy Search

"Mom, I want you to see this." With care I placed the red-covered 1986 edition of the World Book Encyclopedia on my mother Inez's twig of a lap. She sat in the corner of her favorite room in the green tweed power-lift recliner, with her feet up. When Mom purchased this home fifteen years earlier she had claimed the space as her office/den instead of keeping it a front bedroom, as intended. The room's large window let in the afternoon sunshine as the panoramic view opened to the comings and goings of the gated Stonebridge community in Fresno, California.

Despite the day's brightness, she glanced toward the brass floor lamp beside us. "Why don't you turn on that lamp?" I leaned over and switched on the light.

Inez reached out for what I held in my hand, a large round magnifying glass fit for Sherlock Holmes, retrieved from the side cabinet. She said, "Now what am I looking at?"

With the encyclopedia opened to a map, I secured the pages and pointed to the small letters that formed the name *Forget.* Inez turned, and readjusted her glasses as she looked through the magnifying glass positioned over the Canadian province of Saskatchewan.

"See, go up from the North Dakota border, about three-fourths of an inch. You are looking for the village of Forget. It's spelled F-o-r-g-e-t, but I think it is pronounced *For-sjay* in French. Do you see it?" Inez craned her neck once again, not yet finding the name.

"If you go straight up from North Portal on the Dakota line . . ." I placed my index finger beneath the spot I wanted Mom to see. "Your father and his family entered the States using this border crossing. North Portal, Saskatchewan and Portal, North Dakota are two aligned cities on either side of the US–Canadian border. Forget is just about 70 miles north of the border."

Mom smiled. "Now I see it. Forget is just south of Highway 13. Looks like there's a lot of small villages around it."

"Yes, there are more than two hundred and fifty small villages in Saskatchewan. The last census listed Forget with only forty-five people. But for some reason it served as a rally point for the David family as they transitioned from France to Canada, then to the U.S."

"Oh really? I never heard of the place," said Mom.

"I first noticed 'Forget,' documented in November of 1908, as the place the older David siblings—Alice, Edouard, Henri, and Leon—resided before crossing into the United States. They listed their Uncle Regis Barthelon as a contact person in Forget, Saskatchewan. Bainville, Montana was their stated destination."

Inez repositioned herself in her chair, "I can't imagine how you found all these facts."

I had to agree with my mother. In little more than a month, I had discovered David family information while using online genealogy sites available through the Fresno County library system. I approached each bit of genealogical data as an archeologist, brushing away bits of debris until the desired treasure was exposed. Much of the David story was found to be true, although my research indicated that their American trek started earlier than we had previously thought.

The phone rang. Inez scowled, "Let the answering machine get it. . . . I'm receiving so many telemarketer calls these days."

Nodding, I retrieved the encyclopedia from Mom's lap. I took the magnifying glass from her hand and said, "Edouard, the oldest brother and apparent farmer of the family, arrived in April 1906. He traveled with a group of French farm laborers bound for Canada. Because of their contract, they came through New York Harbor rather than stopping at Ellis Island. The men continued overland to Winnipeg and on to Forget.

"In May of the next year," I scanned my notes, "that would be 1907, your father—Henri—his mother Josephine David, and five of his siblings arrived in Québec via the *SS Parisian*. I'm not sure how Uncle Regis Barthelon was related to them, but I discovered his name, as well as the names of his wife and son, on the same ship manifest."

Sitting back in the burgundy leather chair, I paused, then said, "It appeared the family played a game of tag as they alternated their travel from France, to Forget, and then on to Montana."

Mom looked over at me. "So, the David family didn't arrive in Canada together?"

"That's right. At some point, Josephine and the three younger children returned to France only to travel back to Canada with their father, Louis, as passengers on the *SS Corinthian*. They arrived at the Port of Montréal on November 1, 1909. Instead of going to their stated destination of Forget, they continued to the US border crossing at Portal, North Dakota, then on to Bainville, Montana."

A white, box-shaped mail truck trimmed with red and blue passed in front of the window. I continued, "No doubt, they became aware of the intense advertising that targeted European immigrants for free fertile farmland in the eastern Montana high plains. Also, the permissible homestead acreage doubled from the previous 160-acre limit to 320-acres."

Inez nodded, "I believe I've heard of that. Some sort of Homestead Act, wasn't it?"

"Yes, the United States Enlarged Homestead Act of 1909. The homestead boom spread across the West, but more people claimed land in Montana than anywhere else."

Inez's eyebrows knitted together in thought, "Gosh, I guess I had it all wrong. I believed they settled in Scobey, but it sounds like everyone went to Bainville."

I smiled at my mother, "I suppose the parents and the younger children met the four older siblings in Bainville. About the same time, Uncle Regis Barthelon and his family passed through the border crossing of Portal, North Dakota. They also settled in Bainville, Montana—just like the Davids.

"But not all the family stayed in Bainville. The 1910 US Census showed the two brothers, Ed and Henri, working in Dawson County, Montana, some 105 miles southeast of Bainville and just west of the North Dakota state line."

I picked up and fingered my research cards. "You know besides Ed and Henri, I couldn't find census listings for your grandmother, aunts, or other uncles in either Montana or North Dakota. I even checked the equivalent 1911 Canadian census. No luck.

"However, I believe I found your grandfather in the 1910 census of Warm Springs. It's one of the townships in southwestern Montana, part of Deer Lodge County. A fifty-year-old Louis David is recorded there. The name, age, and French nationality matched your grandfather. A list of inmates . . ."

"Inmates?" Mom sat forward. "What does that mean?"

I chuckled, "At first I feared it meant he was a criminal, or perhaps mentally ill when I noticed the institution listed as The Montana State Insane Asylum. I considered ignoring the entry and not claim him as a relative. But after further research, I believe he was in treatment for tuberculosis. The Montana State Hospital also served as the tuberculosis sanitarium."

"Teresa, I'm just thrilled with all this information you have found." Mom sat back in her recliner; her smile beamed brighter than the sun's rays streaming into the room.

~

Train Ride from the Snake Pit

Entering the train, Henri nodded his head in approval at finding a vacant seat. *Yes, that should give my long legs enough room to stretch out.* With a weary sigh, he tossed his pack onto the empty, worn leather seat and lowered himself into the aisle space. The attempted visit with his father at the sanitarium had left him spent and tired. *Maybe now I can get some needed rest.*

"Tickets, please." The conductor came out of nowhere. He punched Henri's voucher and said as he handed it back, "Going to Dawson County, huh? You'll be with us most of the day. I've got a cousin just setting up a homestead in Dawson. He says the area is known for its dryland grain and splendid hoof stock. You a homesteader?"

Henri smiled. "I'm one of six farm hands working at the John Simpson Ranch, but I hope to have my own homestead someday soon."

As the conductor faded into the next car, so did Henri's cheerful mask. *Someday soon? Not likely. Not with Papa's illness.*

The train ride offered rest and time of reflection for Henri. It had been less than five months since his parents and younger siblings emigrated from France to America. Soon, Papa had night sweats, weight loss, and fatigue. Shock came when his coughs produced mouthfuls of blood. The government authorities were quick to pound on the door and pressure Papa into entering treatment at a tuberculosis sanitarium.

While visiting his father at the hospital, Henri had first mistakenly entered the Montana State Insane Asylum. He could not forget what he had seen and heard. Whether feeble-minded or insane, all the patients wore tormented stares. The assembly—lacking peace or quiet—was in constant movement, like a snake pit. When an attendant discovered Henri, he was directed to the chief medical officer's office.

"Mr. David, please sit down," said the sanitarium doctor. He pointed Henri to a scarred wooden chair. "Tell me what you know about your father's illness."

Henri said, "We call it consumption. After all, it seems to be consuming and wasting away Papa's body. No?"

"Yes, you are right," answered the doctor. "It is called tuberculosis and frequently nicknamed TB for *tubercle bacillus.* Other people may call it Koch disease, Wasting Disease, or the White Plague. Whatever the name, TB is a world-class killer. Do you know this disease claims a quarter of European adults and is the leading cause of death in the United States?"

Henri shook his head. The doctor continued, "It is caused by a germ—called a '*bacillus*'—too small to be seen. This sickness floats on air when a person, like your father, coughs, sneezes, or talks. Even though tuberculosis is contagious, it's not easy to catch from a stranger. A person is much more likely to get tuberculosis from someone they live or work with in close contact, in a setting without fresh, circulating air."

Leaning forward in his chair, Henri's face and body tensed with the strain of concentration.

The doctor pointed to his own chest as he explained to Henri, "When the bacilli germs enter the body, they set up in the moist lining of the upper part of the lungs. They form a ball around themselves. This ball is called a '*tubercle.*' Most people exposed to TB never develop symptoms because the bacteria cannot live in an inactive form in the body. However, TB bacteria becomes active if the body's immune defenses weaken."

Henri found his voice to ask, "What does that mean?"

"Immune defenses weaken when a person is physically run down, malnourished, or elderly, or has contracted a serious illness such as cancer. This can mean the start of tuberculosis. The tubercles break open and the bacilli invade lung tissue as infection spreads through the lymph nodes into the bloodstream, and to any organ in the body. In their active state, TB bacteria kill the tissue of organs they infect and prove fatal if left untreated."

The doctor leaned against the edge of the desk and continued, "The treatment we employ here at the Deer Lodge County sanitarium includes bed rest, a strict, nutritious diet and clean air. But we continue to do research. In fact, I'd like you to take part in a new study we just started doing. It is called the Mantoux skin test."

"Okay . . . but when can I see my father?"

"Oh, I am sorry, Mr. David. Tuberculosis patients are not allowed visitors. It is against our hospital policy."

The train bumped along the tracks, jostling Henri's thoughts. Overwhelming helplessness and guilt caused his present fatigue. It could make a grown man cry, especially if the man was the patient's son. Parallels between the asylum and the TB sanitarium continued to plague him. His father's medical refuge resembled a prison. *Papa isn't an animal to be caged and kept from his family.*

He could only pray Papa's time in that pit would be short. Henri absentmindedly brushed his inner left arm, the site of his skin test. A large, reddened lump formed where the nurse had injected a small bubble of tuberculin protein.

The gentle rocking of the train lulled Henri to drowsiness. He cocked his Panama hat over his eyes and extended his legs as far as possible. Before dropping off to sleep he thought to himself *I'd never let them lock me up in a place like that. . . .*

Dryland Farming

The "free" deal offered in the 1909 Enlarged Homestead Act had a catch. The prairie lands, once thought useful only for grazing, had proven valuable for agriculture, but lacked water access and presented irrigation challenges. Much of the area, a semiarid environment, received less than twelve inches of moisture per year. Settlers from previous Homestead Acts had already claimed the best parcels along rivers, streams, and other waterways.

An unusually wet cycle lasted from 1909 to 1916, just long enough to lure thousands of homesteaders, like Inez's relatives, to the Montana Plains. Grain crops grew beyond expectations in this unusually wet weather. Initial planting yielded bumper crops, but with each year the outcome became more of a gamble, due to the minimal amount of rainfall. Dry-farming or "dryland farming" conserved the limited moisture by adopting techniques of deep plowing. However, this practice displaced the virgin topsoil of indigenous, deep-rooted grasses that naturally helped trap moisture and soil. Thus, dirt and crops were vulnerable to high winds and drought.

Henri, Inez's father, was not passionate about farming. Nevertheless, he toiled for years at dryland farming whether as a farm laborer, a ranch hand, or a homesteader. He migrated first to Saskatchewan and then to the Montana areas of Bainville, Dawson, Scobey, Four Buttes, and Wolf Point. The American dream touted ownership of land whether one had a farmer's heart—or not.

~

The Maternal Side of Inez's Family

While research into David genealogy helped put order to our family story, much remains veiled. The accounts of Louis and Josephine David, Inez's paternal grandparents, still escape us today. Other David relatives were woven in and out, throughout the tapestry of Inez's lifetime. However, these were mere threads when compared to the solid strands of steel that made up her maternal relationships.

Inez's mother, like her mother before her, shared the Doyon and Turcotte family history by telling stories of relatives' personalities and circumstances. Where the David family members were latecomers to North America, the other side of her family helped build Québec settlements and establish local Catholic dioceses.

Family nuns and priests recorded Doyon/Turcotte genealogy. In 1990, Aimee Rose Doyon Jaynes, one of Inez's maternal aunts and a genealogical pioneer, compiled information in a booklet titled *The Doyons.* She recorded twelve generations of the Doyon family, starting with their arrival in New France (present day Québec) in the mid-1600s. Aimee included the history of Inez's maternal grandparents, Louis Cerinus Doyon and Rose Aimee née Turcotte, along with the genealogy of the maternal branches of the Turcotte and Provost lines.

In 2001, Inez's oldest daughter, Lynda, attended a medical conference in Québec. At the end of the visit, she decided to squeeze in a whirlwind sightseeing trip of the area. Armed with Aunt Aimee's

Doyon booklet, she and her friends thought it would be fun to check out the Doyon/Turcotte family history before returning home.

The unique land pattern arranged in narrow strips along the banks of the St. Lawrence River, sparked Lynda's attention and curiosity. Called *seigneuries,* these thin, elongated plots extended inland. She thought at first that this had been to furnish each farm with water access.

However, Lynda discovered that these land parcels were remnants of a French feudal land distribution system carried over to New France settlements in the 1600s. The system provided the occupant farmer and his family with the basics of food and shelter, while the French noblemen owners reaped the monetary rewards. This arrangement continued until 1854.

In one of Québec's oldest cemeteries, La-Visitation-de-Notre-Dame Cemetery at Château-Richer, Lynda came upon the gravesite of Jean Doyon—her tenth-great-grandfather. At the nearby ancestral farm, Lynda proudly viewed a plaque written in French honoring the patriarch, Jean Doyon, and his wife, Marthe Gagnon Doyon: *Hommage à Jean Doyon et Marthe Gagnon—Ancêtres des Doyon d'Amérique,1644; Site de la ferme ancestrale.*

Aunt Aimee's booklet mentioned Sainte-Famille, Île d'Orléans. Lynda found the small island rising in the middle of the St. Lawrence River near Québec City. Old Norman-style houses, churches, and shrines dotted the island. Raspberries grew in abundance. Serene vineyards and pastures gave off a delightful earthy essence.

Lynda was not prepared for her reception at the Île d'Orléans visitor center. When she inquired about her Turcotte heritage, the elderly woman behind the desk became thrilled to the point of apoplexy at the prospect of sharing her information. Lynda suspected such a request had not been made of the lady in the past 50 years.

The woman produced copious Turcotte information. Then she directed Lynda to a life-size statue honoring Abel Turcot, a farmer and miller instrumental in establishing the Île d'Orleans in 1650. He was also our grandmother's maternal patriarch. These days, his name is synonymous with the famous Abel Turcault Ale, a full-bodied roasted-caramel Scotch ale distributed by the Île d'Orléans Microbrewery.

Uneducated, Abel Turcot wrote his last name many different ways over the years. Versions included Turcault, Turcaud, Turkot, and Turcat. The spelling "Turcotte" surfaced in Québec in the early 1700s. Perhaps, spelling the name this way created the impression of a stronger French heritage.

Lynda enjoyed her day of discovery. She found the family patriarchs of the1600s were respected and honored. The grandfathers were pillars of the community in New France and provided great contributions and service to the Catholic church there. Lynda felt proud that, above and beyond their importance to her family, both men were significant in Québécoise history.

~

The Lumberjack and the Rosebud

"On your way, Doyon," called the foreman. He slapped the side of the wagon. "This is the final run of the day. See you at the lumberyard."

Louis Cerinus Doyon flicked the reins. The wagon, heavily laden with logs, pulled away from the Maine forest. A light dusting of snow began to fall.

Left on his own, the 23-year-old drove along, free to reminisce about the previous spring. *For a time, my dreams came true—I was part of Buffalo Bill Cody's Wild-West show. Qu'est-il arrivé? What happened?*

The most famous man on the planet in the years around 1900 was William Frederick "Buffalo Bill" Cody. He used his status as one of the colorful figures of the Old American West to organize his popular cowboy-themed wild west shows. Cody's legendary standing as a Western figure earned Louis' respect. The creator of Buffalo Bill's Wild West show was not just a showman or an actor/entertainer. He was renowned as a Pony Express rider, a buffalo hunter, a Congressional Medal of Honor recipient for valor as a U.S. Army scout, an entrepreneur, and the founder of Cody, Wyoming.

A white snowshoe hare bolted in front of the wagon path. Louis steadied the reins before the horses could become spooked or prance sideways.

"Don't get nervous," Louis murmured to his horses. "It's just a *petit lapin.*"

Returning to his thoughts, Doyon mused, *I wanted to be like Cody. To do something bigger and better than lumberjacking.* Louis had started out tending the show's livestock until he proved his sharpshooting abilities. He even exhibited talent as a performer. However, all the promise and thrill stopped with the end of the performance season. The return to lumberjacking proved to be humbling, even though it had been his family business since the mid 1600s.

In 1644, the family patriarch, Jean Doyon, arrived at the Canadian colony of New France, near the gulf of the Saint Lawrence River. At the age of 25, Jean signed an indentured contract as a laborer. Over three years, he developed into an expert pit sawyer.

With this skill, his honesty, and a reliance on his Catholic faith, Jean Doyon became an esteemed pillar of the New France settlement. His descendants thrived in Canada and the United States. The Doyon name still inspired respect, even though Louis and his father were far down in the birth order and considered a lesser branch of the Doyon lineage.

Ambitious and not afraid of hard work, Louis Cerinus desired to be someone someday. He also yearned to prove his worth as a Doyon. Oh, he had heard the whispers behind his back—"Arrogant S.O.B Frenchman."

Certainly, his dark, handsome features gave every impression of being a Frenchman. Nevertheless, his maternal grandmother had blond hair and blue eyes and was rumored to be a Castilian Spaniard.

With a laugh, Louis thought to himself, *Why not be arrogant? I'm young and strong and good looking . . . and a Doyon to boot! Besides, the girls never complain.*

Attracting the opposite sex was not a problem. *Don't all the young girls bat their eyelashes, flirt, and giggle when I walk by?* Women considered him a great catch for matrimony. Their fathers also encouraged marriage once they saw his sturdy wagon, the fine team of horses he drove, and how he saved his money.

The wagon jostled at a rough spot on the road. The piled logs shifted but remained secure. Louis' thoughts drifted to the pretty little *coup de rose* (rosebud)—17-year-old Rose Aimee Turcotte.

He had noticed the eldest daughter of Evangeliste Turcotte at Mass during his last visit home to Québec. He fancied Rose's cultured ways that, perhaps, resulted from her fine French education. His sisters spoke highly of her singing, fashion design, and needlework talents.

The Doyon and Turcotte families were long-time acquaintances. Though rumored to be of Scottish heritage, Mr. Turcotte was a successful French chef in Québec and an influential contributor to the Sainte-Anne-de-Beaupré Shrine.

Maybe it is time to think of settling down. Rose Aimee comes from a good Catholic family. That's important to me—in fact essential.

The lumberyard came within view. After pulling into the encampment, Louis jumped out of the wagon to help unload the timber. The sky darkened, and the dusting of snow turned into wet, heavy sleet.

Another worker yelled over the wind. "Glad to get that load put away before the brunt of the storm hits."

Louis, distracted, nodded his head. "I'm going to the paymaster to see what's due me and head north for Christmas," he replied. Without hesitation he stepped into the full force of the sleet and wind.

It was easy to forget the cold, lumberjacking and wild west shows when he could think about a *coup de rose.*

~

The Dream

Seventeen-year-old Rose Aimee Turcotte nibbled at her lower lip in concentration as she perfected the penciled lines on her sketch pad. *There, that's how I want the bodice to look.*

The ingénue stretched her neck and rolled her shoulders. It had been a challenge to capture the dress design on paper before getting ready for Christmas Mass.

She flipped through the sketch book and smiled with contentment. *I'm getting a nice collection of drawings.*

For as long as she could remember, Rose had created outfits for her dolls. Ideas came from the Montgomery Ward catalogue, known as the "Wish Book." Mama allowed her to cut up old catalogues to fashion her own designs for her paper doll models. Soon she developed the sense for proportions needed in dress designs.

Rose did not like designs with hoops, petticoats, or obvious corsets. Her style emphasized a woman's natural figure in comfortable clothes. She strived to incorporate texture into her designs, by using silk, lace, and embroidery.

A gentle knock roused her from her daydreams. Her mother peeked into the room and said, "*Mon chéri.* I have some exciting news. Remember my good friend who designs in Montréal?"

Rose's eyes widened as she nodded.

"Well, I wrote to her all about your love for fashion design and Rose . . . she's invited you to live with her while you further your design education."

Giggles of glee broke out as the two swayed side-to-side in a mother-daughter hug.

"Oh Mama! Montréal! That makes me so happy . . . but what will Father say?"

The two women did not have long to wonder. Evangeliste Turcotte, flushed with excitement, bustled into Rose's bedroom. "Here you two are. I'm late getting home because as I left the restaurant, I ran into Leon Doyon's second son, Louis Cerinus. My, he's an impressive young man, and what a fine pair of horses he drives. Anyway, he asked about you Rose, and said he was looking forward to seeing you at Mass."

Rose scarcely heard what her father said. She could not contain her joy while her own news bubbled out. "Papa, I've been invited to stay with Mama's friend in Montreal . . . to study designing."

Evangeliste's pleasant mood darkened as he addressed his daughter, "Don't speak nonsense, you know your mother isn't well. I would never agree to have you go so far away . . . now let's get ready for Mass."

He ushered her pale and solemn mother out of the room. It was then that Rose noticed the gray silk scarf draped at Mama's neck to conceal her growing goiter. Her abnormal neck swelling and bulging eyes broadcast volumes about her illness.

Rose turned from the closed door. Her designs lay on the floor—forgotten and trampled.

The following spring, on May 12th of 1902, Louis and Rose celebrated their wedding at the bride's home of Sainte-Rose-de-Watford, in the province of Québec. Rose clutched her Bible while Reverend Father J.P. Veilleux performed the wedding ceremony.

Rose's father had not wanted his daughter to leave her home in Sainte-Rose-de-Watford to study dress design. However, the newlyweds did leave the area to set up their first home in Jackson Pond, Maine, 110 miles south of St. Rose. Louis continued in the logging industry, where he harvested small, thin pine and birch trees for pulpwood to make paper products. Later he worked in the paper mill.

Louis loved and honored his "*coup de rose.*" He expressed his love with his pet term of endearment, "*sumava,*" which may have been French-Canadian slang for "little mother." Whenever possible he treated her to her favorite indulgence of strawberries and cream.

Even though Louis provided for Rose as best as he could, life proved hard and challenging for the young couple. The work of a lumberjack was not only difficult and dangerous, but also irregular work with low pay and temporary housing. Often, living conditions were primitive and isolated. Louis expected better of his life—after all, he was a Doyon.

Rose put away her design book after marriage. She later told her daughters that not attending the Montréal design school was her one regret in life. Yet her dreams of designing were not easily extinguished . . . and sometimes dreams do come true.

The Birthing of Leona

Inez writes, July 11, 2003:

> *"Today I am thinking of my mother, [Maria Emelia] Leona Doyon who was born on April 6, 1903 in St. Rose de Watford, County Dorchester—Province of Québec, Canada. Her parents, Louis Cerinus and Rose Aimee Doyon were living in Jackson Pond, Maine but traveled up to Québec to be near her mother when the time came for the birth of their first child. Evangeliste and Rose Délima Turcotte, [the grandparents-to-be] lived in an isolated, wooded area of Canada, far from medical help.*
>
> *"When my Mother was born, she was a hard birth for my poor little Grandma. It was a very dry birth and labor [went on] for several days."*

Louis Doyon tapped his right foot with nervous energy against the floor of the wooden porch. If he had a pocket watch, he would have consulted the passing of time, every few minutes. Instead, he observed the elongated shadows cast against the barn as the sun began to set in the western sky. Unable to sit any longer, Louis sprang to his feet to pace back and forth on the front veranda.

Evangeliste Turcotte smiled, "It takes time for babies to be born. I should know, we've had nine of them."

"Well, this is taking too long," snapped the father-to-be. "I'm supposed to meet a man about some work early tomorrow—and he's on the other side of the river."

He continued, "The midwife said Rose's water sac burst three days ago. The contractions were piddly and not getting anywhere. Now the baby is coming butt first and the contractions have stopped altogether. Rose is growing weaker by the moment. *Sacré bleu.* That darn midwife is not willing to do what's needed."

Evangeliste's face clouded and he asked, "And what is that, pray tell?"

"I'll show you," said Louis as he jumped off the porch and ran into the barn. He emerged minutes later, grasping a contraption in his hands.

"You're not planning to use that hog puller on my daughter, are you?"

With a sober look, Louis answered, "I've delivered piglets, calves, and foals—and something needs to be done to get this baby born."

Louis could not be contradicted. With a commanding presence, he stepped into the birthing room, hog puller in hand. Evangeliste heard raised women's voices mixed with Louis's before a silence ensued. One loud slap, then another before a baby's lusty cry pierced the quiet.

Delighted with her baby girl, Rose said, over and over, "Our baby is beautiful and perfect." Louis only saw that the baby's legs continued to fold up to her chest, in the same positioning as while in the womb. She could not be held in the usual way. With disgust, he watched Rose struggle to diaper and dress the baby. The legs sprang back to the deformed position before the task could be completed. It would continue that way for another six weeks.

Louis had been so sure the baby would be a boy and not a girl. Prior to the birth, he even decided to name the baby Leon, after his father, who had died six months before of typhoid fever. Begrudgingly, Louis allowed the baby to be named Leona.

Later that night while preparing for bed, Louis sighed to himself, *Well, at least I'll make my meeting tomorrow.*

~

Prayers at the Shrine of Sainte-Anne-de-Beaupré

Nine months after delivering her first baby, Rose contracted smallpox, the viral disease characterized by crusting pustules and extreme high fevers. It was not uncommon at the time for anyone to fall ill with this infection. Without an effective treatment or known cure, smallpox could become deadly if other medical complications developed. Death occurred in about a quarter of cases.

Rose remained delirious with high fevers and near death for many weeks. In addition, she had another condition complicating matters: She was in the third trimester of her second pregnancy. Rose's baby boy, Emery Ovide, was born on May 6th, 1904. Unaware of his birth, the little mother was so ill that she was given last rites and taken to the shrine at Sainte-Anne-de-Beaupré parish for prayers of healing.

The family received the miracle they prayed for. Rose did not die, and her condition slowly improved. She was still recuperating in June of the next year when she had her third baby, Laura Marie. Smallpox had weakened Rose's general health, yet over the next 17 years she carried ten more pregnancies. Saint Anne remained her special saint throughout her lifetime—until her death at the age of ninety-eight.

One unusual consequence resulted from the high fever and smallpox lesions. After her illness, to the delight of the children in the family, Rose's nose and face became very pliable. She could lick the tip of her nose with her tongue.

Family stories said that her husband, Louis, took it upon himself during Rose's illness to re-sculpture her nose when a huge puss filled pox remained on it. It is said, he took out his pocketknife and cut off the pox and then shaped her malleable nose with his fingers.

The great surprise—the nose looked normal.

~

A Day in April

The horse-drawn wagon carrying a man, a boy, and a girl stopped at the corner crossroad of the logging town of Saint John, New Brunswick.

In a curt manner the father said, "Leona, take this shopping list for the general store. I'll pick you up when I'm done with the blacksmith." He handed a paper to his slight nine-year-old daughter. A gentle breeze, fragrant with woodlands and balsam fir, ruffled through the girl's wavy auburn hair.

Accepting the list, Leona hopped down from the wagon and moved aside to avoid splatters from its wheels. She navigated the slippery ice crystals forming over the mud puddles that half melted in the balmy 60-degree temperature of the previous day.

The matching brown horses spirited the wagon down the road towards the blacksmith shop. The stoic, pale face of seven-year-old Emery looked back at his sister.

Reaching into her sweater sleeve, Leona retrieved a white hankie with embroidered lilac flowers, knotted to secure a coin. Both the fancy-work handkerchief and the five-cent Canadian coin—a mixture of silver and copper—were gifts from her dear Grand-mère Turcotte.

Leona's ninth birthday occurred on April 6th, well over a week passed. This would be her first chance to buy something with her birthday money.

As the first grandchild, Leona shared a special bond with her grand-mère. Looking at the embroidered hankie she thought, *I sure do miss Grand-mère and St.-Rose-de-Watford.* She swallowed the urge to cry. *No. I won't allow sad feelings.*

Nevertheless, as she headed for the general store, Leona's thoughts dwelt on how things used to be when she lived near, or with, her grandparents in province of Québec. Her father often traveled the length of Canada as a lumberjack. After smallpox left her mother frail, he returned the family to St. Rose for the delivery of each child—seven births in ten years of marriage. The arrangement worked well for the family.

This time was different. Her father moved the growing family far from Québec to the timberlands of New Brunswick. They lived in a logging camp along the Saint John River. The area, known for the logging industry, had many saw and pulp mills that dotted the maritime province.

That was good for Father, but it left me miserable and homesick for Québec—besides, Mama is again pregnant. Leona took a deep breath and stood tall. *No matter, we'll get along fine.*

Inquisitive, quick-minded, and mature beyond her years, Leona was ready to take charge of any situation. She would have the help of Alexina and Laura, her five- and six-year-old sisters, to run the household.

As Leona approached the general store she saw crowds of people congregating in small groups. She weaved through the groupings to catch snippets of conversation.

"Struck an iceberg" . . . "Supposed to be unsinkable" . . . "*Titanic*" . . . "Not enough lifeboats."

No one noticed the auburn-haired girl tucking her birthday coin and hankie back into her sweater sleeve—not on that day in April of 1912. The tragedy was not easily forgotten—not for the world, not for the nine-year-old girl.

One of the worst sea disasters in history had occurred. The SS *Titanic* had struck an iceberg in the North Atlantic, and sank about

375 miles southeast of Halifax, Nova Scotia. More than two-thirds of the passengers, an estimated 1,500 lives, were lost.

The closest port to the accident, Halifax, served as the collection center for the catastrophe. Many residents of Saint John considered Halifax to be their neighbor, given that it was located less than three hours away by waterway. Once the loss of life became known, people and ships from the Saint John area joined the recovery effort. Lumbermen, such as Louis Doyon, farmers, and shopkeepers stood ready to help.

Ships from Saint John set out, stocked with embalming supplies, undertakers—two of them women—and clergy. Due to health regulations, only embalmed bodies could be returned to port. Approximately 328 recovered and preserved bodies were brought to Halifax and nearly 120 badly damaged bodies were buried at sea.

Leona remembered the discussions of the disaster, as the aftermath accounts went on for weeks. Recounted stories of the tragedy became the only topic in the stores, around the neighborhoods of Saint John, throughout the New Brunswick province, and across the world.

Reports indicated one steamship, the *Parisian,* turned off their radio for the night after having contacted the SS *Titanic* at 10:30 P.M. The *Titanic* struck the iceberg an hour and ten minutes later. Even though the two vessels were within 50 miles of each other at the time of the accident, the *Parisian* was unaware, and thus unable, to respond to the distress calls of the *Titanic.* Once the catastrophe became known, the *Parisian* went out as a rescue ship. It returned without any survivors.

Eight years after the sinking of the *Titanic*, Leona learned that her future husband, Henri David, had traveled from France to Québec on the SS *Parisian* in 1907.

Anchors

Leona and her family did return to Sainte-Rose-de-Watford to see her beloved grandparents one last time. The purpose of the visit was bittersweet, as Louis Doyon had decided to move his family to the Montana territory of the United States. This visit proved to be a final goodbye to her Grand-mère Turcotte.

To take a small part of Sainte-Rose-de-Watford with them, ten-year-old Leona and her mother, Rose, picked six of Grand-mère's beautiful violet pansy flowers as a remembrance and pressed them in Rose's big blue Bible.

With ceremony and a sense of hope, Leona planted the seeds from an apple core before she left St. Rose. She fancied that if a seed grew into a future tree, her heart would always be anchored there with her grandparents.

Then the time came to say goodbye and board the train. The slight smell of peppermint and mothballs lingered in the air after an embrace with Grand-père.

Grand-mère, pale and weak, breathed heavily with any exertion due to her heart ailment. Around her neck, even in the June warm weather, she wore a gray scarf to hide the growing goiter. The older lady's ample bosom mashed against Leona face with their hug goodbye. Both whispered "*Je t'aime, au revoir,*" before Leona turned and ran to the train.

Over a century later, the pansies were framed and displayed in the homes of Leona's granddaughter and great-granddaughter.

~

The Adventure

In Aunt Aimee's 1990 booklet "The Doyons," the 1913 family adventure was retold from the remembrances of her mother, Rose Turcotte Doyon:

> *"Many Canadian friends of Dad's were migrating [sic] to the United States, to Montana where they were offered homestead land to start farming in the wide-open spaces of Eastern Montana, at Scobey.*
>
> *"Dad's brother-in-law, Lorenzo Provost was already in Montana and writing of the great opportunities and anxious to have his wife and family join him. However, he forgot to mention all the inconveniences, hardships with cold severe winters, lack of money to buy farming equipment and housing for the families.*
>
> *"Dad was tempted so he sold his good team of horses, his wagon, and all personal property and packed up to leave for Montana. He also arranged for Aunt Felicine [née Doyon] Provost and her seven children to travel along with us. That must have been quite a sight, one man with two families.*
>
> *"At this time, we lived in St. Camille, County Bellechase, P. Q. [Province of Québec]. After Dad sold his possessions we moved to St. Rose and lived with Grandpa and Grandma Turcotte for about three weeks. Grandma was quite ill with heart problems and an enlarged thyroid. It was very hard for Mother to leave and move so far away. Grandmother died about a year after we moved to Montana.*

"In June 1913, we left Canada for the United States. Dad took charge of two families each with seven children, all about the same age. The oldest, Cousin Joe Provost, about twelve and I [Aimee Rose] was less than a year old. No one able to speak English except Dad, and not too good at that.

"We left St. Rose and boarded a train in Québec City. It must have been a long tiresome ride. Almost a week. The trains were not the modern trains of today. They were slow, dirty, warm, and inconvenient in so many ways. At many stops Dad jumped off to buy food and milk for everyone. I still have a little granite kettle that Dad bought to heat the milk for me.

"Our Port of Entry was Port Huron in Michigan. Imagine going through customs with all that luggage and a gang like that. From [there] it was on to Chicago—where another change of trains took place, then on to Scobey, Montana.

"The families were dirty and exhausted when they arrived. They were met at the station by Uncle Lorenzo and friends in big wagons. [We traveled] for twelve more miles over bumpy country roads to the homes of friends . . . [and] stayed for a considerable length of time until Dad was able to make arrangements for a homestead. With the help of neighbors [Dad] built somewhat of a home to move his family into.

"The first few years were very difficult with many hardships and problems to overcome. Fortunately, the Canadians had all settled close by. They formed a regular French Community which provided help, encouragement, and social life for everyone. All the women and children spoke only French, this made it very difficult for the children especially when they started school.

"Consequently, the family had an extremely rough life once they arrived in Montana. All lived in one room and an attic, where they slept on beds of straw. It is hard to conceive what terribly poor conditions they endured with such harsh winters and not a lot to eat."

Our Writing Adventure

"What have you been up to, Mom?" I asked during a phone call from my home in Bakersfield, California.

"Oh, the usual . . . except I've been doing some writing."

"What have you been writing?" I asked.

Mom hesitated, "You know, doing what you asked—putting down some of my thoughts and memories."

Years had passed since we began our discussion of what an interesting childhood my mother, Inez, had led. Whatever her reasons, we started on our own adventure. With intention, I spurred her on. Each time Mom began to go down her memory lane, I would tease her saying, "Have you written that down?"

We hit a gold mine in historical treasures with what Inez penned from her remembrances. One example was when she wrote the following thoughts about her mother, Leona, and her life in the early Montana years:

> *"My Mom was a bright little girl and a fast learner as well as a hard-worker. She did go to school a short time—perhaps three years—off and on. But she did get enough education to receive a certification of having an eighth-grade education. She had lovely handwriting, she knew math well and had fine composition.*
>
> *"I think, however, how hard her life was for her. She would work with her father in the fields and never stayed at the house to*

learn to cook or other things young girls learned. She was his 'hired help.'

"She would work with as many as a six-horse team and was not allowed to wear men's trousers, which could have protected her so much better. She said she was badly irritated from the dust that came up under her dress. I have a picture of her taken when she was 14 years old with a large team of horses. They did dry land farming in that prairie country. She worked so hard and was so thin, the neighbors worried about her. But at that time, no one dared turn him [her father] into the authorities.

"My grandfather [Louis Doyon] was very strict and downright 'mean.' He always had a mistaken idea that anything the other kids did wrong was her fault because she was the eldest and was supposed to set the example. Very often she was punished for something that occurred that she never even knew had happened. He believed in whipping with a long whip used on cattle, called a 'Black Snake.' He would whip her until she bled and would pass out.

"Although she never in her life told me she was sexually abused, she implied it many times. I'm sure the man was mentally ill. From the behavior he showed, he had to be. One time my mother said he beat a horse to death by tying the horse tight and beating its head with a heavy chain until he killed it. She said she saw him do it."

~

A Composite of the Montana Leona

"Moo-o-o-o, moo-o-o-o."

"I hear you Buttercup. You're next after Bessie."

Fourteen-year-old Leona sniffed and rubbed her chafed nose on her sleeve, as she milked. Between the cold morning and the dusty barn hay, her red nose matched the buffalo plaids of the oversized woolen overcoat she wore. Black rubber boots, a gray wool skirt, and a brown knitted cap completed her ensemble.

Milking came early at the Doyon homestead and Leona milked every day, twice a day—morning and late afternoon. It was said women made the best milkers—maybe because of their small hands and great patience. Leona's hands remained undersized. However, since coming to Montana, the seldom-used muscles of her forearms and hands grew strong and mighty. They served as effective tools for the task of milking. She milked three cows in little over 45 minutes.

With each alternating squeeze of the teats, streams of milk splashed in rhythmic cadence into the metal bucket. *Right hand—gently clamp teat between extended thumb and first finger. Squeeze downward middle finger, ring finger, pinky. Release. Left hand—clamp. Squeeze downward middle, ring, pinky. Release.*

Once in the quiet and peaceful cow barn, the demands of the day and the constant chatter of her siblings faded away. Milking time gave her the opportunity to ponder obstacles, as well as reflect on things in her life.

Escaping into a daydream, Leona worried about a feature of her appearance. Lack of a figure, a slight overbite, and even poor eyesight—all of these Leona could bear, but her freckles—*Mon Dieu! Mama never had such freckles. Why do I?*

What started as a dusting of freckles had blossomed into a crop of brown spots. Time in the sun, plus her naturally pale skin and red-highlighted hair, only encouraged more freckle clusters on her forehead and cheeks, and across the bridge of her nose. *To think, I didn't even notice those freckles until cousin Joe Provost teased me about them.*

The rhythmic cadence of milking continued. *Clamp. Squeeze. Release. Clamp. Squeeze. Release.* Milk frothed as it hit the inside of the metal pail.

Truth be told, Leona loved to spend time outdoors. She lived on the prairie, tended the livestock, and considered herself all Montana cowgirl. Horseback riding became a favorite pastime and Leona developed into an expert rider and a crack-shot markswoman. Now, she thought, she must take extra care to protect her skin. Grand-mére Turcotte's words of wisdom to avoid the sun came to mind: "A true lady is never freckled or tanned."

Leona tried everything to rid her skin of the invading brown spots. She no longer saved her money for ribbons or candy. Every coin she scraped together went towards clearing her skin of unwanted freckles. *That Pond's Vanishing Cream I found in the mail-order catalogue is really working.* She sniffed. *At least I never had freckles on my lips like my brothers.*

The cow's now-empty udder hung wrinkled and soft. Leona washed and dried the deflated milk sac. *Really, I'm glad Father still needs me as his field hand. It gives me the freedom of being outdoors and grants me a peculiar sense of pride.*

Many able-bodied men signed up to go off to the Great War. That meant hired hands were a scarcity. *I wonder if Papa could make a go of the homestead without me.* Being needed was an ace up her sleeve, but she also knew her father hated his dependence on her.

An application of Bag Balm to the udder completed the milking. Finished with Bessie, Leona struggled to rearrange the extra skirt material in her way before she moved on to the next cow. *No, I don't mind working outside, but I do mind this darn skirt Papa demands I wear. It gets dirty or wet, or requires extra time to untangle.* Leona stretched her stiff back and legs as she rose from the wooden milking stool.

"Okay Buttercup, it's your turn." The bovine looked at her with big soft brown eyes. Leona placed the metal stanchions around Buttercup's neck to secure her in the stall. With the cow restrained, Leona washed the udders and patted them dry. She positioned the three-legged stool alongside Buttercup and crouched down lightly, ready for anything. The Jersey cow, with a brown nose and a sweet looking face, was her favorite breed. But she knew all cows were capable of kicking or tail swishing any unsuspecting milker.

Leona leaned her head into the cow's body. Gently she bumped the milk bag to encourage the letdown reflex before grabbing the two fore teats. A quick test squirt into a cup served to check the appearance of the milk. *Clamp. Squeeze middle, ring, pinky. Release. Clamp. Squeeze middle, ring, pinky. Release.*

Her daydreaming returned with the rhythmic swishing of milk streams against the side of the bucket. Leona thought back on how her three years of schooling had come to a halt that previous spring. Her father restricted her formal education when he realized she could read and write English better than either of her parents.

Father thought I had enough schooling and said I was needed at home. . . . I know I'm quick with figuring math and could yell out the answers before the rest of the kids. Leona beamed to herself with pride. *And didn't I win the big spelling bee in Helena?* She had traveled by train to the capital for the state contest and brought home the first-place trophy.

Leona's three closest-in-age siblings did not fare so well in school. Emery and Laura struggled, relying on their native tongue of French-Canadian instead of perfecting their speech in English. *I wonder if being born while Mama had smallpox made it harder for them to learn. And Alexina is smart enough, but too nervous and shy—too timid to do well in school. But Papa did get his scholars.*

A younger sister and brother—Sedonia (Sid) and Doria—toddlers at the time of their immigration, grew up bilingual in French and English. When both excelled at the local school they were chosen as novitiates for the Catholic ministry and sent away for schooling. Sid, six years Leona's junior, entered the convent and sisterhood. Her brother Doria, seven years younger, entered the seminary to study for the priesthood. *What a proud moment for my parents,* thought Leona.

But a sourness agitated in her stomach. Leona did not have much use for the Church or for religion. Her family was religious. Leona was not. *What really goes against my grain is how the priest and nuns ignore me and my best points. They are too busy making over Sid and Doria's piety and scholastic abilities.*

She knew it would be a bad idea to express her opinions about the Church to her father. He could easily go out of control, lashing out at her as he often did to an animal. *It's best to look happy and stay clear of him, especially when he has that certain look in his eyes.* What scared Leona was the possibility she possessed some of these same traits.

Finished with her morning milking, Leona cleaned the equipment and prepared for the later afternoon milking. Her family members were awakening, and she could hear them getting ready for the day. She knew they would be wanting the fresh milk for breakfast. But as Leona handed the milk over to her sister Laura she thought, *How can they drink this stuff?*

~

Over Ice Cream

"Here's your ice cream. Enjoy!" I placed a small glass dish with two scoops of butter pecan in front of my mother, Inez. She had just eased herself into her favorite stuffed chair and placed her wooden cane within reach. Her footing had become less sure over the last several months as her dowager's hump interfered with her balance.

We were in Mom's front room sanctuary as we passed the time until Public Television's Masterpiece Theater came on. Her new Samsung 42-inch flatscreen TV sat muted in the corner of the room, while flickering images of the news and commercials played on the screen.

While we waited for our program, I started on my ice cream and continued our discussion of the Doyon family's exodus to Montana. "Aunt Aimee mentioned Grandpa Doyon built a makeshift house once the family established themselves in Montana."

"Yes," said Inez, "the place started out to house two adults and seven children. I was told my grandfather took wagons and a group of men to Plentywood to get the wood for the house."

"You're kidding me," I scoffed. "The name of the town was Plentywood? . . . Plentywood, Montana—where Grandpa Doyon was able to get enough lumber to build a house with an upstairs attic?"

Nodding her head, she added, "It took them three days to haul the timber back to the homestead."

Images of the eastern Montana plains characterized by grasses, cacti, and sagebrush—but few trees—flashed in my mind. I expected the homes to be dugouts, made of sod cut from the grasslands. We were talking about 1913, not the 1800s, and yet I assumed obtainable timber in the Scobey area would be scarce and costly.

"You don't think they cut down the actual trees and prepared the lumber for building, do you?"

Mom shrugged, "I wouldn't have a clue. I got the idea he oversaw the building of the house himself—he always viewed himself as a jack-of-all-trades. I guess he had the knowledge and skills as a lumberjack to cut down the trees and prepare the timber for building."

I reached for my cell phone and googled Plentywood, Montana. I read sections from the screen, "It's about 45 miles away, almost straight east from Scobey. I don't know what kind of lumber they would have used, but poplar and pine are listed as abundant there. . . . It says rocks and sod were used to insulate and fortify the rough planks against the winds. I guess the gales often blew down the homestead shacks. Also, most people stuffed straw and newspaper between the boards to keep out the cold winter winds."

Inez concentrated on her ice cream, then said with a sigh, "It's hard to conceive what dreadful conditions they endured—such harsh winters and not enough to eat."

"I read that the Montana homesteaders enjoyed a wet cycle of about seven good years with bumper crops from 1909 to 1916. This probably ended just as your grandparents were getting established. Then, all hell broke loose: drought, famine, and economic depression."

Reaching for my notebook, I pulled out the paper I wanted. "This guy, William Alexander wrote in his diary, after a 1923 Fourth of July picnic in Culbertson, Montana. It left quite an impression on me. He described how people had changed in ten years of homesteading:

> 'In 1913 people had just come to Montana. They were well dressed had plenty of money they were hopeful, spirited, and energetic. In 1923 every face looked careworn. The sociability was gone. In its place was a look of reserve and suspicion.'

"Sad stuff, wasn't it?" . . . I hesitated before broaching another subject. "Tell me more of what you know about your grandfather, Mom."

"Louis Cerinus Doyon." Inez shifted her position and leaned forward before saying. "He wasn't a drinker and was quite religious . . . a definite authoritarian. According to my mother, he expected his kids to take off running when he told them to do something. If they dawdled, or even walked in a normal pace, he would kick them in the butt and yell—'Run'."

My eyes opened wide, "Wow, that sounds nutty to me. And yet, no one else in the family had issues with him, except your mom?"

"That's right," nodded Inez. "They admitted he was strict, but they didn't believe he was any harsher on others than he was on himself. The rest of the family actually admired and respected him as a hard worker . . . and even considered him a great father."

"Mom, I'm a bit confused. Did Grandpa Doyon exhibit a mean spirit to your mother, but not to the rest of the family? Do you think she was just too strong-willed?"

Inez readjusted her dish as she spoke, "Yes, according to both of my aunts, Leona was bold and rebellious. She wouldn't back down from a disagreement. Compared to the other children, there's no doubt of her defiance—especially when she believed she was in the right. Perhaps she was too much like her father, in that way."

I remembered something I heard and said, "I suspect a parent will often find fault with the child who has traits and characteristics similar to his own. If he can blame wrongdoings on the child, he doesn't have to recognize and take responsibility for his own negative qualities. All I can think of is that your mother was the family scapegoat."

Inez took a sip of water, "No excuses can explain the mistreatment of my mother by her father except that he was unstable, maybe schizophrenic. I think he romanticized tales of Montana cowboys, the Badlands, and Teddy Roosevelt's pre-presidential adventures."

She continued, "Imagine the adjustment moving from the Northeastern woodlands to such a contrasting harshness of the wide-open high plains. He faced the disappointment that hard work could not alter the weather or save a failing crop. My grandfather must have thought he entered a dream come true when he arrived in Montana—he woke to a nightmare in the making."

We finished our ice cream, and I gathered the dishes. With a slight reluctance I said, "Mom, were you mistreated by your mother?"

Inez shook her head, "No, there was never any ill-treatment from my mother—that's where the daughter differed from the father. I'm thankful she inherited Grandma Doyon's sense of fun. I think the French call it *joie de vivre*."

I went to the kitchen and cleaned up. I returned as the Masterpiece Theater music invited me to join the telecast. *It should be a good show. . . . Too bad all the ice cream was gone.*

~

Joie de Vivre

How did the Doyon side of Inez's family make it through such hard times in Montana, when others did not? The answer may be a simple one: They laughed.

Maybe Rose Doyon's strong faith in God, her gratitude of recovering from smallpox and the prolonged coma it had caused served to spearhead her family into what the French call *joie de vivre* (joy of life). This phrase described the core attributes of her family and their cheerful enjoyment of life. Without a doubt, their uplifting philosophy and happy nature began with "the little mother."

Despite the cycle of drought, poverty, and hunger, Rose and her twelve children interpreted everyday life as a comical puzzle in which to find some element of joy. Mama Rose was the picture of frivolity. Her playful cheerfulness provided lighthearted fun in unkind circumstances and despair. Her children also possessed sunny, uplifting attitudes and laughed at most anything they did. Thus, the laughter, intentional or unintentional, counteracted the sternness of Papa Louis, who seemed never to laugh.

Rose filled the ordinary times with comical drawings, expressive poetry, and lively tunes. She often sang the French Christmas carol, *Il est né, le divin enfant*, He is Born, the Divine Christ Child, and other little French songs. Her fondness for strawberries came out in pantomime. With a devious grin and big eyes, looking side to side, she rubbed her tummy when asked, "Where did all the whole strawberries go from the jam jar?" She did love strawberries.

However, Rose's physical humor excelled while she "danced" the newest family baby on her foot. With stretched open eyes and a wide grin she would sing: "Dee dee—ditty ditty—dee dee—diddle diddle—dee dee—ditty ditty —dee dee dee. "You want to go again?" she would ask. "Okay, here we go." On and on the ride and the tune went until all involved—Rose, the baby, and spectators— dissolved into giggles and peals of laughter. What fun! Leona adapted the dee dee—ditty ditty ride for her children and grandchildren to enjoy with future generations, as well.

Frequent sweeping was a necessity for those who lived on the prairie. With flamboyant ceremony, Rose would stop her sweeping long enough to choose a perfect stalk of straw from her broom—one exactly right to thread through the hole of her earring-less pierced ears. The piece of straw kept the holes in her earlobes from closing, but also served as funny, dangling earrings to be modeled as the newest French fashion.

The Doyon children received their work ethic from their father, but they inherited the Turcotte "funny-gene" from their mother. The mundane became animated. With goofy expressions and toothy grins, they laughed with hilarity over body function quirks of farts, burps, and hiccoughs. They jigged and danced about to lively tunes or strutted around sporting an askew hat, with a newly found feather stuck into the brim for flair. They simply grabbed every opportunity to lift their mood to laughter.

The children even found their own avenues of joy while sweeping. Or, perhaps, it was Rose who taught the children to stop their work just long enough to plunge the end of the broom handle into the molasses barrel for a quick sweet treat on the sly. Yes, there was always something to enjoy, smile, or laugh about, and time enough for *joie de vivre.*

Part Two

Montana Years
1917–1928

~

Draft Registration

An early Model T Ford came to an abrupt stop in front of the wooden side-board building that served as the Scobey courthouse. Henri and Leon David, dressed in starched white shirts and gray slacks, jumped out of the automobile and hurried into the building.

The round, beefy face of the Registrar, Roy Shiffern broke into a huge grin. "Hello, my French friends. . . . Where have you been? I thought you two forgot about the registration."

"Oh, *oui,*" said Leon. "We got a late start, then we found the Model T had a flat tire. Of course, we had to clean up once again."

"Of course," chuckled Roy.

In the midst of European fighting during the Great War, the United States passed the Selective Service Act which required men between the ages of 21 and 30 to register for military service. A draft, by way of a lottery, was to follow. The legislation occurred six weeks after the United States declared war on Germany. Congress set the mandatory registration date as June 5, 1917, and the David brothers, in this age group, responded to the first registration.

Roy rubbed his wire-rimmed spectacles with a cloth handkerchief before situating them on his face. He then continued, "We had a record number of registrations and ran out of the forms. . . . I'll just use a blank paper and fill in your answers where they should go.

"Henri, you go first. State your full name, your age and birthdate."

"Henry August David, and I'm 26 years old. I was born on March 8th, 1891."

"I know your home is Scobey, Sheridan County, Montana. How about your place of birth?"

Taking care to describe his origins with precision, Henri answered, "I was born in Varacieux, Isère, Dauphiné, France." The *département* of Isère was equivalent to a county in the United States. While Henri used the name Dauphiné, the region's official name had been changed to Rhône-Alpes over a hundred years before.

"Have you declared your intention to be a U.S. citizen or are you still an alien?" Roy's voice took on a serious tone.

Henri shot back his answer, "I am still a citizen of France, but I have declared my intention to become a U.S. citizen."

Roy looked on the form for the next question, "Let's see, you are single, and your race is Caucasian . . . you farm your own homestead and are self-employed. Do you have any dependents or claim any exemptions?"

Henri shook his head and said, "No dependents and no exemptions to claim."

Reaching for another page, Roy explained, "In this section, I document your physical characteristics. I'd say you are tall, slim your eyes are brown, and your hair is black. You are not missing any arms or legs or eyes or anything like that.

"I'm to include a paragraph that you certify that you have reviewed your answers and the answers are true. Sign your name and I will witness your signature."

Henri looked over the two papers and nodded his head. Smiling he thought, *Others describe my eye color as hazel or dark gray.*

Roy handed Henri the fountain pen. Perhaps inconsistency existed between Henri's French loyalty and U.S. pride with this declaration. He signed the draft registration with his name in the more-Americanized form, *Henry*, yet his French middle name, *Auguste*, with an "*e*," went unchanged in his signature.

Giving Leon his chance to register, Henri stepped to the window. His thoughts were not of the dusty road outside, but of his older sister who remained in France. *Antoinette, I do hope you are safe. It's been so very long since we have heard from you.*

Henri felt Leon's hand on his shoulder as Roy said, "Well my friends, you both are registered, but it's my understanding that farmers will be exempt from this draft. Your wheat crops are too precious to our troops—they will help us win this war."

None of the David brothers were drafted into military service. Because of the great demand for wheat, the brothers expanded their farming to a larger scale, north of Scobey. Henri's father and brothers obtained their US citizenship. Yet, records were never found of Henri becoming a U.S. citizen.

At the time, Henri became chronically ill with what doctors diagnosed as either pleurisy or pneumonia. Frequent hospital care became a necessity for him. Henri was not known to be sick before this period. Perhaps the illness resulted from the lingering flu of the 1918 influenza pandemic. Bacterial pneumonia often followed the viral infection of the influenza.

"Sssshhhhh"

Inez's journaling revealed a family legend:

> *"I am trying to start back before I could remember. After the First World War (1918), but before I was born (1926), My father was dryland farming, however, he would also go across the border into Canada. According to my mother, he was smuggling wheat."*

During the First World War, the U.S. and Canada believed that the brewing and distilling of liquor diverted precious grain, molasses, and labor from the wartime effort. A temporary prohibition resulted in using the grain to produce more food instead of liquor. However, when the war ended, anti-alcohol groups regarded drinking as a great evil and demanded local, state, and national governments prohibit alcohol outright. The 18th Amendment to the United States Constitution became the notorious U.S. legislation that prohibited the importation, transport, manufacture, or sale of alcoholic beverages.

Was Henri sneaking Saskatchewan wheat across the Canada-Montana border? "Sssshhhhh." Perhaps Henri David was a bit of a rogue—not a cad or a swindler, but his unconventional deeds did have a smidgen of rascal quality. Maybe he thought his lingering lung issues gave him license to flirt with defiance. Or did it just appear so?

In the first decades of the 1900s, the border between Canada and the United States was easily lost in the prairie landscape. A person could have one foot in Saskatchewan as the next foot stepped into Montana or North Dakota, and not know the difference. Without any demarcation to distinguish territories, people could, and did, walk back and forth across the borders any time, unhampered by signs, guards or passports.

At the time, Henri's relatives farmed wheat in Saskatchewan. It was unclear if the border crossing with the wheat was done just once or numerous times, or if Henri had help from his brothers. But if rumor was true, Henri stepped over the line—literally, over the boundary line between the two North American countries with devious intentions. Perhaps, the contraband grain was intended to make whiskey.

With the David brothers' homesteads all in the same vicinity, they worked together and expanded their post–WWI dryland farming income with more enterprises. However, the Montana census, taken on February 3, 1920, placed Henri, his parents, and younger brother, Marcel, living in Roosevelt County in Wolf Point. Perhaps the town of Wolf Point, located 53 miles south of Scobey and about 70 miles west of Bainville, served as a winter respite. The family members were still listed as farmers, yet without indications of where they farmed.

Six months later, something important changed for Henri.

~

Romance at the Rodeo

Inez journaled:

> *"When she [Leona] met my father, Henri A. David, he was so saddened by the conditions she was living under. He expressed caring for her and his family told him, 'If you want this girl, you'd better marry her before her father kills her.'*
>
> *"She was seventeen when they were married (August 7, 1920). He was nearly thirteen years older than her. She said she didn't know anything about love but just wanted to get away from her father [Louis Doyon]."*

"Ha, you might as well marry her—she's damaged goods already. Right?" With arrogance and contempt, Louis Doyon jeered at Leona and Henri. Droplets of spittle from his explosive words clung to his prized handlebar mustache.

When he turned around to wipe his mouth, Leona's eyes shot hateful pitchforks into her father's butt. Her intended, Henri, sat calm and unfazed as he stated in a controlled voice, "*Très bien*, we will be married as soon as possible."

It had been just a few days since the Doyon family returned from the "Granddaddy of Montana Rodeos" at Wolf Point. Papa Doyon, keen on rodeos since his days with Buffalo Bill Cody's Wild West show, made it a point to attend the oldest annual state rodeo, held on the second weekend of July every year.

The three days of fun featured a whirlwind of activities for everyone: a parade, a carnival, bed races, gun fights, pie-eating contests and street dances. The rodeo was world-class with steer roping, bronc riding, and a wild horse race known as the Wild Horse Stampede.

The young adult group of French Canadians, made up of the Doyons and Provosts, encountered the French David family on the first evening street dance of the rodeo. With the backdrop of Missouri River cottonwoods, the giant, orange, prairie moon hung in the dusty purple sky. '*Amour*' was everywhere.

Enveloped in the magic of the evening, Henri and Leona danced. He found Leona fun-loving and high spirited. But he also discovered something else about her. When Henri placed his hand on her back, Leona yelped in pain.

"*Mon Dieu*, what is wrong, Leona?"

With tears in her eyes, she answered, "My father used the black snake whip on me."

Not able to wait any longer, Henri turned Leona and gently raised her blouse to expose a better view. Purplish bruises and wounds of red gashes crisscrossed her back.

When he found his voice, he whispered, "But why would he do such a thing?"

Leona swallowed, "When I came in from plowing the field, Papa said my younger brother forgot to close the chicken coop—being the oldest, I should have been a better teacher for him."

Henri wanted to kiss the wounds and wash them with his tears, but the gaiety of the street dancers demanded frivolity and fun. Instead, Henri took Leona's petite, warm hand in his and led her back into the dancing—all along making plans for Leona's future, as his wife.

Papa Doyon insinuated a disgrace to Leona's virtue. She wed within three weeks of the rodeo, although it did not prove to be a shotgun wedding.

Because Leona's parents were devout Catholics, Leona and Henri were married in the local Catholic chapel. The bride wore white and was attended by her cousin, Alma Provost. Henri's brother Marcel served as the best man. The wedding celebration lasted several days.

Perhaps Leona did not love Henri at the time of their wedding, but she had hopes to find love. What follows is a wedding love song written by Leona and her mother in outdated or slang French-Canadian. Roughly translated it laments how much Leona would miss her mother, but her new husband would now be her protector and champion. It is unknown if the poem was sung or recited at the wedding, or if it was gifted to Henri in private.

These are pictures of the handwritten copy of Leona's Wedding Poem in French.

(1) 1920
Song Called
"The day of Our Marriage"
Or Le Jour du Marriage

Le jour du Marriage
C'est le seul jour aux bonheur.
Le Moment le plus triste
C'est de mi voir parti
Separer de ma tendre mère (Bis)
Pour ne jamais revenir

(2)
Chere époux me sera tu tendre
Comme tu me la promis
Ton serment me fais présence
Dans ton alliance fini
Soit fidele à tes promesse
Conserve moi ton amour
Dans les bras de ma tendre mère (Bis)
Tu m'enlève c'est pour toujour

(3)
Pour moi ma bonne mère pleur
C'est de mi voir parti
Pour les état étrangère
Dans ces dangereux navire

(2)
tu sera le sur la terre
Mon protecteur et mon guide
tu sera mon gouverneur (Bis)
Dan les eaux et les rapids (Bis)

(4)
Adieu donc la Compagné
Adieu donc tous mes ami
Ce soir je vous abandonne
C'est pour suivre mon mari
Je m'en vas prendre l'ouvrage
L'ouvrage avec mon mari
Je m'en vas prendre mon ménage (Bis)
Dieu bénira mon ennui

(5)
Adieu donc cher père et mère
Adieu donc cher frère et sœur
Avec peine je vous abandonne
Je reviendrai vous voir
Je reviendrai vous voir
Avec mon fidele amant
Cessez donc ma tendre mère (Bis)
Cessez donc pleurer pas tant

Leona (Copy)

~

The Threshing Crew

Inez's journal, January 28, 2013:

> *"My father and his three brothers—Ed, Leon, and Marcel—decided to start a large threshing crew in northern Montana on the Canadian border of Saskatchewan. They had a crew with huge trains of threshers—harvesting wheat, barley, some rye and even some wild rice."*

Throughout the harvest season, the David brothers rented out their threshing "rig" business as they moved from grain field to grain field. The operation included combine harvesters, crews of 10 to 12 men, and support wagons, tractors, and horses. The combine machinery blended the steps of harvesting and threshing in a single process. Huge threshing machines separated the wheat kernels from the straw stalks.

Spring and winter wheat crops were harvested in late May to early September. Since the brothers were fellow homesteaders with their own dryland farms, they knew the importance of being available to harvest during the best of conditions. If the timing was off, they were gambling with the farmer's livelihood.

The adage "make hay while the sun shines" was especially true and vital in a wheat harvest. The warmth of the sun helped the stalks dry and separate from the chaff. However, if left too long in the field, over-dried seed heads might break apart, dropping the grain kernels to the ground. It was also wise to get the crop out of the field before the wet season. Strong winds and rainstorms also shattered the seed heads and destroyed grain crops.

The dirty work of threshing grain in the 1920s required long, exhausting days throughout the heat of the summer. The marathon hours and the continuous dust and debris from threshing were not good for Henri's unresolved lung condition. His brothers relinquished the tractor driver position to him because they realized he had become weak and unhealthy.

Dust and hay debris flurried in the breeze of the wheat field. Henri, red-faced, stood legs apart and torso bent forward. He struggled to catch his breath after each series of coughs.

Marcel rushed to Henri. Water sloshed in the bucket he carried to his brother. Offering a dipper of water, Marcel said, "Are you okay? That was a bad coughing spell. You should rest."

Left weak and damp with sweat, Henri managed sips of water between the uncontrolled coughing. He resorted to shallow breathing and splinted his right ribs with his hands to ward off punishing stabs of pain with each lung-expanding-cough.

Henri flopped down to rest next to the tractor where a ribbon of shade offered some relief from the sun. With a slight smile, Henri looked up to Marcel and said between intermittent coughing, "You just want to take over my position, *kahf*. . . as the main tractor driver."

"Oh no. You keep that coveted position," answered the younger brother. "I don't have your focus and concentration. I get bored, my mind wanders."

"*Oui*, you are a dreamer," said Henri as he accepted his brother's helping hand up.

~

Manning the Cook-Car

Inez's journaling continues, January 28, 2013:

> *. . . They [the David brothers] also had a number of cook-cars and this is where Mom [Leona] and Aunt Ella, Uncle Leon's wife, cooked the meals for the threshing crews. Mom talked about making pie shells and just before a lunch or meal, they would fill the pie shells for a nice hot meat pie for dinner."*

A vital part of the threshing crew, the cook-car—sometimes called the cook shack— served as kitchen, dining facility, and headquarters for the entire operation. The standard traveling "shack" measured 8 feet wide by 16 feet long, and 7 feet high. To handle the weight, it sat on a geared, high-wheeled wagon and moved with the threshing rigs and equipment. Daily in these structures, women cooked enough food to fortify the hungry men of the work crew.

Pie crusts, made with lard and flour, were used for both dinner (midday meal) and dessert. Three meals a day were served in the cook-car and two light lunches were taken out to the workers for their coffee breaks at 9:00 a.m. and 3:00 p.m. Making these meals required the stove to be on nearly the entire day.

"Leona! Your pie crusts are about to burn!" Ella brushed her formidable right forearm across her damp brow.

Drawn by the threshing activity beyond the kitchen car, Leona watched half-dozen workers pitch dried wheat shocks into a massive side-by-side train of harvester-threshing machinery. The noisy equipment threshed the grain from the stalks as straw blew out the back of the machine. The grain kernels filtered through a spout into jute sacks. Nearby, two men hand-sewed the grain-filled sacks closed. Reluctantly, Leona turned her attention back to her baking.

The cook-car was hotter than hot. In preparation for the threshing crew's meals, the women had peeled, chopped, stirred, and cooked since early light. Opposites in most every way, Ella and Leona were thrown together as cooks because their husbands, being brothers and partners, were also co-owners of the harvesting and threshing company.

Yet even the hottest kitchen could not melt away the icy tension that existed between the two women.

Ella delivered more criticism. "I hope you remembered to put salt in the pie dough. . . . I swear, any dummy can cook, but I can't trust you to do anything right."

Embarrassed to be caught daydreaming and criticized for her baking, Leona seethed in mute response. In resentment, she scowled with squinted eyes and pursed lips. *I'd rather be anywhere else than in this sweltering cook-car with you.*

Leona dared not utter her next thoughts. *Who does she think she is? Well, I think she is just a bossy Indian!*

In appearance, Leona was slight and fair skinned with curly, auburn hair. She categorized Ella's complexion, dark hair and stockiness as features of a Native American, although that was just speculation. The thought that Ella was of Indian heritage, as well as a devout Roman Catholic, gave Leona more reasons to resent her sister-in-law.

Ella, married over seven years, was six years older than Leona. She ran the cook-car with order and efficiency, just like she organized her home and raised her three children. With the age difference, she tended to treat Leona more like a child than a peer, and did not hide that she opposed Henri's marriage to Leona.

The most apparent difference between the wives showed in their cooking abilities. The belittling became a point of contention between the two women. Ella grew up in Bottineau, North Dakota and developed into an experienced cook while she worked alongside her adoptive mother, to feed work crews.

By contrast, Leona, the teenage newlywed and kitchen novice, had limited cooking experience while growing up. She understood mechanical equipment and was a whiz with a sewing machine, but baking, seasonings, and the timing of food preparation stumped her. Attempts to teach her how to cook did not go well, for Leona was very prideful and downright touchy about her shortcomings.

Before she opened the hot oven door, Leona grabbed a handful of apron material as protection for her hands. Still thinking of outside, she considered, *I could really be a lot of help, if only Henri would teach me how to drive the tractor.*

Leona removed the overly dark-brown pie shells from the oven and placed them on the table to cool. Previously cooked shells stacked up next to the table, one on top of the other, like a totem pole. She grabbed a pie shell and began spooning the mixture of hot meat and vegetables into it. Her slight smile revealed a pleasure in providing such a substantial meal for the workers.

However, after the last pie shell was filled, a clouded notion came to Leona. *Mon Dieu! I DID put salt in the pie dough— didn't I?*

~

Henry

In the second week of 1922 Rose Doyon delivered a baby boy, Maurice Lawrence Doyon, the last of her thirteen children. As Rose's childbearing days concluded, her oldest daughter, Leona (Doyon David) began to show with her first pregnancy.

When the time came for Leona's baby to be born, husband Henri was working with the threshing crew in northeastern Montana. The soon-to-be parents lived in a small claim shanty out in what Leona called the "boonies." After Leona labored for several days, an elderly midwife was called to help with the delivery.

Finally, on June 6th, the baby boy was born. Blue and not breathing, he did not respond to the usual slap on the bottom or the clearing of mucus from his nose and mouth. The midwife placed the limp baby in a pan of warm water, then quickly dunked him into a pan of cool water—no response. Again, the baby went into the alternate baths of warm water followed by the cool water—still no response. Not willing to give up, the experienced midwife said a quick prayer, and with vigor, plunged the unresponsive newborn once more into the warm, and then to the cooler water. This time the baby started to gasp and cry.

The baby weighed well over eight pounds. He received the very French-sounding name of Henry Louis David. Although named for his father, he was not an official "Junior." His grandfathers were both "Louis," and that became the baby's middle name.

Troubles of infancy were not yet over for little Henry. A tight cord of tissue that anchored his tongue to the bottom of the mouth was discovered. This tongue-tied condition did not interfere with the baby's nursing. However, it bothered his Grandpa Louis Doyon, who thought it would affect Henry's speech.

At the age of two months, while Henry was being cared for by his grandparents, his Grandpa Doyon decided to release the prominent cord by clipping it with scissors. The procedure went without any problems. But when Leona returned and attempted to put little Henry to breast to feed, he could not suck properly. He was unable to suck from a baby bottle, either.

The family panicked when the baby cried with hunger, but he could not be fed. Feeding with a cup yielded minimal results until someone offered him some canned Eagle Brand sweetened condensed milk, a special blend of thickened milk and sugar used as the base ingredient for a variety of desserts. Even though the canned milk was diluted with water, Henry loved the taste and became quite roly-poly.

Eventually Henry grew out of his baby fat, but he kept his sweet tooth all through life. And unlike his mother, Henry developed a love of milk—whether sweetened condensed or regular.

Little Henry was all boy. He grew into a rough-and-tumble toddler. The prairie and wheat fields were entertaining and became familiar playgrounds to him. He adored animals the most, but bugs held a fascination for him too.

Mature beyond his actual age, Henry's constant companions were his two David cousins and four Doyon boy uncles. The older boys of both sides of the family accepted and nurtured Henry. After their chores, they taught him how to play Army and Cowboys and Indians. All the while, they referred to Henry as "our little buddy."

~

Family Changes

The David family dynamics started to change. All of Henri's brothers and sisters, except Marcel, were married. Births of grandchildren added to the family. However, the joy of young children did not offset the sad death of the family's matriarch, Josephine David (née Fayard). She died in 1924, at the age of 58, while living in Bainville, Montana.

Josephine and Louis David had probably relocated to Bainville from Wolf Point sometime after Henri's wedding in 1920. Other French relatives, such as Regis and Rosalie Barthelon, also lived there. It may be that the elderly Davids returned to Bainville to be close or to live with Alice, their older daughter. Alice had married Antonio Sala soon after entering the United States in 1908, and she had four children.

Louis David, distraught over his wife's death, wanted to return to his mother country. He never embraced the Montana prairie as his home. He longed for the Alps and the Grenoble area of his beloved France—that is where he wanted to die. To grant their father's wishes, his "boys" pooled their money to buy him passage home to France. He would not be alone. His oldest daughter, Antoinette, and her family remained just outside of Grenoble. His health status during that time is unknown. However, he lived for six more years and died in France in 1930.

The Doyon's side of the family also experienced a type of change. One afternoon, several of Leona's sisters snuck next to their father while he napped and playfully clipped off one side of his big, dark, nasty-looking handlebar moustache. He had worn the moustache for over twenty-five years, and each day it had become more and more disgusting.

When he awoke—*Mon Dieu!* What a commotion of yelling and cursing. When his anger settled down, he shaved off the remaining half of the moustache. That was the end of his facial hair, he never grew it back.

However, no one was punished—with a black snake whip or otherwise—as when Leona had lived at home. Perhaps their father had mellowed. More likely, punishment was withheld because the prank was led by Leona's sister Sedonia (Sid), the novitiate and future Catholic nun, Sister Providence.

One thing had not changed in the Doyon household—*joie de vivre* still thrived, even if Papa Doyon did not always appreciate it.

~

The Ride

Little Henry crouched at the edge of the wheat field. The freckled, round-faced toddler focused his attention on a dead grasshopper covered with black ants. After a minute, Henry reached into his pants pocket and fished out a small, straight twig to poke at the carcass. The pocket held other treasures as well: a bent nail, a small gray feather, a 6-inch piece of string, a half-eaten gingersnap cookie, and a smooth white rock. His dog, Rover, a black and white Border Collie, lay in the nearby shade.

"Hhheennnnnrrrryyy. Time to go." Realizing the call was for him, he brushed three ants from the stick, thrust it into his pocket, and hurried towards his mother's voice.

His mother, Leona, stood next to the cook wagon. One of her hands rested on her hip, the other shaded her eyes as she watched her son scamper towards her.

"Mama, why are we leaving so early?"

"We must go to town to see your papa in the hospital," said Leona. She ushered the boy and his dog into the dilapidated Model T.

Leona muttered under her breath, "Driving a Model T is said to be like doing the Charleston while loading a musket after a big night at a speakeasy. Well, we'll see."

Positioned in the driver's seat, Leona stared straight ahead. Her hands vise-gripped the black steering wheel. At her hesitation, Henry cocked his head to look sideways at his mother, as if to ask a question—but he remained silent.

Leona cricked her neck side to side and shook her hands before repositioning them on the steering wheel. She took several deep breaths. After a while, she sighed and thought to herself: *Come on Leona! You've watched Henri start this Ford hundreds of times. Now it's your turn. Driving a car can't be any harder than controlling a six-horse team, can it?*

A small smile played on her lips before she acted. *At least there's an electric starter.* Copying what she had seen Henri do, Leona first engaged the hand brake. She moved the spark lever, left of the steering wheel, upwards to keep the spark plug from firing. With her right hand, Leona slightly opened the throttle stalk on the right side of the steering wheel, to give some gas, then turned the ignition key to battery. Without delay, she pressed her left heel against the starter button, located on the floor. She advanced the spark lever to adjust the engine timing and increased the throttle.

To her delight, Leona heard a smooth-ticking engine, and switched the ignition key over to magneto to save battery power. With her left hand, she released the brake by moving the transmission lever to the straight up position. Utilizing her hands and feet, along with the gears, pedals, and transmission stalk, she set the car into a forward moving gear. In triumph, Leona aimed the moving car south towards Scobey.

All the while, Leona kept her vigilance, for she had never driven an automobile before. *I'm off to a good start . . . but it only solves half my problems. Now to keep the Ford driving.*

Leona, little Henry, and Rover bounced their way to town. Most of the 15-mile route was unpaved. People usually made their own roads through the grassland, and that was what Leona attempted. Deep ruts formed in the dirt paths, but often these were hidden by debris from the frequent prairie winds. The Model T, durable and maneuverable in most terrains, tended to wobble and shimmy as its thin tires followed the road ruts.

Montana's prairies were deceptive and never as flat as they appeared. Even though a person could see for miles, runoff water often caused hidden ripples and cracks in the landscape. Running water also formed deep gullies that later became dry creek beds. In that part of the country, the French Canadians called this a "coulee," No doubt *coulee* came from the French *couler*, to flow.

Just when Leona thought she could accelerate on a flat area, the Model T hit a coulee section and the vehicle bucked to and fro like a bronco. Lifted from their seats, the mother, son, and dog were tossed back and forth and side to side with each ridge and depression. Clouds of dust were left in their wake. Laugher and squeals filled the car.

"Weeeeeee! Mama, do it some more. That's fun," yelled Henry. Rover joined in with gleeful barking.

After several stalling incidents, and an hour since starting out, the Model T arrived in Scobey. Leona dropped Little Henry and Rover off at her sister's house.

"Tell Papa I love and miss him," were Little Henry's parting words as his mother set off for the hospital.

With precision, Leona drove to the Stinchcombe Hospital and found Henri resting in a six-bed ward. Pale and drawn, his breathing was labored and interrupted by a hacking cough. Despite his apparent illness, he showed improvement from the day before.

"Leona! I didn't expect to see you . . . and you have brought me something."

"Yes, only a change of clothing, but your son sends his love. Let's get you cleaned up before your dinner." Leona gathered bathing supplies for a sponge bath and a shave. With all of Henri's illnesses, she had become quite proficient with the straight razor.

When visiting hours came to an end, Henri said, "Leona, I've been thinking. You should learn how to drive the Model T."

Leona nodded her head and smiled.

~

Living in Scobey

Inez's journal, January 28, 2013:

> *"After my brother Henry was born, my father [Henri] was so ill with lung problems and not getting any better, my parents decided to move into Scobey and bought a mercantile store—with his three brothers. They all had a share of the store's operations and it went by the name, 'David Brothers Mercantile.' That's what they had called it when I was born in 1926. (I still have a roll of two-inch paper tape with 'David Brothers Mercantile' on it). My father was in charge of going to market, shopping and ordering all the goods."*

No longer did Henri drive the threshing machines or farm his homestead. The manual labor of these activities proved too physical and taxing for him and the constant stir of dust and straw debris from grain threshing overwhelmed his weakened lungs. Plagued with coughing, painful breathing, and fluid buildup in and around his lungs, Henri found himself a patient of the Scobey Stinchcombe Hospital throughout most of the year. Sometimes the doctors called Henri's diagnosis pneumonia, other times they said it was pleurisy.

Henri relinquished his dryland farm to his younger brother; later, the homestead would sell for a good price. In time, the threshing company and equipment were also sold. Daniels County Museum in Scobey later displayed the David brothers' threshing machines as part of the area's farm history.

Before long, the four David brothers invested into what was called a "mercantile store"—a classy name for a general store. It may have been the only store in town. If so, this was where people purchased necessities such as food staples, animal feed, seed, and farm implements, as well as furniture, fabric, clothing, and—Henri's favorite items—shoes.

All the David brothers took part in running the mercantile store. They appeared better suited for retail business than for farming. Eduard, Henri's older brother, served as the store's bookkeeper. Younger brothers Leon and Marcel were the shop clerks and took care of selling the merchandise. Henri became the store buyer. When his health improved, he traveled to purchase whatever was needed for the store.

To his delight, Henri could finally wear a three-piece suit to work, with a starched, white dress shirt and fine-looking shoes. The other David brothers also seemed most comfortable in Sunday-best clothes. Leona recalled that the brothers differed from other men in that they preferred to dress this way, even for casual occasions. It raised questions as to whether they truly came from a farming background in France, or from a different lifestyle—one of class and elegance.

Henri and his brothers were particular about how their shirts should be starched and prepared. A shirt was never allowed to be hung after being ironed. They expected each one to be folded—as if processed by a modern dry cleaner—to maintain the creases, even though they were pressed by hand at home.

Buying excursions took Henri to places such as Minneapolis, Chicago, and Grand Rapids, Michigan. He always brought back something special from these trips for Leona. These presents included leather shoes, beautiful leather purses, furniture, and accent pieces, such as a Victor-Victrola record player, a curio cabinet, and a pedestal battery radio. When Henri brought back a treadle sewing machine, Leona taught herself some new techniques and began sewing dresses for herself and her sisters.

For himself, Henri purchased a Panama hat made of toquilla straw—a popular style of the time. This *chapeau* became the signature piece in his wardrobe.

Henri, Leona, and Little Henry moved to the city limits of Scobey and purchased a brown clapboard house with white trim. It was surrounded with a fence, flower garden, lawn, shrubbery, and numerous trees. Were Henri and Leona living beyond their means with these trappings of middle-class Montanans? How could they afford such purchases? Whether it was due to the revenue from the threshing company, proceeds from selling of the homestead, or the prosperity of the mercantile, the couple no longer lived like dirt farmers or resided in a claim shanty out in the boonies.

Returning to Scobey brought more family gatherings with the Doyons and the Davids. However, many pleasant family get-togethers would be upset once the subject of religion surfaced. Leona's father, very opinionated and domineering, was a staunch supporter of the Catholic Church. Henri and Leona were not churchgoers, and no longer had faith in the Catholic Church. Henri, typically easy going and mild-mannered, would often argue the points he thought were wrong with the father-in-law's religion.

Another aspect of the couple's rebellion, may have been in their use of birth control. This enraged Mr. Doyon, for his traditions revolved around Catholicism and a large family. No doubt he questioned Henri and Leona as to why they only had one child in six years of marriage. The younger couple had the modern middle-class view that they should have a choice about how many children they brought into the world.

Leona and Henri used several forms of birth control. One applied method was what Leona called her "pessary." Throughout history different forms of pessaries were used to either blocked the path of sperm going through the cervix to the uterus, or to kill the sperm with a chemical reaction.

In the 1920s pessaries corrected uterine displacement by repositioning the uterus forward or backward. They were made in different shapes and from various materials, such as rubber or brass. However, such devices could also function as birth control, and later were recognized as diaphragms, cervical caps, or intrauterine devices.

Leona described her pessary as small gold ring. It was not known how she obtained this device. It could have been prescribed by a doctor, or perhaps, it came from one of Henri's buying trips.

Working around Henri's progressive illness, the couple made their choices about residence, clothing, religion, and birth control. They appeared to be living their life, as they wanted.

~

Inez Rose David

Along with birth control and smaller families, the middle class in the 1920s moved away from midwives and home deliveries. Instead, many opted for obstetrical care in what was assumed to be the safer care of a modern hospital. This may have been the reason Henri and Leona David's second child, was born at the Stinchcombe Hospital in Scobey, Montana, Daniels County, on August 11, 1926. Leona went into labor while Papa Henri, again ill with lung problems, was a hospital patient.

A cute, dark haired, hospital nurse named Inez cared for Leona throughout her labor and delivery. This nurse made such an impression on Leona, that when the time arrived to name the new baby girl, "Inez" became the chosen name. The child's middle name came from Leona's mother, Rose. The family would pronounce the baby's name as Inès, even though it was spelled I-N-E-Z. Inez weighed 6 pounds and the delivery proved easy—especially compared to the difficult birth of her brother Henry.

Evidently, Inez had such a full head of dark hair that the nurses cut it into a "roaring twenties flapper" hair bob with bangs. It is not known if Nurse Inez had a hand in the haircut, but it came as quite a shock to Leona when her brand-new baby girl appeared with such a grownup hairdo. As it turned out, Inez wore her hair in a similar bob with bangs until she was ten years old.

Inez thrived on Leona's breast milk and put on weight. Papa Henri called her his "little China-man" due to her dark straight hair, her big round cheeks, and her small, dark brown eyes peeking through eye slits. Happy and sweet, she displayed an easy smile that lit up her face. Inez clung contentedly to a knitted gray shawl that went everywhere with her.

Grandpa Doyon prided himself in teaching all the family babies to stand straight legged, like a candlestick, on his one hand. That was until it came to Inez. Try as he might, Grandpa could not achieve the trick with this granddaughter. No one ever determined whether she was too timid or too weak to perform for her grandpa.

The four Doyon "aunties" ranged from teens to early twenties. They went wild for Inez since the last five babies of the family had been boys. The aunties carried, cuddled, kissed, cooed at, and dressed up their living doll at every opportunity. Perhaps all that loving as an infant increased her longevity, for Inez was not a strong child.

When Inez outgrew her baby fat, she developed into a frail little girl. Her baby book notes that she had whooping cough when three years old. Later, she was diagnosed with a heart murmur, and the doctor said she had a rheumatic heart.

Leona discouraged Inez from overexertion when she played. If the toddler did start to run, she would stop abruptly and melt into a squatting position—a common stance taken by children with heart disease. At these times, Leona reported Inez would say, "I tired."

~

The Radio

". . . seven, eight, nine—Tunney is up." Radio announcer, Graham McNamee, shrieked with excitement above the steady roar of the ringside crowd. A multitude of over 100,000 people watched the boxing match at Soldier Field in Chicago on the evening of September 22, 1927 as millions more listened on the radio.

Boxing, a fashionable spectator sport during the 1920s, had also developed a large following over the newly established radio airwaves. One American professional boxer and icon of the era, William Harrison "Jack" Dempsey, held the title of World Heavyweight Champion from 1919 to 1926 due to his iron strength and killer left hook. He was best known for thrilling knockout victories that often occurred in just seconds of the onset of the fight. However, in the previous Dempsey–Tunney match a year before (on September 23, 1926), Dempsey was unable to knockout or defeat Gene Tunney for the heavyweight title. The rematch, scheduled for a year later, was now in progress.

The National Broadcasting Company (NBC) estimated fifty million people around the world tuned in for this fight. Everyone from sheep shearers in Australia's outback, to U.S. marines stationed in Shanghai, to a scientific team on an iceberg near Greenland, to patrons in cafes from Paris to Rio de Janeiro followed the fight over the airwaves. Before long, Scobey residents learned the only radio in town happened to be owned by Henri David.

After dinner, relatives and friends began to arrive at the home of Henri and Leona David on that warm "Indian summer" Thursday evening. Leona attempted to put her children to bed while Henri, still recovering from his most recent hospital stay for pleurisy, welcomed their guests. Soon it was standing room only, as more people arrived at the house. Men, as well as women, gathered in the doorway and leaned in from the windowsills.

Perplexed, Leona looked over at Henri, "Where are all these people coming from?"

Henri shrugged, then hoisted the wide-awake one-year-old, Inez into his arms, "They've heard about our radio." The dark mahogany pedestal cabinet battery radio, recently purchased in Grand Rapids, stood in a place of prominence in the front parlor.

Jack Dempsey lost this rematch although Gene Tunney's second victory remains controversial with the fight coined as "The Battle of the Long Count." A new rule mandated a fighter go to a neutral corner when the opponent was knocked down. It appeared Tunney gained an advantage when he was knocked down with Dempsey's strong left hook in the seventh round.

But the referee, Dave Barry, delayed a good five seconds in the countdown as he attempted to move Dempsey to a neutral corner. Tunney took a nine count before getting up to resume the fight—14 seconds after being knocked down. However, an inconsistency occurred in the next round. When Dempsey was knocked down, the referee started the count immediately even though Tunney did not move to a neutral corner.

The fight continued for the full ten rounds. Dempsey, not used to boxing for a full fight, showed fatigue. Tunney won the match with a unanimous decision and retained his heavyweight title. With the buildup of the second match between these two boxers and the controversial "long count" that resulted that night, the Heavyweight Championship rematch of September 1927 became known, at the time, as the fight of the century.

Leona had little understanding of boxing or what the "Battle of the Long Count" meant. She just remembered sharing the novelty of a new radio with family, friends, and strangers while they gathered for what proved to be forty minutes of history and boxing extravaganza.

~

Travels of 1928

A large Doyon-Turcotte family reunion occurred in Sainte-Rose-de-Watford in the late Spring of 1928. Many of Leona's immediate family attended, along with numerous Doyon and Turcotte cousins. During the gathering, Leona's family met Grandfather Evangeliste Turcotte's second wife, Virginie Laliberte for the first time. The couple had married in 1921 and celebrated their seventh anniversary at the reunion.

Delima Rose (neé Provost), Evangeliste's first wife and Rose's mother, died soon after Leona's family emigrated to the United States. Even though she had a chronic heart condition, Delima Rose's death resulted from strangulation by a large thyroid goiter.

As a little girl, one of Leona's special activities with this favorite grand-mére was to press leaves and pansies from the garden into the Bible. Days before leaving Canada, Grand-mére had suggested to her then ten-year-old granddaughter that they try planting the seeds from an apple core near the Turcotte house. This way Leona could leave something of herself at her birthplace before embarking on a new life.

Leona exclaimed as her car entered the driveway of the Turcotte residence, "Oh, look at my apple tree!" A wide grin appeared on her face when she saw the pink-and white-blossomed apple tree next to her grandparents' house. To Leona's delight, an apple tree grew in the exact spot where she had planted seeds, fifteen years earlier. She knew the tree welcomed her back to Sainte-Rose-de-Watford.

After the Doyon-Turcotte family reunion in Québec, according to captions written on photographs taken at the time, Henri, Leona, and Leona's parents visited with Rose's younger brother, Albert, and other relatives elsewhere in Canada.

The David side of the family was also included in the travels. All of Henri's siblings had gone their separate ways with the death of their mother, the return of their father to France, and the dissolvement of the partnership of the David Brothers Mercantile.

Edouard, still the main farmer of the family, moved his wife from Saskatchewan to a homestead in the plains of Alberta, Canada; later, they relocated to Enderby, British Columbia, to establish a dairy. Younger brother Leon and his growing family moved around from North Dakota to Regina, Saskatchewan, then to Wolf Point, Montana, followed by Klamath Falls, Oregon. They finally settled in Southern California where Leon left farming for the liquor industry. The youngest brother, Marcel, moved to Arizona for his health—it was said he had tuberculosis.

All three of the David sisters had married and moved on from Scobey. Alice lived in Bainsville, Montana, Marthe moved to Washington state, and Lea had established a home in Idaho.

Therefore, with this Canadian trip, Henri and Leona enlarged their excursion to see Henri's brothers, Leon and Edouard in Regina, Saskatchewan. This trip to see Henri's brothers had a greater purpose than mere visitation—it was an act of farewell. Doctors told Henri to move to a milder climate, for his health was in jeopardy.

Part Three

Childhood
1928–1932

~

Klamath Falls, Oregon, 1928

"Mama, the dog likes me." The lad crouched, petting an old brown dog of questionable origin. The freckled-faced, six-year-old boy beamed. Henry never met a dog he didn't love. Leona nodded her head but kept her attention on her toddler, Inez, who chased yellow butterflies in the tall grass.

On the trip west from Montana, the David family stopped in Oregon, south of Crater Lake at an auto-camp that accommodated automobile travelers. The spectacular views of the renowned lake with its bluest of blue water and unknown depth captivated Leona as she thought, *This would be wonderful for the kids to live in a place like this, so beautiful and majestic.*

Henri and Leona were in search of a new home. Scobey doctors convinced Henri his health was in jeopardy if he remained in Montana. Once he understood the implications, he did not delay moving from Scobey. After Inez's second birthday, the family loaded their baggage into a new Model A Ford. Other items, such as furniture, were sold or stored with the Doyons.

The family ventured on the ultimate road trip, along a highway that followed the old Lewis and Clark Trail, which stretched from Montana, across the northern tip of Idaho, along the shared state borders of Washington and Oregon, and on to the Pacific Ocean. Possibly, the Davids' search for a new residence coincided with visits to Henri's siblings: Lea in Idaho, Marthe in Washington, and Marcel in Arizona. However, with an undecided destination, Henri and Leona believed they would recognize the right place to reside when they came across it.

Klamath Falls, Oregon, 1928

It had been a smooth trip, except when a suitcase fell and crushed Henri's beloved hat. To his dismay, the large Panama straw hat, prominent in the previous spring and summer's photographs, was ruined. It seemed laughable to Leona at the time, but a premonition gnawed at her peace of mind—*Is this an omen of things to come?*

Inez squealed as a butterfly dipped towards her. Yet, an uneasy feeling crept over Leona. She looked around, in hopes of seeing her husband. *What's taking Henri so long? He didn't sleep well last night, and he seems very pale this morning.*

She directed her son, "Henry, watch your sister for me."

Seeing only one person in the area, Leona approached a large, doughy man in soiled work clothes with a toothpick in his mouth. Her concern triggered a mixture of French and English, "*Excusez-moi Monsieur, mon mari*—ah, my husband went in to use, ah—*les toilettes*, a long time ago. Could you see if he is well, *s'il vous plaît*?"

The man looked right though Leona, continued to chew on his wooden pick and walked away. *Did he not hear me? Was my French accent too strong to understand?*

With no time to waste, Leona drew near the entrance to the bathroom and rapped quickly on the door. "Hell-o. . . . *Est-ce que tu vas bien?* —are you all right?"

Without waiting a moment longer, she yanked the door open to reveal a pale Henri passed out on the hard dirt floor. But the shocking sight was the blood clinging to his chin and staining across the front of his white, starched shirt. Henri's eyes fluttered open, only to spew more blood with each cough.

In dreamlike action, Leona called out for help. From the previously deserted area came willing souls in response. A park ranger stepped forward, loaded Henri into a car, and drove off to the nearest hospital, in Klamath Falls. Leona followed with the children in the Model A Ford.

After a medical evaluation, Henri was admitted to the hospital for the hemorrhaging of his lungs. Leona and the children were directed to stay at a boarding house close by, to wait for Henri's recovery—if he would recover.

Leona studied Henri's face—so pale and gaunt as he lay in the hospital bed. *Oh, Henri, how many hospital stays have there been in our eight years of marriage? Yet, you've always refused to give into those frail lungs of yours . . . and you never remain hospitalized a minute longer than required. Will this time be different?*

The somber doctor exited the hospital room. Henri lay in his bed, looking out the window. *What do I do now?*

Leona entered the hospital room, coming up to Henri to squeeze his hand.

Henri masked his worrisome thoughts and focused on his wife. *Leona is full of color. She seems well rested and excited.* "You look happy, *mon cheri.*"

"Yes, I am. I've just come back from seeing Edna Zetzman's farm. You know, the one I said was for sale."

"Edna Zetzman? Who is she?"

"Don't you remember, I told you about the woman I met who works at the boarding house where the kids and I are staying. She has a farm on about 300 acres of land, a little outside of Klamath Falls. She needs to sell it fast . . . the asking price is good."

"Leona, I'm not in any condition to run a farm . . ."

"Well, I knew that's what you were going to say. Edna told me her husband was disabled in the War— that's how he got the land—from some sort of homestead grant for war veterans. Anyway, they have had hired help all along, and never had any problems. Besides, I know a lot about farming and such.

"Oh, Henri. . . . You've got to see this place. It has so many appealing qualities. The land has been cultivated for crops such as alfalfa, oats, barley, and has several grain silos. There's a lovely, big house with a nice yard and barns—the main barn, a dairy, horse corrals, sheep pens, enclosures for chickens and turkeys—with the animals to go with them. Of course, there's pasture for the livestock."

Henri pushed up on a forearm, "That sounds very nice, but . . ."

"That's not all. There's a big, established vegetable garden. And berry patches—with bushes of gooseberries and a yellow variety of raspberries, and small pond that forms from the runoff of the drainage ditch. The kids will be able to ice skate when the pond freezes in the winter."

"That's the point, isn't it, Leona. The main purpose of relocating was to live in a better climate."

"I know, but Edna said Klamath Fall's nickname is 'Oregon's City of Sunshine,' because the sun shines 300 days of the year.

"I want this place, Henri. I like Klamath Falls and feel at home here. And Edna and I are already good friends." Henri thought as he searched Leona's face. *She is still young and full of spunk. She's been a good wife, never asking for much . . .* "I'll think about it and have a look when I get out of here. Okay?" Leona hugged Henri with exuberance.

By mid-September, once Henri's illness crisis abated, the Davids purchased those 300 acres of the Zetzman property. Located in Klamath County in South-Central Oregon, the farm was eight miles southeast of Klamath Falls, and less than 15 miles from the California-Oregon border. The surrounding landscape offered the Cascade Mountain Range to the west of the property and the high desert to the southeast.

Besides the basic farm, the property possessed its very own hill less than a half mile from the house. Uninteresting and arid, "Miller Hill's" summit peaked at an elevation of 4,491 feet. It remained fallow with only stunted trees, scrub and sagebrush. At the time, the parched hill did not appear to be useful for anything, except as free range for the ground squirrels.

The farm site had manmade features that would prove to be important in the future. A newly completed wooden bridge connected the farm to the main road. The bridge passed over the large diversion canal planned to run alongside the west side of property. Another addition included the recently built Klamath Falls Municipal Airport (later called Kingsley Field), with a gravel runway and one fixed-base operator. The airfield was north-east of the farm. Despite the enthusiasm for flying in the 1920s, the airplanes approaching the airport were inconspicuous as lazy flies on a summer day.

A strong friendship developed between Leona and the previous owner, Edna Zetzman, a matronly lady some 15 years older than Leona. Mrs. Zetzman, as Inez always addressed her, became a great source of information, and answered many questions about the surrounding area.

"What was the need for so many big canals around here?" asked Leona when Mrs. Zetzman came for a visit to see how the family was adjusting.

"Oh, because we had too much water in one place and not enough in another. There really wasn't any available grassland for livestock. Instead, the pioneers found lakebeds and wetlands, so they started digging canals to help drain the water from the land. Haven't you heard of the Klamath Reclamation Project?"

Leona nodded, "Isn't that where water is routed into California and Arizona?"

"Yes, the Project drained miles of former lake beds and wetlands of the Lower Klamath Lake to supply irrigation water for farms in the Klamath Basin, as well as to other states."

Edna took a swallow of her lemonade, then continued. "But mostly the marshes were drained to reclaim nearly 200,000 acres of farmable land to be offered as homesteads. As I told you before, my husband received this homestead because he was a veteran of the Great War. The good part—the area still has plenty of waterfowl and deer to hunt."

"By the way," said Leona. "Why is the lake named Klamath Falls? We haven't seen any classic falls, like Niagara Falls."

Mrs. Zetaman shook her head, "You're right, it used to be more of a bubbly and unstable current—like a rapid. But since they built the dam across the river in '21 the rapids are only seen when water flow is high."

Young Henry stood in the kitchen doorway listening to the womens' discussion. "Excuse me, Mrs. Zetzman, what is that mountain called?" He pointed southward.

Mrs. Zetzman, scrunched up her face in delight, "Well honey, don't you know that's Mt Shasta, the second highest volcano in the Continental United States? It's about 70 miles from here, into California, but we can see it almost every day of the year because of the Klamath sunshine. . . . My word, I sound like a textbook. I hope you enjoy viewing her as much as I do."

With a laugh, she continued, "Yes, I always thought of 'Shasty' as my special companion. Things can get lonely out here sometimes."

~

Oregon Life

In the summer-like autumn, the David family settled into their new life. Some of the household baggage and furniture left in Scobey arrived by train. Henri, pale and weak, rested in the shade of an oak tree as Leona busied herself with organizing the arrival of their belongings.

The serenity of the setting was short-lived. The construction of the planned diversion canal brought enthusiasm along with the busy network of equipment. Trucks, large shiny-painted bulldozers and dredging machinery dug and moved earth from the channel onto the canal bank. The droning of machinery, smell of diesel and men calling out to each other, excited the fancy of children and adults alike.

Even though young, Inez clearly remembered the construction of the canal. Perhaps, the special gifts given to the children by neighbor, Joe Wright, anchored the memory. She was given a tiny bulldozer, while her brother received a larger metal dredger, a toy replica of the actual machine. The six-year-old boy spent blissful days in the dirt playing with this favorite toy.

When completed, the Diversion Canal, 50-60 feet deep, ran swift and sure alongside the David property. It served as a defining feature to the David farm and a not-so-small part of the Klamath Reclamation Project. Time in Oregon fell into a routine with young Henry enrolled at the local grammar school. However, he found it a distressing time. He was a newcomer who spoke with a strong French accent. The teachers had little understanding or patience with him, while the other children made fun of his speech.

To make things worse, Henry pouted one day at school saying in his French accent, "I want to go home and play with my *topee*." Perhaps this was what he called his toy dredger, or he was speaking about his spinning top (*la toupee*). However, the shocked, indignant teacher told Leona he said, "I want to play with my peepee"—poor Henry!

Inez had troubles of her own. She favored the use of her left hand more than her right one. This was totally unacceptable. No child of Henri David could be left-handed. He persisted in breaking Inez from being a lefty. Eventually, she learned right-hand dominance in writing and general use. However, she found it easier and more natural to use her left hand to pour liquid or powder into a glass or a bowl. As she matured, she operated the right and left hands equally well—thus ambidextrous. Later she learned that her brother Henry was also ambidextrous. It was not known if he started life with left-handed tendencies, as well.

With Henry in school and no other children to play with, Inez became quite lonely. She gravitated to the farm animals, especially the chicks and lambs. This is what Inez wrote of her reminiscences during that time:

> *"Just a short little excerpt that I remembered my mother (Leona) spoke about me as a small child shortly after coming to Klamath Falls. I was a little over two years old and our nearest neighbor had a few sheep. He gave us one little lamb my mom called a 'Bummer.' I'm not sure whether that was the name for a small lamb or just one she used.*

"Anyways, one day as all little children will do, I put my face down to his and he started licking my face and soon he was licking me to the point he took my breath away and I passed out. Here I was out cold, and my poor mom didn't even know what happened. I loved that little 'Guy' though. I have a picture of him as a bummer and later as a beautiful full-grown sheep. I cherish both of those snapshots."

~

One Cold Night

Inez journaled:

> *"Not long after our family settled into the little farm in the winter of 1929, we had a terrible disaster. This was in February—in Oregon and this is an extremely cold part of the year. Again, I don't remember, only hearsay. . . . By then my folks had acquired a few head of cows to milk and they proceeded to go out and milk them."*

❂ ❂ ❂

It had been five months since the purchase of a farm outside of Klamath Falls, Oregon. A February cold snap had developed.

Leona reached for her red, buffalo plaid coat that hung in its place on a hook near the front door. The coat just cleared the hook, when Henri's hand reached over Leona's shoulder to pluck his worn brown work coat from an adjacent hook.

She looked up to her husband and asked, "Are you sure you're up for this? It's awful cold out there."

Henri, with a crooked smile said, "If we both go, the milking will get done faster."

Young Henry piped in, "I'll help too!"

"Yes, you're developing into quite the little milker, aren't you, son?" said Henri.

Leona frowned, "What will we do with Inès?" Hearing her name, the toddler ran to her daddy, holding up her blue mittens.

"She wants to go with us, don't you, *Mon chaton*." Henri swooped up Inez and tickled her cheek until she giggled.

"But the cold . . ." Leona's concerned, creased brows lessened when Henri gave a quick wink.

Henri said, "Let's bundle Inés up and take her with us. We will all milk the cows together." Leona put the kettle to boil and pulled several rubberized, hot-water bags from the drawer to fill.

The smell of smoke. Something wood was burning.

A glance out the dairy door revealed an inferno where a home once stood. Consuming flames hissed, popped, and snapped—eager and hungry. The flicking fire waved, flared, and devoured more.

Horses neighed and cows mooed their distress.

The sight registered as unbelievable. Columns of thick gray smoke billowed into the sky and swallowed the crisp air. The fierce fire continued teasing the house's solid frame. Wooden beauty crackled and wilted under the hot breath of the intense furnace.

Blazing orange flames escaped from the house to engulf everything in its path. Fiery tongues ran along the trees and licked the bottom of the wooden fence posts.

Numerous times Henri disappeared into the firestorm, with hands and clothing clamped to his mouth and nose. Searing heat and choking clouds of noxious smoke drove him back. Leona pitched ineffective buckets of water at the taunting fire. From safety the children wailed at the sights of destruction.

Neighbors arrived with buckets and shovels. Nothing remained to be done . . . or saved.

Floating ashes danced in the smoky air and filtered to the ground. The life of the house decomposed into the nothingness of deathlike grayness.

Inez continued her journaling:

> *". . . [The farm had] no electricity so they lighted their home by lamps and lanterns. Their house caught fire when the lantern used in the house had leaked kerosene. The entire home went down since we were miles from a fire station and no real help. My father was only getting over a bout with pneumonia. He tried his best, along with a few neighbors to save the house, but it was totally destroyed. Poor Dad, in the end, he was unable to save much of anything."*

The fire not only destroyed the house and one of the barns, but Leona and Henri were in a state of shock—not able to grasp or believe what had happened. Their home and everything in their household were destroyed: keepsakes, photographs, paintings, cash on hand, addresses of friends and family, financial records, books, clothing. furniture—all burned up. Leona and the children carried the fear of fire for the rest of their lives.

Henri once again entered the hospital. This time smoke inhalation added to his lung difficulties. Their troubles did not end.

~

After the Fire

Inez continued her journaling:

> *"After the fire my father came down with 'double pneumonia' and never recovered. This was after a few neighbors put a few sticks together for a shelter. I remember tarpaper and two-by-four walls. Henry and I would lose all our little toys and marbles through the subflooring in that shell of a house. For my sick father, the neighbors added a screened in porch because by then it was realized he had tuberculosis and needed to be separated from the rest of us.*
>
> *"What a sad time that must have been. It was 1929–30, in the deep days of the Depression. Mom had made ends meet by having a few cows she would milk and sell the cream. She raised a few turkeys and a few chickens, selling the eggs and butchering a turkey, when needed. She was able to buy her groceries from this small amount each week.*
>
> *"Bless her heart, my little mother took care of us kids and a sick man in bed for 11 months without running water, no indoor plumbing in that very, very miserable weather. God only knows how she did it."*

The local doctors in Klamath Falls, Dr. Paul Sharp and Dr. F. C. Adams, advised Henri to seek treatment, including rest and improved nutrition, in a tuberculosis center. Henri decided against institutional care because he did not want to be away from his young family. He held some strong opinions against such TB sanitariums, and determined it was not for him.

Instead, Leona home-nursed her husband with primitive conditions, in a house hastily built by the neighbors. The added screened-in porch provided fresh air, basic shelter, and little else. Medical personnel made scheduled visits for Henri's breathing and sunlamp treatments. Since the household had no electricity, Klamath County provided a generator to run equipment for the required treatments. Inez remembered the disinfectant smell emitted with the use of the medical machinery.

Without running water in the house or access to a washing machine, Leona set up a wash tub and a scrub board in the yard to do the family laundry. Henri was completely bedridden for many months, so that meant laundering all the bedding by hand. She placed the filled tub in the sunshine to warm the water enough for washing and rinsing the clothes. Everything had to be hung on a clothesline to drip dry or freeze dry, depending on the weather conditions. She also did all the necessary bedside nursing care, including the required bed baths, straight-razor shaves, and cleaning up after the use of a chamber pot.

Aside from the breathing and sunlight treatments, Henri was kept as comfortable as possible with pain medication, while remaining isolated on the screened-in porch. Neither Leona nor the doctors could do little else, except try to keep the children from exposure to their father's tuberculosis. As it turned out, Leona, the younger Henry and Inez, were already exposed. All three had positive skin tests but did not develop tuberculosis.

Inez continued her journaling:

> *"We were not allowed to go into his screened-in porch [but] once and a while my brother would put some wooden boxes*

under the window so we could look at him [Henri]. I also have a picture of myself, not much later, on a really big horse. (As to a small child, the horse was a BIG horse.) The picture was taken outside my father's screened-in porch where he spent his last living months. It hurt him to see us little children since he knew it was just a matter of time when he would be gone, and he was hoping we would be able to forget him soon. Of course, we did. I was too young to have memories like Henry.

Besides the concerns for Henri and care for her children, Leona also managed to keep the farm financially sound. However, she needed help with the farm's small herd of cows and its poultry. About this time, Inez became aware of the hired hand that her mom called "Swede." The 1930 U.S. census listed the 24-year-old from Iowa as Howard King. He must have had Scandinavian features, being fair and stocky in build and different from her male relatives who were tall and thin with dark hair and dark eyes.

No doubt, Swede came to the Klamath Falls area by way of riding the rails. People illegally hopped on and off freight trains during hard financial times, as a means of travel and a way to look for work. Men searching for jobs often jumped from the boxcar when the train slowed to take a curve near the property of Leona's neighbor, Joe Wright. Most likely, Joe judged Swede to be a good man to help at the David place.

Swede was used to hard work. He even laughed when he said he worked on a "Honey Wagon" (manure or garbage truck) prior to coming to help at the David farm. But the bachelor farmhand hated the chore of ironing his own shirts. His solution? He cut the sleeves off at the shoulders, thus exposing his muscular arms.

Inez remembered Swede dipped snuff and smelled of tobacco. He gave the empty Copenhagen tobacco tins to her and always had spearmint chewing gum in his overalls to offer the kids. Swede had been hired to help with the cattle and milking, but he was good to and for the children. At such a hard time in their lives, he proved to be a real, physical comfort to them.

After the first week of December, Henri's situation worsened when, annoyed at being bedridden for so many months, he impulsively jumped out of bed—only to plummet to the floor when his legs gave out. The fall appeared to break something loose in his lungs. Spasms of coughing brought up diseased lung. Henri's condition deteriorated and tuberculosis took his life a couple days later.

Here is how Inez describes her memories of her father's death:

> *"Believe it or not, I do remember the day my father died even though I was only 4 years old. His brother Leon, Ella, Leon's wife and their children had come to Klamath Falls to be there when the end happened. It was said that Father became quite agitated that night as he angrily called out to let in his deceased [younger] brother, Marcel who had died earlier that year.*
>
> *"My older cousin, Bea, told me in the morning my dad had died—his passing away was at 3:00 AM December 10th, 1930. We all went to the funeral home for viewing with Mom. I saw him lying in the casket and remembering how he seemed so long to me. Henry went to the funeral, but I didn't. I believe my cousins Leo and Art stayed with me during the funeral.*
>
> *"My father was good to Mom and really cherished her, but unfortunately they only had ten years together and he was ill a big part of that time."*

"Just bury me on a manure pile, that will be just fine." With a cheeky smile, Henri had joked before his death when the subject of funeral arrangements arose. As it was, Leona arranged for his resting place in a Catholic graveyard, far north of the farm. However, no money existed for a headstone to mark the grave. At the ten-year anniversary of Henri's death, Inez remembered how her mother, brother, and herself searched unsuccessfully for the location of his grave.

Years later, in the 1970s, while living in Redmond, Oregon, Inez's brother, Henry was notified his father's gravesite was to be moved because of highway construction. Henry arranged for the transfer of his father's rediscovered remains and purchased a headstone to mark Henri's grave.

~

The Prayer

Leona whispered, "Oh God. There's nothing to eat. What am I going to do?" Tears flooded her face as she half ran, half stumbled towards the hen house. One look inside revealed only a few stray feathers, the smell of chicken manure, and a convulsion of thoughts: *No eggs, no chickens, and no turkeys.*

She cried harder as she leaned up against the coop door, forehead on her left forearm. Sobs broke up her question, "What . . . will . . . I feed . . . the kids?" Stepping away from the chicken coop, Leona walked aimlessly in the yard. She could only think about what had happened over the last few days that compounded this situation.

The small amount of money from Henri's life insurance policy had sat secure in the National Bank of Klamath Falls until panic and rumors of runs on the banks surfaced. On her brother-in-law Leon's advice, Leona rushed with him into the bank, entered by a side door and withdrew all the cash from her National Bank account. The money was deposited, that same day, in a savings and loan company.

The feeling of accomplishment perished when the unimaginable happened—all of the money was lost from the savings and loan company. If the money had been left in the bank, where it had been at first, it would have remained safe.

Even though Christmas was quickly approaching, Leon and his family left that morning in haste, after Leona hurled harsh words at them. Yet, she continued to lament with her thoughts: *How could I have taken Leon's advice? Why didn't I leave the money where it was?"*

Stepping away from the chicken coop, Leona continued to walk about the yard. She cried out to the trees, "Wasn't it enough for the children to lose their father? Now all our money is lost. . . . Nothing's left for Christmas."

Wringing her hands, then entwining her fingers as though praying, Leona looked towards Heaven. She again asked, "Lord, what am I going to do?"

"Honk, hick, honk." Calling to each other, a flock of seven Canada geese flew overhead and landed in the pond, several hundred feet away.

Leona stopped crying, swept the tears off her cheeks with her fingertips, and rushed towards the house. She retrieved Henri's Remington pump shotgun; her nimble fingers loaded the gun with five shotgun shells and she headed to where the geese had landed.

More geese flew above her while she crept closer to the pond. A small flock rose from the water. Leona pumped the shotgun, took aim, and fired with a sure shot at the group of fowl. The kick of the shotgun nearly knocked Leona off her feet, but down came two birds—enough to feed her family. She sighed, "Thank you Lord!"

Leona believed her prayers were answered that day—a true Christmas answer.

Leona had faith in God, but she did not consider herself a good Catholic or respect the local Catholic church. She resented the priests who made visits to the farm during Henri's illness. According to Leona, they seemed to "always be hanging around, leering instead of comforting."

One of the younger priests pointed out Leona's destitute position since the death of her husband. He stated, in a matter-of-fact manner, "You know, arrangements can be made between the two of us." He crowded close to her and became, what Leona described as "frisky," before she put him in his place with a shove and a defiant look.

Had Leona overreacted? Gone were the months focused on tuberculosis, with smells of illness and the struggle to delay death. Leona, more fragile than her feisty image would imply, found herself without direction as she made it through those first hours, days and weeks after Henri's death.

Inez journaled:

> *"Times continued to get bad as the months went by. Mom [Leona] never knew anything about business or finances. She didn't even know how to write a check. Strictly a young, [naive] woman with two small children, a deceased husband and no sense of how to care for a family, on her own."*

Prior to Henri's death, the two attending doctors had become aware of the family's predicament. The two children captivated the doctors' interest and the subject of adoption surfaced. Both doctors were married, but neither had children of his own. The plan progressed to the final stages for Dr. Sharp and his wife to adopt Inez. Dr. Adams and his wife were to take Henry. At the last moment, Leona did not sign the release forms for the adoptions.

Perhaps Leona's family pleaded against the adoptions. After the worst of the winter, she leased the fields of the farm to neighbors, leaving Swede to watch over the farm animals. Leona somehow scraped together money to buy three train tickets—for the two children and herself—back to her home in Montana.

Return to Montana, 1931

What a terrible disappointment for Leona and the children to arrive in Montana in the midst of the Great Depression. Montana led all other states in bankruptcies, abandoned farms, and bank failures as citizens packed and left the state. Why was the area in such dire straits?

At first, high-plains homesteading had brought boom times with abundant crops because of favorable weather and ideal conditions. However, drought, grasshopper infestations, and intense range fires from 1910 to the mid-1920s, spread across the plains like the high winds which devastated crops and destroyed communities.

Before the homesteaders recovered, disaster struck with the double blows of the 1929 stock market crash and a second drought with severe dust storms. The period earned the right to the label of "The Dirty Thirties," but became better known as the notorious Dust Bowl of the 1930s.

More distressing, Leona found her mother, Rose Doyon, in a near-destitute situation after Louis Doyon, Leona's father, died in March of 1930. The death left Rose with four young boys, ages 8 to 14, still at home. When she was unable to pay the expenses of the Scobey homestead, a bank foreclosure forced the family from their home of twenty years. Rose's close-knit family of seven other grown children struggled to help her. However, they too were experiencing hard times.

Rose lacked practical or marketable skills. She had married at seventeen as a French-Canadian ingénue interested in music and art. The delicate 49-year-old, with her broken English and minimal money, moved 300 miles to live with Alexina, her married daughter, in Great Falls, Montana. Rose found work as a nurse's aide at a Catholic hospital. However, the four boys—Eugene, Louis, Remis, and Maurice—were placed in the St. Thomas Orphan Home of Great Falls. Not only an orphanage, it was also a Catholic Home that served as a school and a boarding house for children from rural areas. It provided a place for children from broken homes and for those facing family hardships.

With few options, plus circumstances the way they were in Montana, Leona decided to return to Oregon. However, she returned alone. Her children remained in Montana. Henry went with his young uncles to the orphanage home

Inez was cared for by one of her aunts.

Inez's thoughts about those times:

> *"Mom must have thought it would be best to take Henry to the orphanage in Great Falls and be with his young uncles since she didn't know what to do with him. Henry was 8 1/2 years old. He did not fare so well. Life had been hard for this little boy who had lost his father and basically lost his mother too, because he did not know why she left him there.*
>
> *The nuns were hard on those young boys. It was a terrible experience, leaving Henry bitter and resentful. I am sure there was a reason for this decision of placing him there and I truly cannot blame anyone for sure, but my thought is that the Church had a hand in this and perhaps both Mom and her mother were too ignorant to know what to do in such a situation. She was under their influence and since her brothers were there, she thought it would be all right. Obviously, it was not. For this, there is no place to put the blame but for hard times and poor judgments."*

Family stories told how the young uncles had tough times during that period. The nuns were strict to the point of meanness. Students, required to attend Chapel seven times a day, spent a lot of time praying on their knees. The 10-year-old uncle, Louis, had a deformed leg that made it hard to kneel to pray. Not kneeling to pray defied authority. He was routinely punishment with a rod because of it.

Times were desperate, with very few choices. The four uncles never seemed to recover from their experiences at the orphanage. Broken in spirit, aimlessness and depression plagued them the rest of their lives.

Henry fared better than his uncles, although it was not a healthy time for him either. During his stay at the orphanage, Henry became extremely ill with scarlet fever. Tonsillitis followed, requiring his tonsils to be removed. Inez remembered a photograph of Henry, taken at that time, with fever blisters encircling his mouth.

Yet, the David side of the family objected to Henry's placement in the St. Thomas Orphan Home. Uncle Leon and Aunt Ella wanted to adopt, or at least foster, Henry despite the fact they already had four children of their own. According to Cousin Art, "It broke all our hearts that, 'our good little buddy' should be put in such a place."

Inez's journaling continues:

> *"With Henry in the Catholic orphanage, I was taken to live with my Auntie Laura and Uncle Albert Bernard at Four Buttes, Montana which is a little north of Scobey, my birthplace. Where Henry had a time of suffering, I loved being with my aunt and uncle. It was a long time of almost a year we were apart, and I nearly had forgotten him.*
>
> *"Catholic homes at that time were very abusive and as I got older, I understood a lot of what he must have gone through. He never was one to say much, so the unexpressed hurt was just*

burried. I am sure he had deep 'hurts' that he never got over. I never was able to become close to him. I am sure he was jealous because I was still a little girl and made over by my aunts in Montana. I always had a very sad feeling between the two of us. It still hurts when I let myself think of it . . ."

The Lindbergh Baby

"Hey there Lindy, don't you feel glad?

Wonder if that youngster will look like his dad?"

These vivid song lyrics are memories linked to Doyon family gatherings during Inez's Montana stay. The song's subject was about the birth of the Lindbergh baby, born the year before, on June 22, 1930. Three years earlier, Charles Lindbergh, the famous American pilot, flew the first solo, non-stop transatlantic flight from New York to Paris in his *Spirit of St. Louis*. The pilot obtained worldwide celebrity status following his flight.

Perhaps the French felt honored to have Paris as the destination of the historic landing, for the French and those, such as the Doyons, with French Canadian ancestry were especially wild about Lindbergh. Therefore, the birth of this hero's baby had been greatly anticipated, with international public interest that pushed to near frenzy.

The Victrola purchased by Henri during his mercantile buyer days played the record of the song. When Henri and Leona moved to Oregon, they left their record player behind for the rest of the family to enjoy. They knew the Doyons loved music.

Whatever the reason, Inez's relatives cranked the Victrola to play "The Lindbergh Baby Song" often enough for five-year-old Inez to remember the words to the chorus of the song over eight decades later. However, years later she realized that a tragedy had occurred to the toddler's family, the nation, and the world when the 20-month-old Lindbergh baby was kidnapped and later found dead.

~

Auntie Laura and Four Buttes, Montana

Auntie Laura, Leona's younger, married sister, was the Doyon family's third child. Conceived while her mother, Rose, recuperated from smallpox, Laura was a tiny newborn, small enough to fit in a cigar box. Shy, plain, and backward, she dimmed in comparison to her older sister. Leona, clever and outgoing, gave the impression of being sure of herself. Laura did not. In addition, Laura did not possess Leona's manageable, pretty hair but instead had unruly, mousey brown hair that grew low on her forehead and refused to stay neatly parted.

Leona characterized her sister as slow and unable to learn, struggling to catch on to what was being taught at school. Laura did not attend school for long and never really learned to read or write. She spoke mainly French, for her broken English was difficult to understand due to her thick accent.

Their father's response to Laura's difficulties in school was, "Good. She is needed at home." While Leona was taken outside to help in the fields and to do farm chores, Laura remained indoors to keep house, and assisting her frail mother. She also laundered mounds of diapers and clothing from her younger siblings. The family greatly benefited from Laura's skill in cooking.

Laura married Albert Bernard in 1927. They lived on Albert's dryland grain farm west of Scobey, near the little town of Four Buttes, Montana. Albert was a small man, with a long, homely, weathered face. A diligent hard worker, he was also said to be tight-fisted with his money. Even though Albert first seemed a bit scary, he was gentle and kind to Inez. The little niece enjoyed reuniting with her loving aunt and uncle, as the separation from her mother and brother quietly slipped by unnoticed. But Inez did miss her comforting blanket, "Lovey"—a soft, gray, knitted shawl—left in Oregon.

As a 4½-year-old, Inez remembered much of the setting in Montana and her changed life there. The unusual bluffs, also known as "Whiskey Buttes," towered above the prairie town. In the earlier days, the buttes were notorious as a meeting place for the local Indians and those trading whiskey to them. The landscape of rolling prairie hills and the openness of the big, blue Montana sky were an overwhelming experience. She never forgot the feeling of being engulfed in its vastness.

Despite this imposing expanse, Auntie Laura and Uncle Albert's farmhouse offered warmth and coziness. The kitchen, a sitting area, and sleeping areas all had their own spaces in the one large room. A wooden ladder led upstairs to the attic. Inez was instructed never to climb on the ladder or go up into the attic.

Living in a one-room house and cooking with a wood burning stove had its disadvantages. Laura routinely washed the wood walls with strong lye water to clean the interior walls of messy black soot that resulted from cooking. The wetness raised the wood grain, resulting in clean but wavy walls. However, because of Laura's hard work as a meticulous housekeeper, these wavy wood walls were also polished to a high sheen.

Laura had adopted Grandma Rose Doyon's custom of singing whimsical tunes in French. She had quite a repertoire of songs she sang while she cleaned house or rocked in her rocking chair.

The only place Laura sat down was in her wooden, homemade rocking chair. But the strange thing to Inez was to see how Auntie Laura ate her meals at the dinner table. She sat parallel to the table while in her rocker, moving back and forth, as she speared food off her plate with her fork as she rocked forward. She then rocked back and forth as she chewed and swallowed the food morsels. She speared another forkful on another forward rock and continued the whole process throughout the meal.

As months went by, Inez noticed how other things differed from her home in Oregon. One of the first routines established for Inez as a member of the Bernard household included prayer. Inez's own bed was a small cot positioned across the room from the adults' shared bed. Every night, the aunt, uncle, and the little girl knelt, three in a row, against the big adult bed to recite their prayers in French. A small, simple crucifix adorned the wall at the head of the bed.

The sounds of the prairie farm proved scary to Inez, even though the youngster was accustomed with Oregon country life. The Montana prairie's sounds provided ammunition for imagination—especially at night.

~

Thumping in the Night

Woo-o-o-o. . . Woo-o-o-o. . . Woo-o-o-o. The strong winds howled and shrieked, then moaned in the prairie darkness. Across the room, Uncle Albert's snores came in intermittent snorts and gasps.

Thump. Thump. Thump. Something pounded against the wall right outside Inez's sleeping cot.

What's that? Little Inez strained to listen. *I wish I had my Lovey.*

Thump. Thump. Thump. *Is that a monster coming in to get me?* The child pulled the bedcovers over her head.

More blustery prairie winds flung dirt, debris, and sagebrush scratched against the house. A gust of wind shook the little house, the attic door rattled. *Has the monster gotten into the attic?*

Thump. Thump. Thump. Again, the sound pounded against the outside wall. Inez's heartbeat pulsed in her ears. Her mouth, dry as paper, tasted of dirt.

A ghost-like figure in a flowing, white flannel nightgown loomed near the cot. When it spoke, she heard Aunt Laura ask, "*Ne dors-tu pas?* Are you not sleep-ing?"

"I'm scared," said Inez, still holding the bedcovers to her mouth.

Thump. Thump. Thump. With a gentle smile of understanding, Laura said, "*Oh petit*! That's just *Tante's* silly ol' mop blowing in the wind and making all that noise. It won't hurt you."

Laura sat down next to the child and started to hum one of her French tunes as she petted the girl's hair. Inez felt herself relax and soon she drifted off to sleep, even without the comfort of her "Lovey" shawl.

~

Birthday Photograph

Laura did her best to keep Leona connected to Inez. Although money was tight, the sisters arranged for a photograph of Inez on her fifth birthday. Each woman received a keepsake picture celebrating this milestone. For the occasion, Inez wore a sweet pale pink cotton dress with a large, white scalloped-lace collar. Additional birthday presents included a gold heart-locket necklace, with matching bracelet and a child's watch with a rectangle face.

"Oh petit! said Aunt Laura. "Your mama sent money for a picture for your birth-day. How fun that will be.

"First, we cut your hair a little and clean you up." She pulled out sewing scissors from her dresser. She perched Inez on a chair and wrapped an embroidered tea-towel around the child's shoulders. With care and concentration Laura dedicated herself to the task.

"There, we've cut your hair pretty, *No*? And with a lock of hair for a nice little keepsake to give your Mamma . . . and yes, one for me.

"I'll help you with a fast wash before your uncle comes in." The washrag in Laura's hand cleansed the girl with precision. As Laura tidied up, she directed Inez to dress and put on her socks and shoes.

"But Auntie, my shoes are too tight to wear."

Laura reached for the outgrown Mary Jane-style shoes Inez held. "Here honey, let *Tante* see. . . ." She stretched for the scissors. "*Oui*, just a little snip here, with *Tante's* scissors and the shoe is once again comfortable."

An endearing photograph resulted of Inez, a proud five-year-old, posed sitting on a bench, with one leg folded under the other. Heart-locket necklace, bracelet, and watch were all in place, while the large, lace collar showcased the girl's beaming face.

On close inspection, the bridge of each shoe had been carefully split. The Doyon sisters knew how to repurpose, refurbish and make do.

~

Blood Sausage

"Laur-ree, you best hurry up," called Uncle Albert through the open kitchen window.

"*Mon dieu*!" Laura pulled her wet, dripping hands from the pan of dishwater and wiped them on her newly laundered apron. Reaching into a neat stack of pots and pans, she located just what she needed—her prized black cast iron skillet and a large mixing bowl.

Albert and his helper were in the process of butchering one of his hogs, and Laura intended to catch the blood from the slaughtered pig. She said as she ran through the door, "We will soon have the blood sausage."

Inez put down her ragdoll and timidly stepped towards the open door. She looked towards the barn, but her aunt disappeared behind it. She wondered, *What is blood sausage?*

Before long Laura returned to the house with her skillet of blood and bowl of hog parts.

"*Tante*, are you going to use blood in the sausage?" Asked Inez, crinkling her nose.

Laura looked over from the stove. The solidified pork blood and meat pieces cooked in the skillet while a large pot of water simmered. Onions and celery caramelized in diced pork fat in yet another pan.

The aunt smiled and said in her heavy French accent, "*Oui*, fresh pig's blood, diced pork fat, scraps of the snout, ears and organs—all goes into the mix. Most everything of the pig is used—except the squeal . . . you'll love it."

Inez decided right then, *Tante Laura may love that dark, seasoned blood sausage but I'm going to hate it —with or without the squeal.*

~

Naughty Girl

Aunt Laura bustled into the house carrying her collection of four brown eggs from the hen house. A strong wind blew the door, banging against the wall. When she turned from securing the door, she discovered her niece, Inez, climbing on the forbidden attic ladder.

"Oh, Inès Rose, you naughty girl! You bad. What I going to do with you?

"Woo-o-o-o, Woo-o-o-o, Woo-o-o-o. Thump. Thump. Thump.

Laura listened to the sounds of the wind, then made a decision as she said, "Hear that scary sound?—it's your Mama, she's scolding you. She doesn't want you to climb on the ladder and hurt your little self."

In defiance, Inez placed her hands on her hips and stomped outside. When she returned, she struggled to drag Laura's mop through the door.

With one great effort Inez positioned the mop head at her feet and said "*Tante*, that scary sound isn't my Mama scolding me! Remember, it's just your silly ol' mop hitting the wall."

Laura could not help from laughing and embraced the youngster.

When the hug was complete, Inez said, "*Tante*, I'm sorry. I won't climb on the ladder anymore."

And she never did.

~

Remembering Henri

Laura was fourteen when her sister, Leona, met and married Henri David. Laura always had a strong fondness for the man she felt was so very kind to her. Her devotion remained strong as shown many years later, in the 1970s, while visiting California with her sister, Sid (Sister of Province).

A discussion came up between the two Doyon sisters with their niece, Inez, about Henri's physical characteristics. Sid even added, ". . . in reality, Henri was an ugly man due to his, 'brown-speckled' skin."

However, beauty is in the eye of the beholder. Immediately and hotly, Laura refuted the statement by saying in her heavy French accent, "No. No. It's not true—Henri was a wonderful maan. . . . I luv dat maan."

Albert and Laura never did have any biological children of their own. At one point, Laura suffered from a condition known as "milk leg" — inflammation, pain, and pallor resulted from clots that blocked the channel of the main vein of the thigh. Historically, this condition occurred during pregnancy or shortly after childbirth. Although, it was never known if pregnancy was the reason for Laura's milk leg.

For Laura, the care of Inez had many heartstrings: to her sister, to a favorite brother-in-law, as well as to a sweet niece in need. Time came when Laura had to give up Inez and return the child to her own mother. Aunt Laura later told Inez, "It broke my heart to give you up."

With Laura's nurturing love for babies and children, she prayed for children of her own. A few years later, Laura and Albert were able to adopt their own baby.

They named the little boy Henri.

~

February 1932

Inez's journaling, 2003:

> *"Then one day news came that Mom had remarried, and she wanted us to come home to Klamath Falls, Oregon."*

"Inès, Inès." Aunt Laura called to her niece and waved the letter she held. Her joy, enthusiastic but forced, masked her breaking heart. "Your Uncle Albert has brought good news. Your mama has sent tickets for you and your brother to go back to Oregon."

Laura questioned Albert in French, then said to Inez, "You have a new daddy. . . . He's a good man. He doesn't smoke or drink. . . . His name is Mr. Dooo-toon."

The upcoming trip brought a whirlwind of activities: cutting Inez's hair, washing, pressing and packing clothes. Everything blurred together until Laura and Inez were at the station, boarding the train. The smell of burning coal, along with the sounds of hissing steam and wailing train whistle renewed memories of the previous journey, taken with her mother.

After a short train ride to the Montana town of Wolf Point, the niece and aunt walked several short blocks to a tavern near the railroad. An over-the-door bell jingled as they entered the near-deserted tavern. The large wall mirror showcased the neat rows of glassware stacked on a shelf behind the shiny wooden bar. A stagnant mix of whiskey, cigarettes and furniture polish hung in the air.

A familiar man bent down to the girl. He laughed as he asked, "Inès Rose, do you remember me? I'm your Uncle Leon." Inez felt a little catch in her chest. She thought. *He sounds just like my papa.*

Leon invited Laura and Inez to sit at one of the wooden tables while he stepped behind the bar. "It's a little early for my usual business, so I'd like to make you a treat."

He cracked several eggs into glasses, splashed in milk, added vanilla, and stirred the concoction together. Topping the drinks with generous sprinklings of nutmeg, Leon said, "This is my special eggnog, *bon appétit*!"

He placed the frothy egg drink in front of Inez. She cautiously sipped her first taste of the drink. Her eyes widened with joy. She licked her upper lip, savoring the nutmeg. "I like this very much," she said, licking her lips again.

Before long, it was time to board the train for Great Falls, Montana. Inez and Laura spent the night at Aunt Alexina's house, where Grandma Doyon also lived. They enjoyed a pleasant evening together as they shared a meal, talked, and listened to the Victrola record player. The next morning, the aunts packed a leather satchel with food for the trip before going to the orphanage to collect Henry and his clothes.

Crowds of women and children filled the halls of St. Thomas Orphan Home. The women wore the characteristic religious habits of black veils, headpieces and long flowing garments that reached to the ground. Contrasting white collars and white cloth around the face concealed the nuns' hair, ears and necks. The children, subdued and orderly, wore clean but ill-fitting clothes.

Aunt Laura spoke with one of the nuns, then pointed to a chair. "Inès, you sit here, I'll be right back." With that, Laura and the nun disappeared into the crowd.

Inez wiggled on the uncomfortable wooden chair in front of a desk where a stern looking nun sat writing in a book. The girl looked about the room. She recognized a crucifix, much larger than the one hanging above Aunt Laura's bed. Along the walls were bookshelves, statues, and paintings. The smell of cleaning solution wafted through the room.

The nun finished her writing and closed the book. She took a long, appraising look at Inez. She asked in a coarse voice, "Are you a good little girl?"

Inez slowly nodded her head and watched as the nun revealed, in her hand, a small golden stickpin, in the form of a crucifix.

"I'd like to give you this crucifix—but you must promise that you will become a nun when you grow up. Will you do this?"

Inez wanted that stickpin. Once again, she nodded and in a hushed voice said, "I promise."

While Inez admired her gift, a thin, pale boy, in high-water pants and carrying a rucksack, approached with Aunt Laura. The boy's freckled face and shock of reddish-brown hair did not match his serious expression. He seemed somewhat familiar to Inez. Then she realized why. *Oh, that's my brother . . . that's Henry! I'd forgotten all about him.*

Henry, now nine years old, ignored Inez, but watched with interest while Aunt Laura and the nun at the desk signed discharge papers. With no time to lose, the two children and Aunt Laura made their way from the convent to the train station.

The whistle warned of the train's departure. Aunt Laura hugged Henry before handing him the brown leather satchel. She drew Inez to herself and embraced the little girl as though she would never let her go. Nudging Inez and Henry towards the open train doors, Laura said a sad but simple, "Goodbye."

A solemn Henry grabbed hold of Inez's hand and led her to their seats. He placed the all-important bag of food at his feet. Thus, the two little nomads—9½ and 5½ years old— began their journey to Oregon, on their own.

The train pulled away from the station. Inez searched through the window, but she could not see Aunt Laura anywhere. The engine picked up speed. Shapes of houses and barns along the tracks blurred by. Before long, the scenery displayed wooded areas and fewer houses.

Inez's tummy growled. "Henry, I'm hungry."

Henry considered her words, then reached down to retrieve the stash of sandwiches, hard boiled eggs, pickles, fruits, crackers, and cookies. Like a miser, Henry dealt out the morsels of food. In a stern tone he said, "We can't eat it all at once."

When nighttime came, a porter with coffee-colored skin prepared the sleeping berth and said, "There you two go, sleep tight and don't let the bedbugs bite."

Inez put on her flannel nightgown to get ready to sleep. Henry reached out and lightly pinched her upper arm and said, "You sure have gotten fat . . . and you talk funny." She had acquired Aunt Laura's heavy French accent and benefited from the excellent cooking during the yearlong stay at Four Buttes.

The next days and nights were more of the same activities. The view alternated from towns to wilderness. The children ate from their food supply and rested at night in their sleeping berth. When the train approached Washington, the porter told Henry, "You're going to transfer trains at Seattle," and he gave Henry instructions how to find the correct one.

After the engine came to a stop, Henry picked up the leather satchel, took hold of Inez's hand, and led her out of the train. A crisscrossing of railroad tracks that stretched through the railroad yard faced the children. He did not hesitate as the two, hand in hand, picked their way, in a transverse fashion, to the other side of the railroad yard. Amid the smoke and smells of resin and oil, Henry found the correct train to Klamath Falls. Inez's chest swelled with pride when she saw how Henry knew where to go in that enormous train yard. She thought, *What a big man my brother Henry is now.*

Henry and Inez arrived in Klamath Falls after a severe February snowstorm. Meeting them at the train was their mother, Leona, and a tall, slim man with light brown hair. She introduced him as Charlie Dutton, their new stepfather.

The snow drifts piled around the train station, nearly a foot-and-a-half deep, and over thigh-high for Inez. To reach their parked Model A Ford, Leona picked up and carried Inez. Charlie did not hesitate to snatch up his stepson, not realizing the boy was rigid with humiliation.

Henry had safely shepherded himself and Inez across the country. To have a stranger, who was taking the place of his father, carry him to the car like a baby was almost too much for Henry to bear. But he did so, in resentful silence.

Soon after the siblings' arrival to Klamath Falls, a portrait was taken to mark their return to Oregon. The children gained some celebrity status when the photograph, along with the story of travelling by train alone for a four-day trip, was printed in the local newspaper, *The Klamath News.*

February 1932

The leather satchel, kept through Inez's formative years, stayed with her in travel, marriage, and motherhood. She found the bag was the perfect place to keep her family photographs. An added bonus occurred each time she opened the satchel— it smelled of bananas, apples and hard-boiled eggs—the fragrance of Inez and Henry's 1932 train trip from Montana.

~

Charlie and Popcorn

Nebraskan old-timers tell a legend of one particular summer. It got so hot that the corn in the fields started popping right off the stalks. The poor cows and pigs, thinking it was a snowy blizzard, laid down and froze to death.

Jack, the farmhand, chuckled. "The good part is you can eat all the popcorn you want.

It was the spring of 1910 in rural Nebraska. The statement jarred the near thirteen-year-old, Charlie Dutton, out of his daydream. *What did that guy say about popcorn? I didn't know these crops were popcorn. Maybe it won't be so bad after all.*

The farmhand discussed the farm routine. He showed Charlie where to bunk in a makeshift shed. But the youth could not concentrate. He missed his grandmother, his younger brother, Dewey, and his Colorado home, where he had lived for the past ten years.

Living in Denver was no longer an option for Charlie, so he set out to find his estranged father, Chris Kettlehut in Otoe County, Nebraska. When he did find him, a cold and awkward reception confronted Charlie.

His father took him aside and said, "Sorry boy, you can't stay here. We just don't have room or food for you."

Inside the house, talking and laughing could be heard. Neither Charlie nor his father said anything until Chris rubbed the stubble on his chin and said, "Tell you what, I know a guy who could use you as a farmhand . . . to help milk, plow the fields, and harvest the cornhusks."

"I don't know how to plow, or harvest, or even milk," said Charlie, in a slight voice.

The father's eyes widened, "What have you been doing all this time?"

"Going to school, in the city," the boy answered.

"Well, I guess you're done with that school stuff. . . . Farming will teach you everything you need to know."

After a long silence Chris asked in a lowered voice, "Have you seen your mother lately?"

Charlie nodded. "At Grandmother's funeral. . . . She's the one who told me I belonged with you."

"Your mother always was telling people what to do. She is one strange woman . . .. What happened to Dewey?"

Charlie said, "Mother took him with her."

"Yeah, she always favored him." But when Charlie's face paled, the father added, "Before you know it, she'll be dumping him on one of her sisters. . . ."

Chris threw away the stick he had picked up while talking. "Well, I best get you settled in at that farm. It's a ways from here and I need to get back before milking time."

Dumping a sack of potatoes took more care than Charlie's transition into farming. A handshake between Chris and the farmer sealed the boy's fate. Charlie did not even speak with his new boss.

His father's departing words rang in Charlie's ears, "This will help make a man out of you."

Charlie's head bowed to his chest in a defeated stance, remembering his talk with his father. *He didn't even want me and now he's farming me out to strangers.*

The teenager realized the farmhand was speaking to him once again. He forced himself to listen.

"Say, don't you have any work clothes?" Jack wrinkled his nose as he scanned Charlie's expensive but old-fashioned attire: buckled Mary Jane shoes, socks to his knees, large collared, white shirt, and brown velveteen knickers.

Charlie didn't dare speak because he stammered when upset or nervous. He shook his head so his light brown hair, cut bowl style, swished like a mop.

Jack gave a cheerful slap on the boy's back, "I'll lend you some of mine until you can buy some—'course you'll have to roll the cuffs up a bit. . . . And don't worry, we'll make a man out of you."

Charlie McKinley Dutton

Born on May 6, 1897, he signed all legal documents as Charlie—never Charles or anything more formal. His middle name, McKinley, came from the newly elected 25th United States President, William McKinley. Charlie and his younger brother, Dewey, went by the surname Dutton, which was the maiden name of their mother, Cora May Dutton.

Divorced after three years of marriage, Cora May Dutton and Christoph (Chris) Kettlehut, soon found other mates. Chris remarried, fathered ten more children, and continued to farm south of Lincoln, near his birthplace of Palmaya, Nebraska. Cora became involved with Samuel Franklin, a Palmaya neighbor, and relocated to Iowa.

Cora "didn't like little boys." She did not want her sons in her new life, either. Charlie's grandmother, Mary Dutton, took in the two brothers and raised them in Denver, Colorado.

Grandmother Dutton appeared to be affluent. It was possible her wealth resulted from an inheritance from her father, a Colorado miner. A collection of professional portraits taken several times a year, from 1900 to 1910, showed the brothers, Charlie and Dewey, wearing expensive-looking clothing. Perhaps the photographs were a grandmother's attempt to keep a relationship between the boys and their aloof mother.

When Charlie was about twelve, this grandmother became too ill to continue serving as his caretaker. He traveled to Nebraska hoping to live with his father. But, because of the size of his father's current family, there was no room or money for Charlie. Instead, his father "farmed out" Charlie to work on a popcorn farm in Nebraska.

Charlie learned this type of corn, that popped to a white fluff when heated, had been cultivated for hundreds of years by American Indians. They shared the fluffy food with early American explorers. Popcorn became a popular crop for homesteaders to grow. Nebraska, with its favorable growing climate, developed into the nation's leading popcorn producer.

The popcorn plants grew well even in poor soil, but had few natural defenses against weeds, insects, and diseases. The crops required constant vigilance and care by those tending them. But the additional work resulted in a better cash crop than regular corn or wheat, as popcorn became one of the few luxuries families willingly purchased during financially hard times. Therefore, the popcorn business thrived while other enterprises failed.

During the year Charlie worked on the farm, his main food staple became popped popcorn with milk. He ate it three times a day: morning, noon, and night. Charlie later said, "There I was, eating from my bowl of popcorn and milk as I smelled the fried chicken meal being prepared for the farmer's Sunday dinner." Nevertheless, Charlie acquired a taste for his popcorn concoction, and he frequently ate the milk and popcorn mixture throughout the rest of his life.

After his time on the popcorn farm, Charlie worked numerous odd jobs in different locations but nothing held him in Nebraska. When he discovered that other drifters hopped on freight trains without paying for the travel, Charlie began riding the rails too. Jumping onto a moving railroad car was a dangerous and illegal practice, but Charlie never had any trouble traveling this way.

Riding the rails, Charlie arrived in Oregon in 1913. He was 16 years old. At the time his mother, Cora, was believed to be living in Klamath Falls. He may have also been drawn to Oregon because his two aunts, Bertha and Katherine, lived near the Portland area. The two aunts, 9 and 12 years old when Charlie and Dewey were taken in by their grandmother, held special sister-like bonds with Charlie.

Charlie likely rode the rails when he visited San Francisco in the Spring of 1915. There he attended the World's Fair, officially named The Panama–Pacific International Exposition which showcased the completion of the Panama Canal. The Exposition allowed San Francisco, labeled "The Jewel City," to show the world how the city had recovered from the earthquake of 1906.

The 635-acre fair stretched between the Presidio and Fort Mason, along the northern shore of San Francisco. The size and design were truly remarkable. Later Charlie said of his adventure, "I camped in the park at night and got around to seeing most everything."

An airplane flying through the Palace of Machinery, the largest structure of the exhibition, demonstrated the size and scope of the building. The Horticulture Palace had a glass dome larger than Rome's Saint Peter's Basilica. The Tower of Jewels reached 40 stories skyward. Over 100,000 pieces of multicolored cut glass sparkled from the tower by day and were illuminated by intense electric lights at night.

Other featured structures included the Palace of Fine Arts, the Japanese Pavilion, and Festival Hall. In addition, visitors were able to view the Liberty Bell, on loan from its home in Philadelphia, an exhibit on the telephone, and light shows at night. When the evening fog came in, 48 electric spotlights in seven different colors illuminated the sky to look like the northern lights. Charlie commemorated his visit with the purchases of three different souvenir postcard/folders with 30 photos of the featured buildings and a map of the exposition.

After the San Francisco Exposition, Charlie returned to Oregon. Not much is known about him, except he qualified for a special license to drive lumber trucks. Three years later, near the end of the First World War, he was drafted into the U.S. Army. However,

Charlie contracted a severe case of influenza before he could report for duty.

This illness, known as the "1918 flu pandemic," or "Spanish Flu," spread throughout the world. About one-third of the world's population was infected by what was considered one of human history's deadliest of natural disasters.

Most influenza strains in the past had attacked children, the elderly, and the weak. In contrast, young adults, previously strong and healthy, were the ones who died during the 1918 pandemic. More U.S. soldiers died with this influenza than were killed in the battles of the Great War. By the time Charlie recovered from the flu, the Great War was over.

In 1918, Charlie encountered another disaster. While in Klamath Falls, he met a woman with the same name as his mother—Cora. Charlie was twenty-one and Cora was eighteen when they married in 1919. Unfortunately, Cora Gray proved to have many of the same characteristics as Charlie's own mother, Cora May, as described by Inez in her journaling in 2003:

> *"Charlie had a daughter, Wana and a son, Orin from his first wife, Cora. When Charlie and Cora divorced, Charlie took custody of the two children. This was due to the fact that Cora liked to party and drink and was an unfit mother to care for the children [ruled by the court]. When they were two and five years old, Cora basically kidnapped the children by telling a lie to the housekeeper who was babysitting them while Charlie was at work.*
>
> *We're talking about times when no one had money to follow up or have help to get them back, so he had to leave them with their mom—not knowing where they had gone."*

~

Charlie and Leona, Klamath Falls

Leona had a plan when she left her two children in Montana in the Spring of 1931. She returned to the Klamath Falls area and began attending a local commercial college that trained students in such things as office work and bookkeeping. However, she lost interest in the business world when, at a local dance, she met Charlie Dutton.

He was the Deputy Sheriff of Malin, a small Oregon town about 30 miles south of Klamath Falls, near the California/Oregon border. Charlie must have seemed quite the catch to Leona. He was 35 years old, tall, slim and very handsome, especially in his deputy uniform. He did not drink or smoke, and most importantly, he liked children. Charlie told her that he had two children of his own, although he had not seen them for five years. They were with their mother, in an unknown location.

Besides being in law enforcement, Charlie had acquired knowledge of farming, driving lumber trucks, carpentry, and painting, and had all the abilities of a general handyman. Being a hard worker, he taught himself whatever skills he needed, whenever he needed them.

Yet, Charlie tended to be backward and shy. He brought up the idea of marriage by saying, "Well . . . would you like to put . . . you know, our 'things' together?" Leona thought that was hilarious. They married on September 4, 1931, about nine months after Inez's father died.

Since Leona still retained ownership of the small farm outside of Klamath Falls, Charlie was pleased to move to the farm and help her work the established homestead. However, the farm remained in Leona's name.

Part Four

School Days
1932–1940

~

Oregon Years, 1932–1935

Coming back home to the Oregon farm, Inez encountered a familiar, yet different, look—everything was painted. Once he came to the farm, Charlie's mantra seemed to be, "If it doesn't move, paint it."

Married five months earlier, Leona and Charlie had accomplished much in their determination to put things right on the property. Charlie used his skills as a jack-of-all-trades on, what Leona referred to as "a house of just sticks put together." Neighbors had hastily built the shelter for the family after the fire in 1929 destroyed the home and barn. Because of Henri's illness and death that followed, no repairs or improvements had been done.

Charlie restored Leona's property with needed carpentry, painting, and general handyman work. The dwelling, with renovations and tender care by Charlie, proved durable for years to come. All were completed, despite the lack of money, during the hard years of the Depression.

Young Henry again attended classes at Summers Elementary. Homework, chores, and personal interests occupied his time. He did not allow Inez to enter his realm. Perhaps, he was still wary of the time his sister, as a three-year-old toddler, became angry that he would not share what he was doing. She bopped him on the head with a toy hammer and left a scar.

Having recovered from his illnesses while in the Montana orphanage, Henry milked and did other farm chores. Inez was not taught to do these tasks. Leona did not expect her daughter to milk and do heavy farm chores, as Leona, herself, was required to do in her childhood. Henry thrived in Oregon, but Inez became sickly. She lost the plumpness she gained at Four Buttes and instead grew weak and puny. Therefore, the extent of Inez's outside chores was limited to weeding and helping to tend the vegetable garden.

However, the results of Leona's good intentions tended to isolated Inez from the rest of family. With all the activity going on around her, she became nearly invisible and insignificant. Inez missed the constant company of her doting Aunt Laura in Montana. So, even though her new father was kind and loving, it took time to adjust to the changes in her family.

Here is how Inez described country living in 1932:

> *"After Mom married Charlie, he somewhat remodeled most of the house, but never did anything to the upstairs room where we slept. As long as I could remember it was always the same, just one big room (with a secured ladder for the entry)—no true closets—just cretonne (flowered, rough material) curtains and sheets hanging on a rope, as dividing the room—half for the folks and the remaining half for Henry and me.*
>
> *"We used gas lamps in the house until we received electricity in 1935 and then Mom did have an electric stove (retaining the wood burning stove, as well)—but never did have indoor plumbing. We continued carrying fresh water to the house after pumping it by hand. Of course, no plumbing meant no indoor bathrooms—just outhouses.*
>
> *"As it was said before, Mom raised chickens and a few turkeys. We had plenty of meat. In the fall Dad would hunt wild game. He always got his geese and ducks, as well as pheasants.*
>
> *"Mom maintained a huge garden and all summer we would pick and pick and pick green beans, peas, corn, and berries—strawberries and raspberries. I remember shucking and cleaning cobs of corn all season long. Then Mom canned and canned and*

canned vegetables, berries, and meats. She relied on a pressure cooker to help make her meals. At least we had canned vegetables and meat that sustained us during the slim years.

"Charlie loved fruit, although except for berries, we had to buy all the fruit—like peaches, plums, pears, cherries—which was very extravagant for the times. But Mom canned and canned and canned, those too. We always had a supply of raisins, prunes, and dried figs, shipped from California. Mom baked bread and churned the butter. In reality, we really did eat quite well—with a balanced diet.

"We never had many cows, perhaps 20-25 at a time. Mom and Henry did most of the milking by hand. Our family usually used heavy cream on most anything we would use regular milk on today. The skim milk, we gave to the hogs or calves. Can you believe that? We didn't consider it any good without the butterfat. We separated the milk from the cream and kept the cream to sell for sour cream. This was done by collecting the cream into large metal milk cans. The new cream was added to the old. Believe it or not, it was truly sour cream (spoilt was more like it).

"Charlie moved the structure of my father's isolated screened-in porch and fashioned it to the back of the house. This was used as a cold storage. It wasn't an icebox or refrigeration, but rather resulted in a cooler room with an 18-inch sawdust floor and walls. It was the best we could do at that time and regulations were not as strict, like now.

"It was lonely in the country for me. Henry, being four years older, was no company for me. I 'imagined' a lot. I had a make-believe-friend who I called 'Laun.' I would play for hours in the yard with my 'friend.' Dad had a grinding wheel that I sat on and peddled. So I peddled and peddled, imagining I was traveling somewhere and never left the yard.

"With imagination the lumber ends and pieces from the 'box factory' [where Charley worked] became our cars, trucks, houses, bridges and road system—really just as good as modern-day toys. Of course, one had to take care that her prize toy didn't end up heating the cook-stove fire."

~

Elementary Schooling

In the autumn of 1932, after her sixth birthday, Inez entered first grade at Summers Elementary, where Henry already attended. Oregon did not offer a kindergarten, so this was Inez's first time in any type of class or school setting.

Klamath County provided school bus services for those children required to travel the roadways to get to school. Even during the summer season, the country dirt roads developed deep, hazardous ruts. Those same miles became more dangerous during the severe, cold Oregon winters.

Threating frost and frequent snowstorms could run from September to early June, Oregon's all-time low temperature occurred during Inez's first winter attending school, February 1933. The temperature in northeast Oregon dropped to -54 degrees F when a frigid outbreak brought a surge of Arctic air into the area.

To get to the nearest school-bus stop, the children trudged three-fourths of a mile across an open pasture. While still dark, Henry directed the way with a flashlight. To help the kids get to and from the bus stop during the harshest weather, Charlie fashioned a large square wooden box upon a sled that he hitched to several horses. Thus, he ferried the children through the storms.

So went the weekday task of getting to the bus stop. What did that truly mean? Only after questioned about these experiences, did Inez describe it this way:

"First, I put on white, cotton, long-john underwear, ones with the 'trap-door' at the behind. Since I was small, the underwear would be much too big. So much so, that I had to fold up the material of the arms and legs into cuffs. This formed lumps in the garment, when long woolen socks were pulled over the underwear legs, onto the thighs. This developed more lumps to contend with. A sweater was added before covering the lower half of the body with a pair of Henry's wool or twill overalls. The overalls were cuffed up, as well. I never had the luxury of a snowsuit. I just had Henry's hand-me-down overalls.

"Snowsuits were not available until I was in junior high school, around 1938 or 1939. Then, the snowsuits kept girls dry and warm as they wore the suits to school. The girls still had to change into dresses or skirts, once they arrived at school. Young girls were not allowed to wear long pants to school.

"Black, rubber galoshes were secured over the shoes which were now snug and uncomfortable due to the thick, knobby socks. The galoshes were useful trappings to help protect the feet from the wet weather conditions. These were not the cute and colorful over boots of nowadays. My galoshes went only up to my ankles—not much protection from the elements when the snow and water splashed up the side of the leg. While walking, hunks of icy snow often collected in the cuffs of the overalls. Some children wore leather boots, but I never did have a pair. Donning a coat, mittens and a stocking cap, I was ready to make my way to the bus stop.

"Our neighbors, the Shoemayers lived close to the road and bus stop. Their home remained our pre-bus stop sanctuary, throughout our school years, even though their children were much older than Henry and me. However, the refuge had an obstacle.

"The direct route to the house went through the Shoemayers' corral. Going around the fences and gates required too much time and effort. So, through the corral we went. This involved squish-squashy steps into the enclosure, sinking deep into the

muck of mud and manure. With our sights on the house, we balanced our bodies so not to fall into the yucky muck, while withdrawing the back foot out of the mud. All the while, we could feel and hear the accompanied sucking threats of the mud, attempting to pull off our galoshes.

"When Henry and I cleared the corral, we washed off our galoshes of the muck. We shed our outer garments and placed them to dry by the heater in the Shoemayers' house. At the same time, our freezing bodies warmed up. Once dried and warmed, I redressed in my required skirt or dress for school. We then walked the distance of about a block to the actual bus stop.

"Riding the bus was pleasant and a social time for me. When I got into the bus, the older children comforted me and warmed my cold hands. Other times they would offer me gum or candy to make me forget about the cold.

"The buses never seemed to have trouble with the roads or the weather. 'Hip', the one and only bus driver for the entire time I rode the bus, was a very nice man. He was especially helpful and watchful for all the students riding the bus.

"After school, the reverse procedure would take place. If a late afternoon snowstorm developed before I got home, Charlie met me at the Shoemayers to accompany me home. It was rather hard for me to walk in the snow up to my knees. He walked ahead of me, having me step in where he just stepped. If there was a strong wind with sleet and snow, I was instructed to wrap my arms tightly around Charlie's waist, from behind, and step where he stepped. This conserved my energy and made it a little easier for me to walk home."

Lack of maturity, partnered with a long bus ride, may have contributed to other kind of vulnerable condition for Inez. Her strict first-grade teacher held to the rules about students not leaving the classroom to use the restroom during class time. One day Inez had to urinate before the lunch break. She saw other children's urine puddles left on the classroom floor—so when she realized she could not hold her urine any longer, she "let loose" . . . what a relief it was . . . until she looked to survey the damage. Much to her shock, over the end of her desk she saw someone's red mitten floating, like a sailboat— back and forth—in her huge puddle of urine.

Further journaling, 2003:

> *"The very cold winter caused frostbite to my feet. Large welts appeared on my legs and even though I was dressed warmly, my feet never seemed to get warm. All winter my feet were numb—they never did thaw out."*

Whenever asked, Inez described her early school days in terms of the condition of her feet. Maybe, she inherited her father's bad feet. Or perhaps, foot damage resulted due to exposure to the cold climates in Oregon and Montana, while wearing too-tight shoes. Whatever the cause, Inez suffered from chilblains, painful, ingrown toenails, and compromised circulation throughout her life.

Boarded Out

INSUFFICIENT ATTENDANCE FOR GRADING. So read Inez's end-of-the-year report card for first grade. After all the effort to get to the bus stop, the harsh weather and frequent cold viruses contributed to her missing too many school days. It flagged failure—Inez would not advance to the second grade.

Klamath County launched into action for a solution to provide the children with a proper education and overcome their bus-stop issue. The County paid for room and board to house the children closer to the elementary school. The next school year, both Inez and Henry stayed through the worst of the winter weather with the Olsens, a childless couple who lived across the street from Summers Elementary school.

Mr. Olsen was the principal of the school and his wife also had training in education. Inez started out the year repeating the first grade. However, after only a couple months of Mrs. Olsen's tutoring, Inez was promoted to the second grade with her regular age group. Later, she won the second-grade spelling bee and received a little autograph album.

The Olsens were firm, but good to the children. Each of them had memorable characteristics: He stuttered so badly that his eyes rolled back in his head when he attempted to overcome a difficult word, while she had a "churchy" appearance, dressed plain, wore no makeup, and pulled her hair back severely.

Once Inez returned from a weekend at home with a special treat of red nail polish on her fingernails. Mrs. Olsen became so upset that she filed off the surface of each nail with a metal file until every speck of red polish was removed— a very painful and degrading action for such a young child. Yet, Mrs. Olsen also had gentle and nurturing qualities. Inez remembered the older woman made taffy one evening and the group enjoyed the novel experience of a taffy pull. When Inez developed a bad cold, Mrs. Olsen gave her hot lemonade to drink and introduced her to another memorable experience—Vicks Vapor Rub applied to her chest.

So set the pattern for Inez, boarding with other families in order to go to school during the frigid winter weather. After the first year, it was decided eleven-year-old Henry was strong enough to withstand the winter elements. He stayed at his home and caught the school bus a mile away, as before. By remaining on the farm, Henry again became a great help with the milking and many other farm chores.

~

3rd and 4th Grades, 1934–1936

Inez's journaling, 2003:

> *"I keep flashing to other times. I do remember living with Julie Reginatos in my third grade. I remember she was a darling little blond girl, a year ahead of me in school. Her mom was divorced (and I'm not sure how long). The family did not live far from us except she didn't have to walk through snow up to her knees to catch the bus, but rather the bus went right by her door."*

For some reason, each new school year brought a different host family for Inez. During third grade, Inez moved in with the Reginatos, who lived at a dairy close to the bus stop. The daughter, Julie, attended the Catholic school but both girls traveled on the same bus to their respective destinations.

Each host home posed challenges with different situations and circumstances. Trouble arose when Julie, used to sleeping with her mother, refused to accept the intended plan for the two little girls to share a bedroom. This issue made for constant tension. As is so often the case, the crowd of three was hard for Julie to understand and embrace. Her demands for attention meant that Inez was inevitably left out of many household activities. The divorced Mrs. Reginatos tried to be fair and kind to Inez, but Julie remained jealous.

Other changes that year required yet more adjustments for Inez. The school district transferred all the incoming third graders from

Summers Elementary School to Altamont Elementary. Both were little country schools, across the street from each other.

Fourth grade for Inez began with a brief stay with a Seventh Day Adventist couple who she remembered drank Postum (an instant decaffeinated powder mix) instead of regular coffee. The couple's relatives from California shipped a crate of persimmons during Inez's stay. Her first bite of the fruit proved awful to her young taste buds.

Whether it was the persimmons or something else, both sides must have felt the strangeness of the relationship. The next month she moved into Klamath Falls to stay with yet another family, the Holstens. This time she was close enough to walk to school. However, it also meant a complete change to a different school. Summers and Altamont Elementary schools were little, old-fashioned country schools, whereas the new school, Mills Elementary, proved to be large and active, as well as academically challenging for Inez.

Somehow, she missed being taught math. Problems such as 6+7=13 were foreign to her. Inez felt so dumb when she fell behind the rest of her class, she swore she never learned these calculations. Inez adapted by counting imaginary fingers, as fast as she could, to figure up the correct answers. Physically counting real fingers violated school rules.

Living with this new host family had positive benefits. Mr. Holsten ran a confectionary-grocery store—that meant candy and sweets stocked the shelves. He was very generous and often allowed her to pick out a candy of her choice. The Holsten's older son and his girlfriend also gave Inez candy. What a treat for a little country girl!

One particular night, while Mr. and Mrs. Holsten went out for the evening, the son and girlfriend babysat for nine-year-old Inez. She was really enjoying the young couple's company, but before she knew it, the clock showed it was nine o'clock—her bedtime. Once in bed, Inez found it hard to fall asleep because it was still light outside. The next morning, she discovered someone had advanced the clock several hours ahead of time. Inez must have been cutting in on the young couple's smooching time.

Inez remained relatively healthy throughout the school year, despite her increased candy intake. Then, she contracted a severe case of *rubeola* virus (regular measles), with the complication of a painful ear abscess. She returned home to her own bed and missed the last two weeks of fourth grade. To Inez, this infirmity was the worst of all her childhood illnesses. Antibiotics were not yet in use, and the ear infection probably contributed to deafness in her right ear.

Maybe being so sick inspired spiritual thoughts in Inez. She started to have private prayers at bedtime. Prior to that time, bedtime prayers were said in rote fashion, in the presence of an adult, such as her mother or Auntie Laura. However, without any formal, structured religion, Inez took it upon herself to never go to sleep without having her special discussion with God—a practice she has kept throughout her life.

~

Who the Heck Was Grandma Farley?

Colorful, eccentric personalities bring fun and spice to the landscape of daily life—unless those characters are relatives, or considered to be relatives. Charlie Dutton brought two such individuals into the unsuspecting life of Inez.

The day Inez and Henry arrived on the train from Montana, they were taken to meet an unusual person—Cora May Dutton Kettlehut Franklin. In 1932, she went by Cora Farley, although the surname of her most recent husband, or boyfriend, was Frost. Charlie's priority on that day was to introduce his two new stepchildren to his mother.

Mother and son had reconnected, though Inez never knew exactly how. All was forgiven for Cora's abandonment of Charlie as a toddler and his brother Dewey as an infant, years before. Perhaps, Cora lived in Klamath Falls first and was the reason Charlie moved from Nebraska and settled in Oregon. The 1930 U.S. Census of Klamath Falls listed Charlie Dutton as residing with Cora Farley.

Through the next twelve years, Charlie's mother blended into Inez and Henry's lives. It was rather a shame to have Grandma Farley around instead of Inez's Grandma Doyon, for they differed completely from each other. Grandma Doyon was short, soft and round, loving and cuddly. She wore colorful clothing and pearl jewelry. She smelled sweet and inviting. Grandma Doyon spoke in French endearments. In contrast, Grandma Farley, a tall, bony woman, stood hunched over, stiff and aloof. She smelled of mothballs and only wore clothes in her favorite color—green.

As the years went by, Henry and Inez realized that Grandma Farley was a weird lady.

Whenever the family stopped by to take her out to lunch for a sandwich, the first thing out of her mouth would be, "Let me wash my feet." Nothing else ever seemed to merit a washing, except her feet.

Most of the time, the woman went around without her dentures, allowing her nose and pointed chin to nearly touch. She resembled a witch in the truest form. Oh, she did have a set of false teeth. They were reserved for the special occasion of dining out. She would put in her teeth, right after washing her feet.

The false teeth did not fit right. In front of everyone, and to Henry's disgust and horror, Grandma Farley struggled to remove those dentures during mealtime as she ate her food. It was not a pleasant sight.

Inez enjoyed seeing Grandma Farley's front yard, for it was unlike any other front yard she had ever seen. Instead of organized flower beds, all sorts of flowers bloomed where the grass should have been. It looked like someone had sprinkled flower seeds at random, and that's probably what Grandma Farley had done.

The flowery welcome was a cruel joke. When one went into the house, he or she would be confronted by the smells from the toilet mingled with mothballs. Cora feared moths damaging her things. She did have several nice wool blankets thrown over her couch. As for the toilet, Cora didn't flush because she believed it would raise the cost of her water bill. The overpowering smells were not the only problem with the residence. Piles of magazines and newspapers stacked everywhere in the house. It could only be assumed Cora read all those magazines and newspapers.

Cora, a true-blue Republican, through and through, did not vote for FDR or his New Deal. Yet, being financially well off and owning several properties did not keep her from collecting her "due" from the relief lines of the times. She took advantage of what was offered and frequented the government relief centers for staples, such as beans, rice, and cornmeal. The bags of food piled up in her house until

Cora gave some to Charlie's family. The food had the pungent smell of moth balls and even seemed to taste like mothballs. Surely Cora never used much of this food herself. Her diet consisted of peanut butter and crackers with coffee—lots and lots of coffee.

Teenage Henry once said with indignant fervor, "Do you think I want to give anyone the idea she is related to me? No thank you." This gave Inez license to avoid any encounter herself with Grandma Farley. Whenever a chance meeting occurred on the streets of Klamath Falls, Inez steered her friends the other way. She would tell them, "Come on, I don't want to speak to that lady."

At these embarrassing times, Grandma Farley could be seen mumbling to herself. No matter the season, she sported a knitted stocking cap on her head. All the while, she clung to a large leather diaper bag—the satchel for her grandson, Orin, born fifteen years earlier. Those things might be in fashion nowadays, but to Henry and Inez it made the woman even more odd. The family never considered Grandma Farley mentally ill. They just considered her contrary—just like she had been all of her life.

In 1955, Inez inherited a hideous green couch that belonged to Grandma Farley. Even though the divan was in good condition, it only stayed a brief time in our house. I don't remember that it smelled of mothballs, but it was stiff and uncomfortable—just like I imagined Grandma Farley.

All my life, I heard my mother joke about "Grandma Farley" and the washing of her feet before going anywhere. I gathered she was different from most other people, but I was surprised to learn the extent of her eccentricities. I must say, she brought contrast and discussion into our family life. And we may say, "There but for the grace of God, go I." But after all was said and done, I felt the same way as my Uncle Henry: "Thank goodness she was not related by blood."

The Saga of Orin (Brown) Dutton

Grandma Farley was not the only memorable character who came into Inez's life with her mother's marriage to Charlie Dutton. This is how Inez describes her stepbrother:

> *"(Very important scribbling: Here I am after how many months and maybe years since I last picked up a pen.). I'm thinking of a time in the fall of 1934, when my brother Henry and I stayed out in the country with our neighbor, Scotty and his wife, for about six weeks while Mom and Dad (Charlie) went on a road trip to Arizona. They drove their newly purchased Chevrolet, to see his father in Nebraska and his brother Dewey in Colorado. Through family members, Charlie discovered his children were living in Nogales, so the car trip was extended into Arizona.*
>
> *"Charlie's daughter and a son, Wana and Orin, were with their mother (Cora Gray) since she snatched them at the ages of 5 and 3 years old, while he was at work. What a thrill for Charlie to find the kids after so long. It had been eight years since he saw them last. They were then 13 and 11 years old and went by the last name of Brown—The name of the fellow Cora married after Charlie and her were divorced.*
>
> *"Wana had a boyfriend, and she did not want to leave Arizona. But Cora decided to have Orin come home to Oregon to live with us for a while. Truth be told, she was glad to have the boy leave. Orin had a history of getting into trouble and proved to be a handful for Cora.*

"My mom (Leona) told of how the pleasantry of the return trip back to Oregon quickly deteriorated when the group stopped at a fruit stand, along the Arizona road. Orin discovered a new fruit he had never seen before—pomegranates. He insisted on eating the pomegranates in the back seat of his father's new car. When he was told not to do this, he snuck tastes of the juicy fruit when the older couple was not looking. Needless to say, Leona was furious over the mess and stains the pomegranate juice made to the new car upholstery.

"With the slow correspondence in those days, we didn't know when the folks were coming home—no telephone, no way to know. Well you can imagine the amazement Henry and I felt when we walked home after getting off the bus. Here was this cute, little, eleven-year-old, blond kid with big brown eyes sitting on the corral fence—the fence to the bullpen.

"Although the bullpen was built sturdy with railroad tie lumber, being physically close to the bullpen was a dangerous thing to do. Not too long before, one of the neighbors (Joe Wright's father) had been found dead in the bullpen, gored to death. So, there sat my stepbrother Orin, big as you please, in such a dangerous place—but oh so daring!

"That was a day I'll never forget. From then on, life seemed to center around Orin. What a guy! He was different from anyone Henry or I had ever known. He was so full of mischief. I can't start to tell you. Whatever he learned in Arizona was so much different from us dumb old, 'Brush Runners' (a derogatory name for people from Oregon.) There wasn't anything Orin didn't know, and he didn't mind sharing it with us. Oh, my!

"Henry was twelve and a half and I was almost eight. What a very impressionable time for us. We became three crazy kids that almost drove my mom crazy.

"Orin was wild and bold—everything Henry wasn't. It was Orin's idea to ride and race young steers like horses. One time he wagered he could fart non-stop from the house to the

barn—Henry lost that bet. But Henry earned back his money, for Orin was willing to pay anyone to do his chores.

"At that time, I was taking dancing and acrobatics. Everything I learned Orin did too. Here was Henry, awkward as the dickens and here was Orin, smooth as satin. Orin could do handstands, backbends and everything I brought home—he could do cartwheels, whatever. And he would mock anything I could do in dance, including tap dancing. What a time that was.

"Then there was the time I broke my arm and Mom thought it was basically Orin's fault. The three of us kids were scuffling around. Orin wanted to do the 'cannonball'—where someone lies on his or her back with their knees bent upwards, so a person sits on his feet, and he gives them a real shove through the air. That's what happened to Orin and me: I sat on his feet; he gave me a real shove upward; I went flying through the air and landed on my butt with my arm back behind me!

"My arm snapped like a stick and my mom came running, for she could hear it break from across the yard. I remember holding out my arm and the part below the elbow just hung there limply. Mom positioned the arm in its place thus setting the bone. The doctor later said it was good it was done earlier because the swelling would have inhibited the bone being set correctly as it should have been. Mom was so mad about the broken arm—of us playing so rough and of the cost for the medical expenses. As it turned out, the first doctor only cast the arm up to the elbow; however, follow up examinations found the broken arm was healing in a twisted position. The second doctor fashioned a different support for the arm after the cast was removed. This time it was not plaster of Paris, but metal frames covered with bandages, with a metal protector for the elbow. I also maintained the arm in a sling for six weeks until it finally healed. So that was the end of my acrobatic career.

"If Orin wasn't in trouble at home, he was in trouble in school (due to stealing money at school.) Orin usually went by the last name of 'Brown,' unless he got into trouble and then his last

name was 'Dutton.' I can't remember how long it was, but he spent quite a bit of time with us. He was probably with us for a year or a year and a half. Then he moved to town with some of his mother's folks in Klamath Falls.

"Later, when Orin was about seventeen, he and another guy got into trouble for taking a couple of under aged girls over the California-Oregon border. The border was only twenty to thirty miles south of Klamath Falls. It was called 'White Slavery' at the time! Anyways, he had a choice of jail or military. He chose the military in 1941—and he went into the Oregon National Guard. Lordy, Lordy, when he came home on leave in his military uniform, he was a DOLL! (Orin wanted me to write while he was in the service, but Mom forbade it so there was no corresponding between the two of us.)

"He married a girl from the state of Washington, whom he had met when he was stationed in the service at Fort Lewis. They had two children, Kathy and Dennis. From then on, I don't know much except that they were divorced, and he later married again.

"Orin reminded me of my 'cannon ball flight' that broke my arm the last time I saw him in 1981 when Charlie died. (Orin's parents, Charlie and Cora, died a few days of each other—Orin was on his way to Charlie's funeral when he was notified of Cora's death in Oregon.) Orin passed away a couple of years after our last meeting in Fresno, California.

"This was the saga of Orin (Brown) Dutton."

~

Electricity to the Farm, 1935

By the 1930s, many people in the United States enjoyed electricity in their homes. Inez became accustomed to the amenities of electricity and indoor plumbing while residing in different homes for school. However, when she returned home to the family farm, she instead had kerosene lamps, an outhouse, a wood-burning stove, and buckets of water to haul.

The lack of electricity in the area was not really a financial issue. Rather, the geographical barriers and the farm's location complicated the establishment and maintenance of the electrical lines. Then, in 1935, the U.S. government extended electrical services to the lone holdover in the area—the David/Dutton property.

Thirteen-year-old Henry held a half-filled metal milking bucket in one hand, as he patted the rump of the milking cow. "Well Daisy, that will do for now."

Henry was not one for small talk. But he did love his critters, and that included talking to the milking cows. He laughed to himself. *Better to talk to a bovine than to my dumb sister, Inez.*

Many of the farm chores fell to Henry since his stepfather worked long hours at the lumber company. He and his mother milked 9 to 10 cows twice a day, every day, during the lactating season. It took close to an hour to milk three cows. He reasoned to himself, *Mom said I milked as fast as she does . . . but if we had an electric milking machine, like our neighbors, we could milk all our cows in twenty minutes and get twice as much milk.*

Henry walked out to the water pump to wash. A dusty, black sedan "government car" drove up the lane leading to the house. Leona came out of the kitchen to meet the vehicle. A man, looking out of place in his three-piece gray flannel suit, exited the automobile.

"Good day. I'm looking for the owners, Henri and Leona David."

Leona wiped her hands on her apron and offered her hand to the stranger. "I'm Leona David, well . . . Dutton now. Henri died four years ago, but I still own this property."

The man flashed a forced smile, "Well ma'am, it's your lucky day. According to our records, you are the last farm in these parts without electricity. So, if you sign on the dotted line, the WPA can begin the process of bringing electrical power to your property."

Leona hesitated. "I thought the Works Progress Administration just constructed buildings, parks and bridges. . . . How much will this cost us?"

With a snicker, he said, "Well ma'am you've got it all wrong. The WPA projects change with the needs. FDR promised everyone the chance to have electricity in their place if they want it. Now the federal government recognized its duty to provide the convenience of electricity to rural homes and farms."

Leona took the ink pen from the man and signed the contract.

In a few days, the farm was abuzz with activity. All the commotion was reminiscent of the 1929 construction when the David family moved onto the farm. However, at this time men and dredging machines occupied the farm to focus on Miller Hill, located directly behind the farmhouse. Always thought to be insignificant—except as a place for Henry to hunt ground squirrels—Miller Hill served as the key to this electrical project.

Machines gobbled up the earth from the hill, a scoopful at a time, in search for water. Once they found water, the next step was to channel it downhill through the generator to produce electricity. A gas engine at the foot of the hill pumped the water back up the hill. Runoff water collected in a drainage ditch, forming a pond of sorts that proved to be an acceptable ice-skating surface later in the winter.

During a walk around the construction site, Henry spied something odd. It looked almost like a make-believe fish on a platter. He picked it up and thought: *How did this get here? The crew said the dredging was deeper than 50 feet today.*

When the site foreman walked by, Henry said. "Excuse me, mister. I found this." Henry held up a perfect petrified fish, the size of his hand, on a piece of hardpan "platter."

The foreman said, "Well now Sonny. Whatcha got there?"

Henry replied, "I remember seeing something like this in my general science book. I think it's called a fossil."

"I'll check it out for you," promised the foreman as he took the fish from Henry.

A week later, Henry found the foreman sitting on a wooden box taking a break under the shade of the oak tree.

"Excuse me, sir. What happened to that fish body that was found the other day?"

The man mopped his brow with a red handkerchief. "Oh, I showed it to that newspaper reporter sniffing around, but he wasn't interested in it. I threw it on the trash heap, and I guess it was taken to the dump."

Henry turned abruptly. He dared not show his temper, but mentally questioned, *How could they just throw it away?*

He continued to search the area in hopes of finding other fish fossils. But he never did.

The digging behind the Dutton home continued to fascinate Henry. However, what excited him the most was the electrical setup and wiring of the actual lines into the house and barn. The subject of electricity ignited sparks of desire for the youth to learn more about the source of energy. Electrical terms became like music to his ears, such magical terms as transformers, meters, cables, conduits, breakers, fuse boxes, and other power-filled terms like hot and neutral wires, current flow, and on-off switches. A new thought entered Henry's mind: *Maybe I can become an electrician when I grow up. Installing lighting and connecting transformers to circuit breakers sound a lot better than farming.*

Henry and nine-year-old Inez watched mesmerized for months while the electricity project brought the family and the farm into the twentieth century. Finally, with the water energy harnessed and routed, the barriers to electricity for the Duttons were overcome. Electricity in the house allowed the family to have an electric stove and a refrigerator. Each room displayed bare, hanging light bulbs that turned on and off with a pull chain.

In the barn, electricity allowed the installation of a modern milking machine and cream separator. These eased the milking workload by helping centrifuge milk, dividing it into cream and skimmed milk. Most of all, it improved the possibility of selling the farm.

Several years later, Henry became a journeyman electrician. He had learned to utilize one of the most important and powerful forms of energy for the betterment of his community and country.

~

Moving to Town, 1936

With electricity established to the house and the milking barns, Leona sold her farm. The 1936 move to within the city limits of Klamath Falls brought many adjustments to the Dutton family. Inez observed the change in scope of living beyond her farm life.

Inez journaled the move to town:

> *"Dad (Charlie) worked at Home Lumber and Supply Company in town. He was paid $75 a month. We moved into a house I loved on Sergeant Street. It had lots of rooms and a quaintness with a music room, a sunroom, a basement, dressing rooms, a pantry with glass doors, a nook in the kitchen with booths, and even a telephone area with a bench. The living room had window seats. It seemed the previous owner kept building on rooms, as he wanted. Henry had one bedroom; my folks and I shared a glassed-in patio, as our bedroom.*
>
> *"This was the most fun time of my life. The place had a lovely gazebo in the yard. I played house from morning until night, in the gazebo, with a little Indian girl from across the street, Charlotte Crane.*
>
> *"Charlotte had beautiful dolls with clothes and everything. She was a year older, eleven, and I was ten years old. Charlotte's father was a representative for the Klamath Indians in Washington D.C. I recall each of Charlotte's family received $15 a month from the U.S. government as a stipend. She had a large extended family that lived with her. Her grandmother*

scared me. She smoked a pipe, and from the corner of the house, watched my every move.

"That year Henry was fourteen and in high school. He stacked wood all summer long to save enough money to buy a second-hand bicycle. At this time, Henry had a dog, Tricksey, a little white terrier. He loved her dearly. Tricksey did not care for me—I think Henry 'sic-ed her' on me.

"Tricksey would tap Mom (Leona), ever-so-gently on the thigh, to beg for the morning bacon. It was shocking that a Dutton dog would be allowed in the house, much less eat with us at breakfast or supper.

"Henry also had Fritz, a white rat that one day moved into Tricksey's doghouse. Needless to say, Tricksey moved out."

❂ ❂ ❂

The journaling continues:

"Holidays were so much more interesting in town. I joined Girl Scouts and enjoyed that until Halloween. Dad told us about how much damage the kids would do during Halloween in his day. So, when girls from the Girl Scouts came to our house to 'Trick or Treat,' my mom threw a dishpan of water on them. Even though I continued with Girl Scouts, I always felt so embarrassed over that situation.

"I did have a wonderful Christmas. This was the first year to enjoy the Christmas lights and decorations of the homes and businesses in town. The hustle and bustle of the holiday season was all around. By playing dolls so much, I wanted a new doll so bad, like Charlotte. However, when I opened my Christmas present, there was a new wig for my old doll. What a disappointment, to say the least!"

Fairview Elementary School

Inez's journal continues:

> *"I went to Fairview elementary school for the fifth grade where I could walk to school and stay with my family throughout the year. By living in town, I could do things I never could do in the country, like having fun roller-skating and playing with friends—or get into trouble.*
>
> *"Sometimes, when Mom worked on Saturdays, she gave me money for a movie and a candy bar. I understood that I was to come right home after the movie. One time after the movie, I got together with another classmate, who was a bad influence on me. We chased after a fire engine, blocks away from our neighborhood to watch the firemen put out a burning house. When Mom came home, she panicked; I was no place to be found. She searched, calling my name, and asking anyone she met about me. When I finally returned home, I knew I was in trouble. I received a spanking a 10-year-old could not forget."*

While attending Fairview Elementary, Inez had the opportunity to perform as one of three dancers in Scotland's national dance—the Highland Fling. The movement required a delicate balance of precision at a vigorous pace, all the while balancing on pointed toes. Executed in 4/4 time, the fling consists of a series of intricate steps performed in place. Especially characteristic was a light step in which the dancer hopped on one foot, while moving the other foot in front and then behind the calf of the leg.

The Klamath Fall Highland Dancers dressed in red and green, plaid skirts, matching garrison caps, and argyle socks. Red suspenders and a white blouse with a plaid sash completed the outfits.

Decades after the actual dance presentation and, to the delight of her children, Inez occasionally did her "fling." It seemed her dancing feet would stir whenever she heard a bagpipe jig. Inez became a girl of ten years old, once again. The only thing missing was her 1936 costume.

All About the Hair

In her younger years, Inez's straight, dark flyaway hair had been maintained in a bobbed style, with frequent haircuts by Charlie. Now that they lived in town, Leona took Inez to a beauty salon to get her first permanent wave.

The permanents of the time worked by running an electrical current through hair that had been tightly wound on spiral rods. An early styling apparatus was called Frederick's permanent wave machine. This large device descended from the ceiling, looking quite a bit like a milking machine as it did. Clamps attached to the curling rods ran electrical power through the rods. The steamy, tedious permanent process took all day. Inez imagined that with curls she would look like popular child star Shirley Temple—but in the end, she still looked like Inez Dutton.

Over several seasons, Inez had three of these types of permanents, but the procedures were always risky. With the second permanent, she sustained burns on her neck and ear. Regardless, she never complained or let anyone know about these injuries.

The bulky, electrical process of styling women's hair changed after 1938. Steam-heated contraptions were no longer needed to set hair into waves. Instead, the curling method advanced to a "cold wave" process that relied on chemicals in lotion form to give the desired curls. This new method was available in beauty salons, but Leona and Inez mostly used the at-home permanent kits.

At eleven years old, Inez started the nightly routine of pin curling her hair with bobby pins. Later, metal hair clips became her beauty tool of choice. Once she got the hang of pin curling, Inez transformed her perceived "problem hair" to one of her greatest assets.

Schoolmates noticed that Inez always had every hair in place, every day of the school year. One of her greatest compliments came by way of the 1942 El Rodeo yearbook. Barbara Halvorsen, an upper classmate, wrote: "You sure can fix your hair darling. I think you are cute too. Good luck."

All was right in the universe if a girl's hair was in place—after all, it's all about the hair.

Changes

Living in town changed the once routine farm life into an erratic time that affected the family's togetherness. Charlie's shifts at the lumber store reflected this. He stayed late into the evening, until the last customer left the store and the day's work was completed. Henry had part-time jobs and his teenage activities often kept him away from home.

Leona went out in the evenings to work as a fry cook at the airport. Released from the demands of farm chores, she now had time for various activities and interests, such as music, sewing and fashion. Still in her early thirties, Leona sought after more fun and entertainment.

Her friend, Mrs. Zetzman, shared her old *Photoplay* magazines with Leona. Soon Leona became a faithful reader of the publication that sensationalized the lives of movie stars. She cut out and scrapbooked pictures from these magazines. Perhaps she wanted the excitement depicted in the movies.

Inez continued journaling about the move to town:

> *"With moving to town, Mom started to have a lot more choices of things to do and pursue. She always fancied herself as being a good singer and she enjoyed singing what she called her 'cowboy songs' with her guitar. One of her friends owned a music store and one embarrassing time occurred when we visited the store where a microphone was hooked up. Mom stepped up to*

the microphone and out came the loudest twang-twangy 'cowboy song,' one could ever imagine. And sadly, the song went on and on twangy, loud, and piercing—all at the same time. Mom was quite pleased with herself when she was done. I was pleased when she was done too!"

Inez addressed what became of her piano lessons:

"I guess Mom hoped I had inherited her musical talent. Somewhere, an old upright piano was obtained, and I started to take piano lessons. The piano teacher had lofty ideas and my first musical piece was 'The Glow Worm.' It is quite complicated with a quick rhythm and much fingering. If that wasn't bad enough, I had started lessons well into the year and a piano recital was scheduled just weeks away. I was very upset and nervous. To make it worse, Mom felt I wasn't learning fast enough, and it wasn't worth the money. So, we stopped the piano lesson and thus, ended my piano career.

Inez also discussed her parents' attendance at a revival meeting:

"Around this time, Mom and Charlie started to feel they should be going to church. Mom did not have much respect for the Catholic Church. Besides, Charlie was a divorced man and not accepted in those days by the Catholics. Every so often they would visit one of the various churches in the area.

"They never really found one that suited them. However, they did tell of one experience at a small church. There must have been some sort of revival going on, because the congregation was worked up to a near frenzy when an extremely large woman fainted.

"The woman's friends seemed to know what to do. They raised her shirt to expose an ample belly and a chilled watermelon was placed on her skin to revive her. With each breath she took, the watermelon quivered and dance on her stomach. Although, she did not resort to speaking in tongues, she did awake with a start to the coldness of the fruit and the revival continued."

More Changes

Even though Charlie followed the world news via radio and newspapers, eleven-year-old Inez was oblivious to the European unrest of the mid-1930s. Yet, the changing circumstances in Germany entered Inez's school life.

Inez journaled:

> *"In the later part of fifth grade, the principle came into the class one day and said we would have a new student, Marianne Lyon. He made a point that we should not make fun of her because she did not speak English. I didn't consider her very good looking as she had a very different look to her. Not until four or five years later, did I realize that she was Jewish, and her family had escaped from Germany.*
>
> *The family had money so later her father bought the existing Le Ponte dress shop in Klamath Falls. As it turned out, we also went to high school together. Marianne was very scholastic and quite brilliant, so was her younger sister. Marianne mastered the English language and moved on to taking Spanish and Latin at the same time. Definitely the brightest girl in our high school, she was also involved in all the activities of school. She even became our graduating class valedictorian.*
>
> *Marianne married one of the brothers who owned Weil Brothers clothing store in Fresno, California. I met the brothers by chance one day at a lunch counter in Fresno."*

~

6th Grade, 1937

Inez describes those times:

"The following year (in 1937) we moved from my beloved house on Sergeant Street with its quaint rooms and lovely yard to a monster of a house on Alameda Street in the Pacific Terrace area of Klamath Falls. This Delaware Brownstone house was probably quite hoity-toity in its heyday but, with our sparse furniture, a feeling of the rooms being cold and empty existed. It was a very large home with the majority of the rooms closed off to economize. Dark wood accents decorated the large living room. There were glass doors to the dining room, a parlor, a huge kitchen, a big stone fireplace, hardwood floors throughout the house, a completed upstairs and even a penthouse.

"I went to Roosevelt school for my sixth grade. Many of the people lived in big houses and tended to be sort of snooty and I felt out of place. We had moved after the new school year had already started. I had become very thin. A note was sent home from school to tell my mother I was too thin; I was eleven years old and weighed sixty pounds. We always had plenty of healthy foods to eat so I'm not sure why I was so underweight.

"The saddest memory of that year was on Valentine's Day. My mother made sure all the class members had valentines. However, I didn't receive even one, in return. This never happened to me before in other schools. The agony of hearing my teacher read name after name for students to come up and receive a valentine, but none for me, was humiliating.

"One girl, Barbara Brosterhaus, lived several houses from ours, ignored me at school when her friends were about. But away from school, she was always eager to dress up in pretend clothes and put on makeup. She enjoyed putting on plays with constructed costumes for each part. Clothing was embellished and enhanced with colored crepe paper. Sometimes, three of us girls played, but usually those times meant that I was the third girl out."

The brownstone on Alameda Street was located in an upscale part of Klamath Falls known for architectural beauty and style. Perhaps Leona felt she moved up to affluence with the purchase of that brownstone. However, the cost for the furnishings, heating, and general maintenance of such a large structure may not have been accurately considered.

When the person who bought their farm began defaulting on his monthly payments, Leona decided to rent three bedrooms out to railroad men, to make ends meet. Their meals were not included, but she did provide linens.

Despite their financial situation, Inez remembered the purchase of a bulky mechanical laundry aid to press the renter's sheets and towels. It was called a mangle and consisted of two rollers in a sturdy frame, connected by cogs and powered by a hand crank. Leona's desire to obtain this machine seemed extravagant to the point of poor judgment.

Meanwhile, Leona and Charlie's marriage, was becoming complicated and stressful. Jealousy over fraternizing with the opposite sex may have been the cause. The true reasons for the strain are unknown. It was not evident to Inez, but an undercurrent of dissatisfaction existed for the whole family.

Blending Charlie's and Leona's families had not turned out as originally planned. Many disagreements centered on having Charlie's children stay with them. Both Wana and Orin were disrespectful of Leona. Wana moved to Klamath Falls when she was in her mid-teen years and proved to be as wild as her own mother. Leona called Wana a "chippie" and felt she was a bad influence on the other kids. Orin continued breaking family and school rules. Wana and Orin didn't want to be part of the family either.

Her mother, Charlie, and Henry were all going their own ways. Inez, left alone a lot, became nervous and easily frightened. The fact that she was so very underweight for her age indicated physical evidence of a child under stress.

Soon the union between Charlie and Leona dissolved completely.

~

Train Trip to Texas

"Look-ie here, look-ie here. What a pur-dy lady who just walked into the train!" The man's Errol Flynn moustache disappeared with his smile when he flashed his yellow, toothy grin. Greased, thinning black hair showed when he half-stood and tipped his hat.

His appearance shrieked sleaziness, yet Leona glowed with appreciation.

Oh, brother. Does she really believe that stuff? thought eleven-year-old Inez.

In late November of 1937, the mother-daughter duo hustled into the last two empty adjoining train seats. Inez was directed to sit in the empty seat next to the window, across from a sleeping lump of a man. Leona stationed herself in front of the smooth-talking stranger as he removed his gray coat jacket. He sported a pair of gray suspenders that stretched against a wilted, stained white shirt. He reeked of cigarettes, alcohol, and sweat, but her mother did not appear to take notice.

A jolting, hesitant movement gave the first sign of the train's forward motion. Inez pressed her face to the smudged glass window. She looked back on the familiar sights of Klamath Falls slipping away. And the adventure began. . . .

Inez did not know the actual reason for the impromptu train trip. Her mother had developed a habit of taking spontaneous excursions and holidays by herself, although this time she was taking her daughter with her. This journey appeared to be a spur of the moment decision by Leona to go see her mother—Inez's grandmother—in Hereford,

Texas. The visit coincided with the grandmother's birthday as well as Thanksgiving. Besides this, Leona's six-year marriage to Charlie, Inez's stepfather, had become rocky. Things were tense at home with emotional outbursts by Leona and silence on Charlie's part.

The train ride from Oregon to Texas in the late 1930s was downright long and boring. People in the train car settled in. The pre-teen Inez escaped in her own little world, away from the persistent crying babies, rumbling train noises and a silly-acting mother. Leona and the salesman—for that is what Inez decided he was—laughed and joked. Inez passively looked out the train window and daydreamed about her grandmother.

It will be swell to see Grandma Doyon again, thought Inez. Her grandmother had visited their Klamath Falls farm during the summer of 1935; Inez remembered the older lady wearing bold colored, printed dresses and pearl earrings. Short, plump, and welcoming, she hugged often and smelled good—like flowers.

Always interested in her granddaughter's activities, Grandma spoke in a laughing, heavy French accent. Even though her English was difficult for Inez to understand, Grandma was such fun with her singing and her playful ways.

Inez's daydreaming continued. She remembered Grandma Rose Doyon, now called Grandma Schwartz, remarried a year before to Fred Schwartz. He was a bachelor friend of the family in Montana before Rose's first husband, Louis Doyon, died. Fred, rumored to be financially well-off, homesteaded around Scobey, Montana but also owned properties in and around Amarillo, Texas.

The tedious trip soon became even worse when Inez overheard a portion of her mother's conversation. The salesman, flirting with Leona, stated, "Such a pur-dy lady like you should be in the movies." He added, "In fact, I'm going to make you a movie star. I have big plans to put you on a white horse with your auburn curly hair flowing down." Leona giggled.

How disgusting! How gullible can Mom be? Inez started to cry. *I'm going to die of embarrassment.*

Heavy rains made the sky gray and the situation more depressing. The train traveled south through California, with frequent stops throughout the San Joaquin Valley. The mournful cry of a train whistle sounded as the wheels changed pitch. Inez watched the train roll to a stop beside yet another depot in another city. Passengers came and went from the train cars, letting in the damp chill from outside.

In an attempt to ward off the cold, Inez tucked her jacket closer to her body and wrapped her arms, crisscrossed, at her abdomen. She shivered until the porter came around to prepare the sleeper coaches for the night. The plan had been for the mother and daughter to sleep together in the berth. However, that evening Inez went to bed alone. Her mother did not climb into the shared sleeping berth until hours later.

The next day, the ride on the train was much the same as the day before, except that the undesirable salesman was gone. Leona, unusually quiet, remained in her seat lost in thought. Inez used the mist of her breath to fog the window and for a while amused herself by drawing tic-tac-toe grids. She played on and off with her fingers but mostly she searched out the window for something different to see. Most everyone napped in their seats as the train chugged along.

Near the Barstow stop, Joshua trees with their outstretched cactus-like limbs appeared on the landscape. California rains were left behind. The locomotive rumbled through the states of Arizona and New Mexico. The view from the train window showcased flat, endless plains with uninviting regions of barren wasteland.

When the train stopped, the drier climate released whiffs of oiled wood, hydraulic fluid, and steam. The smells reminded Inez of her train journey six years earlier. She and her brother traveled by themselves from Montana to Oregon. Their mother and new stepfather welcomed them at the journey's end in Klamath Falls. The thought came to Inez, *That was a time of new beginnings. I wonder, is this the time for new endings?*

When the porter prepared their sleeping coach that evening, Leona and Inez went to sleep together.

~

West Texas

Leona shook Inez from her sleep. "You better hurry up and grab your things, this is our stop, we get out here."

When Inez and her mother departed the train, the depot stood dark and deserted. Just as the morning light crept into the darkness, a red checkered taxi appeared out of nowhere. It was a wreck of a car. Only after Inez got into the cab did she realize all the doors were missing.

With a jolt, the taxi rocketed away from the train station. The taxi bumped and jerked along the 25 or 30 miles of dusty, rough roads that led to their rural destination. Inez braced herself and shivered. She could not get away from the brisk morning wind, as it rushed in from the gaping door frame. She drew up her thin, naked legs and hugged them to her chest.

All the while, Inez feared falling out the doorless vehicle. On the other hand, a greater fear came from the temptation to get just a little closer to the opening, daring her to think, *Wouldn't it be fun to put my head and arms out, against the force of the wind? No, Mom won't go for that.*

The emerging sun revealed nothing to see but endless acres of cotton fields. The region had many popular titles: The Panhandle, West Texas, or the High Plains, and was described as a mesa, tableland, or plateau. In Spanish it was called *Llano Estacado*, which meant Palisaded Plains, perhaps due to the appearance of a stockade or fort. In English, it was generally called the Staked Plains. Slightly larger than the state of Indiana, the territory measured 250 miles north to south, and 200 miles east to west. Therefore, the Panhandle was one of the largest plateaus anywhere in the North American Continent. And with a snicker, the mesa was often described as "85 percent sky and 15 percent grassland."

Inez reflected, *I've never looked further and seen less.*

A wispy layering of fog hung at the base of the cotton plants as the taxi pulled up to a small, unpainted farmhouse, between Hereford and nowhere. Two dogs of mixed breed, a pudgy white terrier mix and a younger black-and-white border collie mix, rushed forward and barked as Leona and Inez departed the cab. Besides the two dogs, Whitey and Blackie, Grandma Doyon-Schwartz and her youngest son, the teenage Maurice, welcomed the travelers to the farm. Fred Schwartz, whom Leona and Inez had not yet met, was absent at their arrival.

For the first days of the visit, the dust blew relentlessly from the fields. Grandma could be found diligently sweeping the Texas dirt out from the house and off the porch. Inez noticed that Grandma seemed older. She appeared worn out in her drab, colorless shift.

Time at the farm grew wearisome for Inez. In truth, she was left numb and dazed from the train ride that had uprooted her and brought her to this God-forsaken place. Her memories of that time were fragmented and vague. Her mother would not tolerate moping around, so Inez put on a happy face, as best as she could. All the while, she shut out troublesome and unhappy thoughts of home.

Inez wished she brought along Pamela, her life-size paper doll. Inez never even heard of the name of "Pamela" before getting the paper doll. Leona allowed the purchase of this doll because it reminded them of Shirley Temple. Pamela was the size of a real toddler and came with additional paper clothes for dressing her up. But Pamela and her wardrobe were back in Oregon.

Maurice occupied himself with his music. Most of the time he sat around, playing his guitar and singing despondent hillbilly songs. He had left a girlfriend back in Montana when the family moved, and he missed her terribly.

The lanky, forlorn teenager had the same reddish, chestnut brown hair, fair complexion, and brown eyes as his sister, Leona. His youthful presence reminded Inez of her brother, since Maurice was only six months older. And just like Henry, Maurice was distant and aloof. The idea came to Inez: *I wonder where Henry is, and what he's doing?*

As Grandma continued to sweep, Inez's boredom persisted until she spied cotton tufts left on the harvested plants. Leona joked, "Inès. If you're so bored, why don't you go outside into the fields and pick some cotton." Inez decided to give it a try. An hour into her labors, Inez's collection of cotton tufts filled only a quarter of her canvas sack—not even enough to weigh.

After a while, the strange location and the people started to become familiar. Inez noticed fun and silliness sparked every so often. Maurice's music became livelier and more entertaining. He made silly faces and unexpected comments that kept the females amused. The animated camaraderie, the laughter and joking between Leona, Maurice, and Grandma pulled Inez into the circle.

Inez's waning appetite improved. Grandma Doyon, although not known for her cooking skills, served a delicious and memorable meal of homemade French bread, fresh-churned butter, and vegetable-barley soup. Inez went back for a third helping.

Later in the visit, a sightseeing trip into Amarillo was arranged for Leona and Inez. Fred Schwartz made a brief appearance to take the two visitors to town. On the way, they viewed another one of his cotton fields outside of Hereford and some of his Amarillo properties.

While in Amarillo, they met Fred's sister and some other adults. The hope of a diversion was crushed when Inez discovered no other children were present for her to talk to or play with. The excursion that day proved to Inez that the metropolis of Amarillo was nondescript, except for the ever-present wind. Later she learned Amarillo was listed as one of the windiest cities in the United States.

~

Spending Time with Grandma Rose Doyon

A granddaughter needs to spend time with her grandmother. Amid the setting of the Hereford farm—the ever-present wind, the parched land, and a wooden shack— the elder, Rose, and youngster, Inez, bonded. In a place that seemed like nothing— came love. Grandma doted on her granddaughter and they both flourished.

How did this happen? The grandma did what she always had done as a mother and as a girl herself. She found fun in the moment and expressed good in every and any situation.

On one occasion, Grandma shared her thoughts about improving her butter-churning chore—something Inez noticed Grandma did a lot.

"Inès. You think this is a good idea?" Grandma presented Inez with a cartoon clipping with a caricature of an older woman churning butter. But instead of churning the usual way, with hands on the dowel, the butter appeared to be churned by a system of weights and pulleys connected to a rocking chair. As the woman rocked, the dowel would go up and down, in like fashion, as it churned the butter with each back-and-forth rock of the chair. Thus, she could churn the butter while rocking—well, in her imagination.

Inez grinned and said, "Grandma, I think that's a swell idea." And she truly did. Inez kept that cartoon clipping eighty years in her scrapbook—a memento of her 1937 trip to Hereford, Texas.

Spending time with Grandma Doyon had a long-lasting effect on the young girl. Inez developed a similar pleasant demeanor that remained throughout her lifetime.

However, life's situations were not all promising for Rose Doyon. Within six months, for some unknown reason, her husband, Fred Schwartz sent Rose packing. He gave her $5 and put her on the train back to Montana. Fred, a confirmed bachelor prior to marrying her, perhaps held high expectations of their union that he blamed her for failing to meet. Maybe he expected Rose to be a better cook and housekeeper for she was not used to such work. In Montana, Rose's children had always helped to lighten her workload.

Her grown children never wanted her to marry Fred in the first place. They were so pleased when he ended the relationship that nothing was ever contested. A divorce never took place, so Rose remained Mrs. Fred Swartz in name ever after. She gently but consistently corrected the speaker when she was addressed as Grandma Doyon. She signed her cards and letters as "Grandma Swartz;" but she was forevermore "Grandma Doyon" to her family.

With the end of the marriage, Rose changed out of those drab, lifeless shifts and returned to her colorful outfits and pearl jewelry.

Rose's fashion-design studies had been cut short in her youth, first by her father and then with her first marriage. She confided in her daughters that this was her life's greatest disappointment. Nevertheless, part of her childlike qualities remained, as she held on to her design dreams.

Sometimes dreams do come true. With the introduction of the Barbie Doll by the Mattel Toy Company, a demand for chic clothing to dress the dolls developed. Barbie's adult, fashion-model figure evoked a woman's choice in her career and her lifestyle, as well as in her wardrobe.

A seed from that past desire for fashion designing sprouted. Even though Rose's studies were long discontinued, her aspirations became a reality while she was in her mid-seventies. Rose was commissioned to design, and hand sew one-of-a-kind Barbie fashion ensembles for a local Montana toy store. Thus, the ambitions of her youth had come full circle.

~

Back Home

One day when Inez woke up, her mother informed her they were returning to Oregon. Inez did not look forward to the return trip to Klamath Falls any more than she had leaving Oregon in the first place. She dreaded the upcoming unrest and uncertainty.

The return train trip was tiresome and familiar. The good part was the lack of any flirting salesmen to entertain her mother. But it was still a boring train ride—until they entered California.

Heavy rains and flooding throughout the state threatened the progress of the trains. Due to floodwaters in the area, passengers were required to disembark the train at Stockton. People crowded into the lobby of a nearby hotel because no rooms were available.

During the long miserable night people milled about. Some were sick, coughing and sniffing could be heard throughout the cold, drafty lobby. Inez passed one old man who appeared to have an ear infection. He had a soiled piece of cotton in one ear, but drainage still dripped through the inadequate barrier. Inez felt the bile rise in her throat. *Yuck, what's that stuff coming out of that guy's ear?*

The next morning, passengers waded through puddled water to board the train. The flooding made for an unforgettable exit from Stockton. For many miles, the water streamed out from both sides of the train as it pushed forward along the watery track. Excited and mesmerized by the sight, Inez thought, *Wow, look at that shooting water. This feels more like a boat cruise rather than a train ride!*

After the display of train waterworks, the ride home was anti-climactic. Exhausted from the lack of sleep the night before, Inez and Leona dosed through the remainder of the trip back to Oregon.

Home again to Klamath Falls—but where was her home? It all seemed a blur to Inez. Prior to their departure for Texas, Leona had moved herself and Inez from Alameda Street to a small house on Crescent Lane. Even though the house remained in the Roosevelt school district with its snooty, high-class girls, there proved to be a good side—Inez made a lifelong friendship.

Inez described the situation in her journaling:

> *"One good thing that came from the Roosevelt school was my close association with Genevieve Peters. She was a year ahead in school, being one year and two months older than me (with her birthday in June). We were like sisters, and she was probably my closest friend ever. Genevieve was an only child of the Peters—John and Cassie (who we called 'Pete').*
>
> *"John met and married Cassie while he recuperated from respiratory effects of poison gas while in the European trenches during World War I. The couple lived in Bremerton, Washington and worked at the Bremerton Naval base until they moved to Klamath Falls in the mid 1930's, when Mom and I met them.*
>
> *"It helped to have such a friendship because during this time things were not going well for Mom and Charlie. The Brownstone house was sold, and a house was rented on Crescent Street, near the Peters' home. The folks' separation evolved into a full-fledged divorce.*

"Soon Mom left for Medford, Oregon where she attended a beauty school to learn hairdressing. I moved in to stay with the Peters and became like one of their family members.

"John was now working for Hodge-Parson wholesale produce. Often, he would bring home produce too ripe to pack for shipping so there was always something new to try. It was during this period that I tasted for the first-time avocados and artichokes.

"Later during that summer, I was included in the Peter's family trip. It was a car trip lasting a little over a week to visit John Peters' brother and his family in Dixon, California."

This time the boarding arrangement for Inez was different from all the previous rooming situations. She already knew and liked this family of John and Cassie Peters and their daughter, Genevieve. They embraced her as their own. What a godsend to have such a welcoming relationship at this vulnerable time for Inez.

That One-Eyed Bastard, Bert Wright

"I hated that one-eyed bastard, Bert Wright." The statement stunned Inez when Henry revealed this to her during his 1971 visit to California. The brother and sister were speaking of past times growing up in Klamath Falls. To have him express such venomous emotions surprised Inez. The subject of Bert Wright, a nondescript guy with only one eye, had never been discussed between the siblings.

The teenage Henry was well aware of Bert Wright. He had taken up with Leona and was a frequent visitor at the rented property on Crescent Lane. The relationship persisted while Leona attended beautician school in Medford.

Henry continued, "You know what was going on, don't you? . . . No good, that's for sure."

Inez never examined her suspicions of the happenings of thirty-five years before. She had hesitated to respond outright to Henry's tirade. She only knew that Bert Wright was just wrong. *The man didn't even wear a dashing black eyepatch to cover his defective eye.*

She remained protective of her mother, not wanting to face the truth of Leona's actions. However, Inez realized that Henry was right: "No good" had taken place. Her mother was separated from Inez's stepfather, but Bert was a married man with a large family of children.

Inez recalled one summer night while she stayed with her mother in Medford, 80 miles from Klamath Falls. While bedded down in the front room for the evening, she awoke to yelling and loud banging on the apartment's front door. The noise frightened Inez so much that she ran into the bedroom in time to see the naked backside of a man climbing out the window. The banging and yelling ceased. Nothing was mentioned or explained, but Inez never forgot the incident.

During the same time, a questionable set of events occurred. Inez remembered her mother and Bert taking a trip to California to seek medical treatment for Leona's stomach problems. Leona always suffered from "female troubles," but this seemed to be something different—perhaps an unwanted pregnancy. Leona returned from the trip sickly, extremely pale, and bleeding. Inez believed her mother nearly died from hemorrhaging.

Leona never indicated any wrongdoing or remorse. She never apologized for her actions or considered how they affected her son or daughter. By pretending nothing had occurred, Inez protected herself and her mother all those many years by ignoring that such things took place.

Inez looked over to Henry. "What are we going to say? It's called family skeletons in the closets."

Henry snorted and slowly shook his head. "Yes. I guess Mom lived her life as she pleased. But I'm glad that one-eyed bastard faded from our lives."

Brother and sister shared a sad smile.

~

Shasta Way and the Return to the Bus

Charlie had been busy while Leona rented the place on Crescent Lane, traveled to Texas, and left for schooling in Medford. He purchased a small plot of land on Shasta Way, in the outskirts of Klamath Falls. In contrast to their previous brownstone house on Alameda Street, Charlie built a tiny house. At first, it had only been one room with an attic. Then he added a bedroom for himself.

Though her parents were estranged during the end of Inez's 7th grade, she and Henry moved in to live with Charlie in his miniature home. Henry slept in the attic after Charlie replaced the simple entry ladder with a staircase. Another small room was added to give Inez a place to sleep too.

When Leona graduated from beauty school, she moved in with Charlie and the children—the family had weathered the storm of disharmony. Perhaps Charlie and Leona were never actually divorced, for Inez did not recall a remarriage.

Life got better and better for Inez. Not only was her family back together in Charlie's little house, but many past familiarities also returned. Shasta Way came within the boundaries of the Midland School District. Rather than attend a school in the Roosevelt district, Inez transferred to Altamont Junior High School. Altamont was located across the street from her original little country school—Summers Elementary—where she started in 1932.

Living at the new location instead of the farm meant a rearrangement for bus pickup and drop off times for Henry and Inez. The Shasta Way house was situated on one side of the district, whereas the farm site was on the other side of the bus route.

However, the bus route still served as the transportation for entire families of the Midland suburbs—from elementary children to high school students. This included Summers Elementary, Altamont Elementary, Altamont Junior High, Klamath Union High School, and various Catholic schools.

"Wait for me." Inez called out before stooping to pick up her fallen lunch pail.

With a scowl, her teenage brother looked over his shoulder and said, "Hurry up, Inès. You're going to make us miss the bus."

The girl's steps chugged as fast as her short legs would go. Her breathing puffed loudly like a train. She caught up with her brother when he stopped at the crossroad. He looked both directions down the wide, yet deserted road, and flicked his hand indicating that Inez should cross.

When she hesitated, he said, "What are you waiting for? The bus will stop over there."

She hurried to the indicated spot. Even though Henry was in high school, they waited at the same bus stop. He still tried to ignore her, but she was not alone and knew he watched out for her.

Inez smoothed her skirt and patted her flyaway hair into place. Fifteen minutes later a large yellow vehicle barreled towards the two waiting Dutton youths. Brakes squealed to a stop. The side door opened with the hiss of air pressure and a clunk.

Henry bounded into the bus, taking two steps at a time. Voices could be heard when he entered. "Look, it's Henry Dutton . . . Hey, Dutton."

Inez climbed the steps with care, one at a time. She was met with her own pleasant greeting as "Hip" Largent, the bus driver said, "Welcome back, Inez." Her face radiated a great grin when longtime friends patted her arms and grabbed at her hands as she worked her way to a seat near the back of the bus.

Julie Reginatos, Doris Phillips, Maxine Copeland, the Lessmister sisters, the Tutor brothers, and Bill Christianson were a few of the happy faces that acknowledged her. Inez knew many of them since the first grade. She came to know the brothers and sisters of her bus mates because they shared the same rural community.

When Inez took her seat, an unfamiliar older boy in a checkered blue shirt, turned to stare at her. He said with a shy smile before he faced forward, "I didn't know Henry had a sister."

Being Henry's sister gave Inez recognition. She later became better acquainted with the older boys on the bus who were her brother's friends. She discovered they were nice to her because they respected and liked Henry. It was one more validation, she belonged—she was one of their group. But Henry never accepted her as such. He considered her his "dumb sister." She was not to talk to him in public.

Familiar surroundings such as the railroad tracks and crossings, the farmland with crops of grain and corn, and pastures with cows and bulls went by as the bus skirted alongside and crossed over bridges of the Diversion Canal. They passed the distinctive Weyerhauser Lumber Yard, at the time the world's largest pine sawmill. Plus, the bus still traveled within a few miles from the California-Oregon border to pick up one family's children.

Even the recluse, with his dwelling in the side of the mountain, remained part of the landscape. As long as Inez could remember, he had lived there. Salvaged bits of wood, tin and metal cluttered the opening of the hermit's cave. All the kids stayed clear of him because of his scary looks, with his wild head of hair, unkempt beard, and ragged dirty clothes.

The ride proved to be a time of socialization and camaraderie for the chatty adolescents. Technically the new kid on the bus, Inez renewed old friendships without disruption. Doris Phillips talked away while someone else asked a question of Inez. The boys sitting catty-corner, poked and teased one another. Inez had missed the playful bus banter between the kids more than she realized. *It was good to be back.*

In the Fall, Inez entered the 8th grade at Altamont Junior High. While life at Shasta Way returned to a stable, consistent existence for Inez and her family, she remembered overhearing the broadcast on the family's table radio of Germany invading Poland on September 1st, 1939.

Two days later, President Franklin Delano Roosevelt announced, on his national radio address, that France and Britain declared war on Germany. FDR advocated neutrality for the United States.

X-ray and School Lunches

"Hold your breath, don't move," said the technician as he ran behind the protective wall. Inez's first experience of getting an x-ray terrified the teenager. The strange and bulky machinery engulfed her. She did not know what the scary equipment might do to her. The technician was about to push the button. Inez pondered, *Will a bolt of electricity shoot through my body? That's what happened in The Bride of Frankenstein.*

"Zzzzzzzzt." She heard the sound of the x-ray and thought, *Is that it? Was that all there was to it? That was nothing. It didn't even hurt.* The technician re-entered the room to adjust Inez's position for a different x-ray view. Once again, the instructions were given. "Hold your breath, don't move." "Zzzzzzzzt."

Inez suffered from excruciating pain in her tailbone. She explained that it felt as if she was sitting on a large, sharp rock. Her discomfort became so persistent that her mother took her for a rare doctor visit. X-rays were ordered to help with the diagnosis. Even though the procedure frightened her, Inez underwent the prescribed series of x-rays after her mother joked, "It's necessary to get to the bottom of your bottom problem."

The x-ray revealed scoliosis of the spine and a congenital pelvic deformity. Instead of the normal shape resembling an upside-down pear, Inez's pelvis was shaped like an elongated crushed ball. The doctor went so far as to inform Leona that Inez might have trouble with childbirth. He discussed the need for medical follow-up when Inez reached childbearing age.

As for immediate treatment, Inez was given very potent vitamin D drops that had an awful taste of strong fish. Leona put the drops in Inez's milk. Inez never liked milk much to begin with and fishy milk was too much for her to stomach. It was never known what helped with the tailbone pain, but most of the discomfort went away as she matured.

When Inez started her menstrual cycle, she put on weight for about a year. No longer considered skinny and scrawny, according to her brother she "looked like Porky Pig." Some of this might have been due to eating the Altamont school lunches. Inez avoided lunches of sandwiches made from Leona's homemade bread. The bread tended to be coarse and dry and not inviting to eat. Thus, she often bought a school lunch for 5 to 10 cents.

Lunches were brought around on carts to the individual classrooms. These meals were tasty, except for ham and large woody lima beans that were served all too frequently. Inez's family never ate lima beans at home, and she did not care to eat them at school either. One time, the lunch meal consisted of fresh maple bars and hot chocolate—what a treat! But they were never served again.

Once Inez experienced an x-ray, she considered radiology as a career possibility. Leona spoke at length with the radiology technician and found the pay was good and the training minimal. The teenager knew her chances of pursuing her dreams of attending nursing training were slim due to the cost of the schooling. Even into her high school years, Inez considered the job as an x-ray technician, but only because it would put her in the medical field.

~

Return to the Farm, 1939

Leona peeled the yellow rubber gloves from her hands. With the back of her wrist, she scooted her wire-rim glasses to their rightful position on her nose. *I've cleaned the place as best as I can. . . . I can't make a silk purse out of a sow's ear.*

Jack Calvin had defaulted on his payments for Leona's farm some three years after purchasing it. That period, from 1936 to 1939 was the latter part of the Great Depression, and Jack could not make a go of the farm. His payments stopped. He just walked away from the land. With little financial choice, the Dutton family repossessed the property and returned to the farm.

Leona opened the back door. She picked up the two buckets of wash water—one in each hand—and made her way to the vegetable garden where she dumped the buckets. With the task done, Leona straightened to view the lovely spring day around her. Even though the rose bushes were still bare, the shrubs of both pink and white camellias blossomed in the shade of the house. Blue crocus, yellow daffodils, and purple iris opened in the sunshine. With delight, Leona recognized her favorite bushes. *There's no sweeter spring fragrance than lilacs in bloom.*

The moments of nature brought nostalgic thoughts. *Can it be eleven years since Henri and I bought this farm? It was such a pretty house . . . before the fire. The rebuilt house functioned, but once sold, I never expected to be back here again.*

Out of the corner of her eye, Leona saw a brown pickup truck slowly moving down the lane towards the house. She turned to see sixteen-year-old Henry driving with a big grin on his face. When the vehicle came to a stop, Leona recognized Babe Reader, a good friend of Charlie's, seated in the passenger's seat. A small girl, about seven years old, also sat in the truck.

Charlie had arranged for Henry to work with Babe on his farm in the Henley area, three miles away. Babe and Henry were combining a driving lesson with a ride home. Henry jumped out of the truck, said his good-byes to Babe, and told his mother, "I better get started on my chores."

Leona leaned into the open truck window after Babe slid to the driver's seat. She cleared her throat and said, "Thanks for teaching Henry how to drive. It means a lot to him."

"I don't understand why Charlie is so dead set against teaching Henry to drive," said Babe.

Leona shrugged her shoulders, "I don't know either . . . guess he's just too protective of his Chevy."

Babe's eyes twinkled with amusement, "Well, Henry can't hurt my old Dodge work truck, that's for sure." He continued, "You have a great kid there. If I had a boy, I would want him to be just like Henry."

The man pushed his hat back off his forehead and spoke in a quieter voice. "I'm grateful Charlie hooked us up. Without a son of my own, I welcome Henry's company." He turned to the girl, "And my little sweetheart here needs to stay out of the sun. Well, good evening to you, Mrs. Dutton."

Leona then noticed how the cute pixie of a girl was dressed in unseasonably heavy clothing. Long sleeves and leggings covered all visible skin except for her alabaster hands. A stray lock of white hair peaked out from the neckline of a large sunbonnet that swallowed the young girl's face. However, not until Leona looked into the child's pink eyes fringed with white eyelashes, did she realize the girl lacked natural coloring to her skin, hair, and eyes—*Oh my, the girl is an albino.*

As the beat-up Dodge truck drove down the driveway, Leona retrieved her two buckets and made her way to the water pump near the barn. As she hand-pumped water into the buckets, she reflected on Babe's daughter: *Here I was complaining about my problems.*

When the Dutton family moved back to the farm in early Spring of 1939, the farmhouse was not a welcoming sight. Everything needed a good cleaning. They found the kitchen in a deplorable condition. Blackened powder coated the kitchen wallpaper. When cooking on a wood burning stove, smoke and soot tended to go everywhere. Without Charlie's meticulous routine to keep the big, black stovepipes cleared of soot buildup, the walls turned grimy. Perhaps the Calvins were not as diligent with the soot upkeep. Maybe the Duttons had become accustomed to the finer and newer kitchens they found in town.

Leona's friend Mrs. Zetzman, who cleaned houses for a living, suggested they try a type of pink gum sponge to clean carbon residue from the wallpaper. Armed with the gummy sponges, Leona, Charlie, Henry, and Inez labored hours over the sooty walls. This time-consuming work cleaned only inches at a time as the eraser surfaces quickly blackened with carbon. Care had to be taken not to leave streaks on the wall. The kitchen could have been refurbished with newly purchased wallpaper, but the family merely made do with what they had.

Even though the house and dairy had electricity, they still lacked indoor plumbing. An outhouse remained for when "nature called," which didn't seem to bother the family. However, the chore of hauling buckets of water for the household needs of cooking, washing, and bathing was not a pleasant one.

Whatever water came into the house had to go out. Charlie attempted to streamline the removal of the kitchen gray water by digging a ditch and installing pipes to drain soiled water away from the house, beyond the garden area. Unfortunately, the system lacked valves or traps, so the exiting water often backed up and caused a great rotten stink. The conditions also formed gases that bubbled and made audible farting noises. At least something brought comical relief to the situation.

The Threatening

Taking a break from gardening, Leona rested against the shovel handle. "Inès, are you tired of pulling weeds? Let's stretch our legs and take a walk."

"That sounds swell." The young girl rose from her crouched position and brushed dirt from her overalls. "I've been wanting to see if anything has changed around here."

The mother and daughter set out to explore the vicinity. The backdrop of a clear blue sky lightened the mood and encouraged them to walk, talk, and laugh.

Leona, in a silly mood, placed yellow wildflowers behind both of her ears. She locked arms with Inez and swiftly walked the girl down the path towards the bridge. They both broke into giggles.

The two strolled across the bridge to the other side of the diversion canal. Pastureland and grain fields blended in the scenery as they walked along the canal bank. The rural community often used the embankment of the canal as a thoroughfare. Charlie drove on the ridge when he had to contend with heavy rain or snow.

Caught up in an enjoyable mother-daughter chat, Leona and Inez lost track of time and of their surroundings. They wandered far into an unfamiliar section of countryside, remote and without any buildings.

Leona tossed away the switch she held, "I better get back to milk the cows."

She turned around and halted with alarm. In the field next to the canal bank appeared a bull—an untethered, big black bull.

In a threatening display, the muscular animal stood broadside with his back arched. When he flexed his neck, hair stood up along his back, doubling his size. The bull lowered his head and shook it from side to side. With the movement, a short, broken chain rattled as it flopped against the copper ring in the bull's nose.

Inez's shock rose to overwhelming panic. The Dutton house was on the other side of the diversion canal. Only a flimsy suggestion of a fence separated the animal from Leona and Inez. Harm could be done. Several years before, one such bull killed the father of their neighbor Joe Wright.

The bull locked eyes with Inez. He pawed the dirt and snorted as he blocked their path home. Inez's hands came up to her mouth. "Oh Mama! Should we run?"

Leona said in a steady voice, "No, we mustn't run." Without shelter or substantial fencing, any attempt to run could be blocked or overtaken by the unrestrained bull. If the animal felt challenged as the "boss" of the herd, anything could happen.

Instead, Leona looked over to the canal and said, "Follow me," She pointed towards some narrow wood planking spanning the 60-foot-deep canal. Inez's heart pounded with fear. She glanced at the length of the catwalk, six feet across the canal.

The foot-wide board, used by crews to tend the diversion canal, provided a route home. Inez could either choose to escape by crawling on the plank over the rushing canal water or be gored and trampled by the massive and terrifying animal. Neither seemed like a good option. So, Inez did what she always did—she followed her mother's instructions.

To position themselves on the catwalk, the two knelt on their hands and knees, in a praying position. This was fitting since they were indeed praying. The plank creaked with the shifting and added weight.

Without any railing to steady their balance, they crawled on all fours over the expanse, at an agonizingly slow pace. At times, Inez's arms and knees trembled. Nothing in her brief acrobatic training prepared her to do anything like this.

The roar of the rushing water confused her senses. An unintentional glimpse revealed the turbulent flow frothing below. Inez became dizzy and sick to her stomach, to the point of despair. "Oh Mama. I don't think I can do this. What if we fall?"

In a breathy voice, her mother said, "Don't look down."

By looking straight ahead, Inez somehow found the fortitude to move herself forward. When Leona made it to the solid ground of the canal bank, she turned towards Inez and helped her to safety. Inez stood, dusting off her hands and knees. The bull snorted and strutted on the other side of the canal.

They had outmaneuvered the bull and defied gravity. Sheer gratitude overcame Inez. Surely the praying had helped—neither she nor her mother knew how to swim.

~

Charlie

The country presented certain dangers never encountered in the city. Inez remembered her stepfather Charlie had his own perils when he returned to the farm:

> *"Charlie used our old work horses once in a while to ride, because he said a saddle pony just ate and wasn't any good for anything else. We had "Doc," a white horse with a very feisty disposition and the most rounded back.*
>
> *"One day Dad was riding him bareback trying to collect some cattle that had gone astray. Doc made a sudden start and Dad slid off the horse's back. Doc turned and stepped right on Dad's chest, leaving a sunken hoof print. Immediately the site showed a bloodshot, black and blue bruise. Poor man, he could hardly breathe and probably broke a few ribs. But again, no visit with a doctor. Until the day Dad died, he had that crushed-in side to his chest."*

~

Hollywood Bound?

"Listen my children and you shall hear, of the midnight ride of Paul Revere, on the eighteenth of April, in seventy-five . . ." The poem, "Paul Revere's Ride," by Henry Wadsworth Longfellow was only one of the poems taught during the late 1930s in the Oregon junior high English curriculum. Other favorite poems of Inez included William Wordsworth's "Daffodils," "I wandered lonely as a cloud that floats on high o'er vales and hills, when all at once I saw a crowd, a host, of golden daffodils . . ." and "House by the Side of the Road," "Let me live in a house by the side of the road and be a friend to man . . ." by Sam Walter Foss.

Such poems offered an interesting perspective on history, life science and ethics. The verses, recited from memory, helped develop public speaking skills and confidence performing in front of an audience. Inez excelled in her memorization and presentation on these assignments.

During her junior high years, Inez participated in several school performances. However, these programs did not require talent in acting or singing. Both Inez and her friend, Genevieve Peters, sang in the Roosevelt Junior High chorus, in the 1938 school operetta, "The Ghost of Lollipop Bay." The featured song, "The Good Ship Lollipop," came from the 1934 movie, *Bright Eyes* and became the signature song of Leona's and Inez's favorite child movie star, Shirley Temple.

The junior high musical production involved more than eighty children. Because of Inez's small stature, she could be found front and center in the newspaper picture published a few days after the show.

Hollywood Bound?

In 1940, the spring of her eighth-grade year, a more mature, full-figured Inez was cast as the lead in another school musical. The Altamont Jr. High School presented the opera production, *Carmen*. This performance might have been forgotten if not for a photograph that marked the occasion in Inez's photo album. Her children asked why the picture showed kids dressed up in Spanish costumes.

Inez explained that the Altamont production consisted of the students singing all of the songs together. There were no solo parts. The featured song was the memorable "Toreador Song."

Inez did not remember how she came to be in the 8th grade operetta. Perhaps her accomplishments of memorization and her presentation of the poems gained the English teacher's notice. With her swarthy appearance, dark hair, and dark eyes, she may have been a natural choice to be cast as the gypsy, Carmen. The male lead for Don José was a cute blond kid named Jeff Welch. He stood a foot shorter than Inez.

Decades later, Inez still sang the words of the "Toreador Song." To the thrill and amusement of her children and grandchildren, the poems memorized in her youth also endured. Whenever an opportune moment occurred, Inez recited these treasured verses, showcasing her acquired culture, if only to her family.

~

Dancing

Inez loved to dance.

Moving to a musical beat was undeniable for her. Syncopation and rhythm got her feet tapping. When music was partnered with dancing, Inez really did shine.

It cannot be known if she was a natural born dancer. Whether or not it was due to genetic influence, Inez did prove quite agile while dancing the Highland Fling. Likewise, her French-Canadian "Doyon dance blood" came to life with the singing of vibrating fiddle strings and articulated brass sounds of Cajun and Dixieland compositions. But truth be told, most any kind of lively melody of the 1940s swing or foxtrot music made her heart dance as much as her feet.

Throughout her life, Inez was especially fond of Louisiana Cajun music and what she called New Orleans Jazz. The sounds reminded her of tunes she heard while living in Montana with her French-Canadian relatives. When the five-year-old Inez returned to Oregon, country music from the Grand Ole Opry often played on the Dutton radio, along with the news and weather reports. Country music and American popular music were said to be influenced by French Louisiana Cajun sounds. It appeared so to Inez.

Inez's desire to dance may have further developed while attending Klamath Falls' movie theaters during the time she lived in "town." Movies such as *Shall We Dance, Swing Time,* and *Babes in Arms* helped introduce the era of dance band music. Big bands influenced the dancing to lively swing music which flourished through the 1930s and into the 1940s.

As Inez matured into her teenage years, she enjoyed a range of social dance situations. She had sincere appreciation for the Klamath Falls community that provided opportunities for dances during prewar and war times. Through such programs, many groups of young people, as well as servicemen and the young at heart found available dances at the Grange hall, the Armory, and the halls of the Eagle Club and the Moose Lodge. Special street dances were held when servicemen came through the area for training. And as ever, school dances were held as well.

Dancing was wholesome fun at its best. The people of the community went out of their way to be supportive to offer such safe and pleasurable amusement. That is why Inez's mother, Leona, guided her daughter towards social dancing. She knew firsthand how isolated a young girl could be when she lived on a farm. Leona encouraged Inez, telling her "It's important you learn to dance."

Leona believed the only way to learn to dance was to actually dance. Practice made perfect. However, simply learning the steps was not the main focus. She took the initiative to stress the social rules and etiquette of dancing. Leona had some rules and strong beliefs of her own, too. Her instructions to Inez were straightforward. If Inez went to a dance, she was expected to stay until the dance was over. There would not be any leaving early because of lack of dreamboat partners. It was about dancing, not looking for love or even a boyfriend.

Inez was admonished not to refuse to dance with a man based on his appearance—even if she didn't like his looks. Leona instructed, "Unless the man is drunk or obviously crazy, I expect you to accept his dance offer."

Inez's gratitude for her mother went far beyond the encouragement to dance. Leona sacrificed her time and energy to accompany

Inez to all the various events. They attended just so Inez could have the chance to dance. Leona herself would not join in. She spent her time visiting with other women, while she waited out the evening on the sidelines.

~

The Grange and Dances

For dancing experience, Leona guided Inez to the nearby Grange Hall in the Midland area of Klamath Falls. It was the best place for her daughter to polish her skills. Long before Inez thought of dancing, her family had participated in the Grange fellowship. Leona had been a member since moving to her Klamath Falls farm in 1929.

The organization encouraged farm families to band together to promote the economic and political well-being of the agricultural community. Through fellowship of like-minded farmers, the Grange encouraged education and maintained community centers for social affairs.

When she turned fourteen, Inez attended an orientation for new Grange members. Families were considered the basis of the association, so once a teenager turned fourteen, they were welcomed into the organization as full-fledged voting members.

During the membership class, Inez learned the official name of the Grange was the National Grange of the Order of Patrons of Husbandry. Founded after the Civil War in 1867, with its roots in agriculture, this organization soon spread across the nation. Members were given opportunities to learn and grow to their fullest potential as citizens and leaders. They believed that community values and informed citizenship strengthened communities and states. Thus, a stronger nation resulted.

The session ended with each new member being interviewed, then quizzed on the mission of the Grange. But what Inez remembered most was the party afterwards, when the participants celebrated with cookies, cake, and punch.

The Grange also introduced Inez to her first Halloween celebration. Partygoers were blindfolded and taken through the Grange basement, which was decorated in a haunted house theme. Moans and groans, clinking chains, and piercing screams were provided. The feeling of spider webs and icy, cold fingers on the back of the neck added to the fun.

Other seasonal theme parties were held throughout the year. However, for Inez's teenage years, the community dances were the most important of all the Grange events.

Inez held vivid memories of dancing at the Grange Hall as she developed, little by little, her social dance abilities. Usually, a rag-tag band played what consisted of a drum, accordion, and piano. Perhaps a string instrument, such as a fiddle, banjo, or guitar, would be thrown into the mix. Waltzes, polkas, and folk dances with a country flavor were the general dances of choice.

~

The Long Walk

Riding the bus, to and from school, remained a requirement for Inez—except for one special day.

On that day, Inez rushed out to the loading area for the school bus. She looked forlorn as the last in the stream of yellow buses turned onto the main road. *Drats! First the darn fountain pen leaked. Now I've missed my ride home.* Altamont Junior High School had let out at noon for their late afternoon graduation ceremony. With no telephone service at the Dutton home, Inez could not call her mother to come get her.

Without asking for help from teachers milling around, Inez accepted her situation. With a sigh, she started walking south, to home. The route from the school to the farm was a good five-mile trek. The daunting obstacle of the railroad yard loomed two miles into the walk. She had been warned to avoid vagrants, as well as the hazardous conditions around railroads.

Memories of crossing another railroad yard, nine years earlier, during her trip from Montana to Oregon, came to mind. That time Inez had her brother to lead her through the maze of tracks, locomotives, and machinery. *I sure wish Henry was here now.*

Water puddles covered the part of the railroad yard where Inez wanted to cross. Most of the puddles could be jumped over. Inez made a game of leaping from one dry area to another, until she faced a lake of a puddle. Fortunately, a long, stray 2 x 4 spanned the water. Inez, with arms spread out for stability, walked heel to toe, as if on a balance beam. When she came to the end of the board, water remained to step over. With one heaving effort, Inez stretched onto dry ground but, in the process, she upset the board, splashing it over. To her surprise the underside of the board revealed numerous protruding, rusty nails. *Boy was I lucky!*

Glad to have passed through the railroad yard without any further problems or encounters, Inez avoided taking the roadway. Cutting across fields and pastures, she saved steps and dodged several other intimidating locations. She did not want to meet up with "the hermit" as she approached where he lived. She selected a path that traveled well around the side of the mountain where he was often seen. Inez kept looking over her shoulder in case she was being followed. *I could swear, I feel him watching me.*

From previous bus rides, Inez recalled other intimidating threats—two bulls, each in separate pastures on her route home. She shuddered to think of the experience of a few weeks before with a bull. *Now, to avoid those bulls.* Determined, she placed herself away from danger of the large animals. Once past the threat of the bulls, Inez could enjoy the loveliness of the day. She started to hum.

The teenager lost track of time as she hiked through the countryside. To keep going she thought to herself. *Put one foot in front of the other—don't stop, don't think—just put one foot in front of the other.* As a formerly weak and sickly first grader, Inez had struggled to make it to the school bus stop. That fragile girl no longer defined her.

Inez neared the Shoemayers' property. *I'm just about home.*

The Shoemayers' place was an in-between rest for Henry and Inez before proceeding to and from the school bus stop. Inez felt trickles of sweat run down her back. *I'm so thirsty. I'll get a drink from the pump before I head for home.*

No one appeared to be around. Inez proceeded to pump water into the dipper, then took a deep drink of cool water. Just then she heard a dreaded sound.

"Cock-a-doodle-do. Cock-a-doodle-do." Inez turned to see Oscar, the Shoemayers' watchdog rooster strutting back and forth. The fowl took his job of protector of the hens seriously. His yellow eyes held mean intent and challenge. Oscar knew he was the cock of the walk. Inez knew she better leave while she could. *But no! Oscar is blocking my way.*

Inez had dealt with Oscar before. She stood tall, clapped her hands with force and in a deep voice yelled, "Shoooo! Who's at the top of the pecking order now?"

The rooster skittered away, stopped near the barn, puffed up, and crowed.

Sweaty and dusty, Inez arrived home tired but with the feeling of accomplishment. Her daunting trek resulted from her sheer determination as much as her physical endurance. No time to dwell on her cross-country triumph, Inez hurried to the front door and met her mother coming out.

"Inès, where have you been? You better get ready for your graduation . . ."

Her stepfather, Charlie, worked that afternoon and missed Inez's commencement. Later, when told of her walk, he could not believe Inez had accomplished such a feat. He was shaken by what she could have encountered—hobos, stray dogs, or a number of other unsafe conditions.

While he was impressed by the distance Inez walked, Charlie had little to say about her educational achievement. His attendance at a graduation ceremony was not a priority for him. He did not attend Henry's high school graduation the following week, either.

Lying in her bed that night, Inez thought of her day. *A special day for me, seemed like another workday for Dad. Too bad he missed my graduation . . . that's just the way things go.*

~

The Summer of 1940

Inez had the whole summer ahead of her. Without school and the friendly bus ride there, the summer loomed lonesome and boring. She tried to spend as much time as possible with her town friend, Genevieve Peters, but the distance between town and farm limited their visits. Mundane jobs such as weeding the garden and helping her mother can any surplus fruits, vegetables, and meats, filled most of Inez's days. Neither chore was very exciting.

Stepfather Charlie's routine of listening to the radio helped ease the dull summer farm life. The radio kept the household informed about the happenings of the day. Economic updates on the Depression appeared alongside reports of race riots in Chicago, Harlem, Los Angeles, and Detroit. President Franklin D. Roosevelt's unprecedented pursuit of a third term became one of the hottest topics.

Yet, the war-related news eclipsed everything else. The Selective Training and Service Act became the country's first military draft created during peacetime. News broadcasts spoke of German and Italian invasions of most of Western Europe. Denmark, Norway, France, Luxembourg, Belgium, and the Netherlands were now occupied by the Germans. Stories told of Britain's resolve in the Dunkirk evacuation and the Battle of Britain. Nazi bombings of London and of British military bases occurred most every night.

But in truth, what captured Inez's attention were the bits and pieces of music, and news of Hollywood stars, and movies. She enjoyed the popular jazz sounds of Benny Goodman and Count Basie and relished any chance she could get to town to see a movie with

Mickey Rooney and Judy Garland, Jean Arthur and James Stewart, or even Bugs Bunny.

Throughout the country, talk continued about the Civil War epic, *Gone with the Wind*, written by Margaret Mitchell. The book topped the American fiction bestseller lists in 1936 and 1937. It was said to be the second favorite book of American readers, just behind the Bible.

The book was made into an Academy Award–winning movie in 1939. Stars included Clark Gable, Vivian Leigh, and Olivia de Havilland. After seeing the movie version of *Gone with the Wind,* Inez decided to read the book. Perhaps, Genevieve bought the book, and then lent it to Inez.

Education was encouraged for Henry and Inez because neither Leona nor Charlie graduated from high school. However, books were not central in the Dutton home. Inez, not much of a reader prior to that time, had only thumbed through catalogs and *Photoplay* magazines from Leona's friend Mrs. Zetzman. Therefore, it was an important step for Inez to tackle *Gone with the Wind* as her first major book to read.

Even though she viewed the popular movie at the theater, it still took her all summer to complete the 1,000 plus page book. Inez methodically read each word in every sentence of the book, line by line. While it took time, she had total retention of what was written. Like setting the type for a printer, she remembered the smallest detail. That was how she read all her books thereafter.

~

Aunt Aimee

"Inès, are you wearing a brassiere?" Her mother scrutinized the teenager prior to her escape. Inez had matured into a shapely woman long before she accepted the role.

Inez crossed her arms in front of her chest, "Aw Mom, do I have to?"

"You know your gong-gongs are getting too big to go without a brassiere." Leona used her pet name for breasts. Where the term came from was unknown, but that is what Inez's mother called them.

Inez cringed and looked around to make certain nobody heard the discussion about her unmentionables.

In the summer of 1940, Inez's Aunt Aimee sent the teenager an unexpected package of brassieres and undergarments. Up until that time, no one seemed to notice that Inez's expanding chest needed support. Somehow Aimee deduced from photographs and family correspondence that her niece was growing up in a hurry.

Receiving anything from her aunts, especially this aunt, thrilled Inez. Throughout her teenage years, Inez dreamed of becoming a registered nurse like her two aunties, Sid and Aimee. Aunt Sid, a Catholic nun, was known as Sister of Providence. Inez loved Aunt Sid but had no desire to become a nun.

On the other hand, Aunt Aimee's life as a scrub nurse on a surgical team in the operating room appeared exciting and adventuresome.

Providing instruments and assisting in operations required quick reactions and anticipation of the surgeon's needs. Surgery within a sterile environment was fascinating and fast-paced—just as Aimee liked it.

Trained for initial nursing at the Canadian Tuberculosis and Lung Center in Ontario, Aimee excelled in operating room techniques. The seasoned twenty-eight-year-old nurse then enlisted as an ensign in the United States Navy Nurse Corp. Military training followed at the Great Lakes Naval Station near Chicago, Illinois. Later, Aimee was stationed at naval hospitals in Philadelphia and in Saranac, New York.

The aunt and niece had not seen each other in thirty years. Making the guest bed together during this rare visit, Inez asked Aimee, "Auntie, why did you send me brassieres when I was a teenager?"

Aunt Aimee chuckled, amused at the question. "Oh yes. I figured I needed new underwear before I started my military career as a Navy Nurse. My brassieres were still in good condition and I thought you could use them."

Inez joined in the laughter, "I sure did need them."

The older woman reached for a pillow and a pillowcase. "Becoming a Navy Nurse was the best thing I ever did. Excellent training and fantastic opportunities."

"I was so proud to tell my friends you were a Navy Nurse," said Inez.

Aimee put the pillow in place. "Well, not many girls from Scobey, Montana had the chance to be on General Patton's neurosurgical standby team when he was injured in Europe.

With surprise in her voice, Inez turned to Aimee, "I didn't know that. Can you tell me about it?"

Aimee gathered her thoughts before speaking, "A couple of months after the end of the war, General Patton was involved in an auto accident in Germany that resulted in paralysis. He was expected to die, but when he rallied, the neurosurgeon, Colonel Spurling, decided to bring the General back to the States to do surgery and further treatment. The diagnosis consisted of spinal cord damage with a broken neck."

Inez smoothed wrinkles on the bedspread, "I've heard those injuries happen when diving into a shallow pool or with tackle football injuries."

"Yes. That type of accident can cause fractures and dislocations to the third and fourth cervical vertebrae. Damage to the spinal cord often results in paralysis. In the General's case, the neurosurgeon must have felt a chance existed to relieve the pressure on the spinal cord."

"But how did you become involved?" Inez asked.

"Well, I was still in the navy but assigned to surgery teams at army medical centers. Along the way, I became proficient in scrubbing for neurosurgeries, surgeries on any part of the brain and nervous system. I wasn't just trained; I was experienced and available. Therefore, I was chosen to be on the neurosurgery team to operate on General Patton.

"We waited on standby, here in the States, to do the surgery. Later we were told that Patton's bags were packed, ready to go, when he died suddenly in the Heidelberg hospital. At first the official cause of death was pulmonary edema and congestive heart failure. A sudden pulmonary embolism was later considered a factor. "

Aimee sighed, "Even though I couldn't help General Patton, I had many chances to make a difference in the lives of sailors and soldiers. . . . It was an honor to serve my country."

~

Getting Ready for High School Days

Having an older sibling had its advantages. One example for Inez was Henry's *El Rodeo* school yearbooks. He earned his own money to buy annuals in his junior and senior years. In covert manner, Inez dedicated every spare moment of her summer to look through the pages of the annuals. Even though Henry had moved on from his high school days, he would not have accepted Inez's action of pouring over his yearbooks. She, of course, could not let her brother see her reading his annuals. She knew the books would have been hidden from her sight forever.

The yearbooks were not only entertaining, but they also gave Inez the power of knowledge as she readied herself for high school. From the time Henry brought the yearbooks home, his sister imagined how it would be when she attended high school. It also added to the information she accumulated from the years of riding the school bus.

The annuals held descriptions of school activities, clubs, and sports with lists of the participants' names. Inez familiarized herself with names to faces, matched student's participation to events, and noted how the girls dressed and wore their hair. Teachers were even considered in her assessments.

For Inez, high school could not start soon enough.

Part Five

High School

1940-1944

~

Mom's Memories

Mom's memories of her teenage years fascinated me. They defined Inez. Like others of her generation—dubbed "The Greatest Generation" by Tom Brokaw—she came of age during the uncertainties of World War II. Yet, she developed the resolve to enjoy her times to the fullest.

Inez's collected memories meant everything to her. Her stories made her four years of high school seem dreamy and full of fun, unhampered by schoolwork, tests, or term papers. She spoke of all kinds of dances: street dances, dances at community halls, ones at the Grange, as well as dances at her high school. She named people from her school bus and homeroom. The stories were spiced up when Mom introduced names of soldiers, sailors, and marines she knew from that time.

My head spun with the attempt to keep everything straight. But Mom's reminiscences were not confused or jumbled. Much like reciting her junior high poems, she conjured up scenes in their entirety whenever she liked.

My mother, Inez, did not escape into fantasy—but I sure did. I visualized her stories as the black-and-white 1940s grade-B movies that I watched every afternoon on *Nancy Allen's Movie Matinee* on KMJ, Fresno's TV channel 24. Yet, I was anxious to untangle all those teenage memories and stories of dances, characters, and fun opportunities that sustained Mom through all these years. I had an investment in her memories; they not only revealed who my mother was, but in turn helped to reveal who I was, too.

Two scrapbooks and several photo albums reinforced Mom's stories. During my sister Lynda's and my pre-adolescent years, we pored over these albums, asking questions and romanticizing Mom's escapades. We looked forward to a time when we too could dance and have fun like her.

But we were shy and studious wallflowers at high school dances—or at least we felt like it. We believed ourselves to be awkward and out of place, convinced we simply were born in the wrong generation.

Lynda and I grew up during the post-Sputnik era. In October 1957, the Soviet Union successfully launched the world's first artificial satellite, *Sputnik I.* Space Age history was changed forever. From that time on, the big push was for American students to excel in science, go to college and beat the Russians to the moon.

I must say, Mom's scenarios seemed suspicious to us, when we compared them to our lives, twenty years later. Party girls of the 1960s usually drank, used drugs, and had loose morals. Lynda joked as she questioned about how Mom stayed a "good girl" with all the beaus, dances, and partying. Delving into the rest of the story brought no disappointment—just the opposite. Mom's character became more endearing, and the value of her cherished memories increased. In the end, we respected how our mother conducted herself in all these situations.

~

Dancing Growing Pains

Growing up had its rough times, and sometimes that was also true on the dancefloor. In her early days of dancing, Inez encountered an unfortunate situation that stemmed from being inexperienced and unaware of basic dance protocol. Inez never forgot the mistake.

At the start of the evening at the Grange, Don Manning asked permission to take Inez home after the dance. This surprised and delighted her. Don was a tall, nice-looking upperclassman with dark brown hair. Her mother, Leona, readily gave her consent for the escort home. In fact, Leona smiled broadly with her approval of the invitation. She knew Don came from an established agricultural family in the Henley area.

After Inez accepted Don's offer he disappeared into the crowd. Several dances went by, then the piano started to play the "Goodnight Song." Not realizing it was the final dance of the evening, Inez accepted the dance with George McMann, a junior high friend. Don came out of nowhere to claim his dance but instead found Inez dancing with George. Not saying a word, Don turned with a jerk and walked out of the Grange Hall.

What a regrettable mix-up. Inez felt terrible over the incident. As time went on, she became more embarrassed for not approaching Don over the matter. Through the next several years, Inez frequently saw Don at the Grange dances. She did not know how to deal with the misunderstanding. She agonized over the right thing to say to take away his hurt feelings. Don continued to avoid Inez with each possible encounter. He either looked the other way or deliberately walked in the opposite direction, without speaking to her. Inez's opportunity for an explanation and apology never came. She carried these sad memories in her heart. Don later died in Africa during World War II.

Even though it was not all pleasantries at the dances, there could be intrigue, hope of romance, and entertainment. However, the entertainment was not limited to music or dancing. Sometimes, disagreements developed into fist fights. The no-alcohol rule in the actual hall did not keep some of the participants from being under the influence. When testosterone and alcohol mixed, the occasional fight ensued.

As soon as an altercation was taken outside, someone would run into the dance hall and call out, "Beef." Young men quickly emptied the dance floor to gather to watch the fight. After all, a guy might learn a fancy "dance step" that could keep him from getting a busted nose or a black eye.

"Pete" Peterman was the usual, self-appointed announcer whenever these Grange fights broke out. He was an older teenager from the Henley area and an acquaintance of Inez's brother, Henry. Average appearing, Pete had sandy brown hair and a medium build. He projected a fun personality and had great moves on the dance floor. His legendary jitterbug steps displayed a smooth blur of activity.

Inez had a crush on Pete. She watched him from the sidelines and dreamed of one day dancing with him. Nothing came of her infatuation. At the time she was thirteen and did not even know how to jitterbug. And no one took notice of her anyway.

Or so she thought.

Other people—specifically boys—did take notice of her, once she started to mature. Inez discovered there had been missed opportunities. Years later, Henry told Inez of several guys from the Henley area who asked him to set them up with a date with her.

Henry snickered, "No way was I going to arrange a date for those guys with my sister."

These would-be suitors consisted of Freddie Beamer, several other guys, and to her amazement—Pete Peterman. Inez never had a clue.

Inez gave the impression of being older than her actual age. For one so young, she had dealt with many unusual challenges while growing up: the illness and death of her father, the separation from her mother and brother afterwards, traveling unchaperoned with her brother on a train from Montana to Oregon, and boarding away from home. All these resulted in a recognized maturity. Of course, her slim, hour-glass figure and eighteen-inch waist might have also mesmerized the guys. Again, Inez never had a clue.

The Klamath Falls area served as a location for maneuvers and training of military units. Thus, servicemen increased in the district. Often, the Armory held programs before the Wednesday and Saturday dances. Inez remembered one Wednesday evening sitting in a musical program prior to a dance. Out of the corner of her eye she noticed a good-looking marine sitting behind her right shoulder. As the group dismissed for the dance, the marine followed right behind her to the dance floor. He touched her arm and Inez turned towards him.

"Would you care to dance?" he asked as the music began to play.

"Oh yes, I would like that very much," smiled Inez as she thought, *He noticed me too.*

He was well built and blond—she had a thing for blonds. He placed his right hand at her waist and offered his left hand as they floated to the dance floor.

The couple only took two dance steps before being interrupted by a tap on the shoulder. Someone was taking the prerogative of cutting in.

The marine shook his head and said, "No, we haven't had a chance to dance yet."

After several more dance steps, yet another marine attempted to cut in. The intruder was ignored, but the dance was destined to end when the first would-be partner returned to claim his dance.

At this point, the handsome marine shrugged his shoulders and walked away. It wasn't the case that Inez was such a hot item. The men outnumbered the women three to one.

To Inez's disappointment, the desired marine vanished from the hall. She always considered him the "marine that got away," for she never saw him again.

Over the next years, Inez danced with all sorts of partners: farmers, teenagers, and servicemen. They varied from young to old, short to tall, and slim to round. Because of the war, men came from all parts of the country. And they brought with them their local nuances to the familiar dance steps. Servicemen from the East Coast thought the Oregon women danced funny, and vice versa.

The more she danced with different men; the quicker Inez adjusted the variation in her dancing. Though everyone had his own style, she became comfortable dancing with most any type of partner.

Inez fulfilled her desire to dance. It is a wonder she didn't wear out her dancing shoes.

~

Klamath Union High School, 1940

Time spent dreaming over Henry's yearbooks finally became reality. Inez manicured and painted her fingernails. She ironed her white blouse and A-line skirt, and then polished her saddle shoes. She shampooed and struggled to pin-curl her naturally straight hair as she readied herself for the first day of school. Inez slept fitfully, for the morning could not come soon enough. Long before sunrise, she bustled out of her bed—her freshman year had come at last.

Since her brother Henry graduated in the spring, Inez trekked alone across the fields to the nearest school bus stop. It felt strange to be by herself, but it did not scare her. Elements of self-confidence and even smugness crept into her thoughts—*I am one of the big kids now.*

The bus approached in a cloud of dust. The vehicle came to a stop, accompanied with gas fumes and squealing brakes. The accordion bus door opened with a clank.

"Good morning, Inez," greeted Hip Largent.

She smiled in response. Hip remained the consistent factor in Inez's bus riding experience. First school-day excitement charged the bus. Inez found an empty seat where a pocket of girls clustered. Busmates called to her, eager to catch up about the summer.

Inez anticipated the arrival at school when Hip drove past the large "K" displayed in white stones on a nearby hillside. He maneuvered the vehicle to a stop in front of the majestic brick high school, built in 1927. Lush trees and lawn showcased the front entry steps leading into the building. Words over the arched doorway identified the bus's destination—Klamath Union High School.

A poster-board drawing of the school mascot, Pelican Pete, welcomed the student body. Student voices, getting reacquainted, surrounded Inez. Upperclassmen including cute girls in red and white Pep Pepper outfits and athletic boys in red letterman sweaters asserted their status. Inez's previous self-assurance evaporated. She fought the urge to scurry through the halls to find a place to hide.

She then started to recognize familiar faces from all the previous schools she attended: Summers, Altamont, Mills, Fairview, and Roosevelt. Hope rose in Inez's chest as she marveled—*I'm going to fit in after all.*

Like many high schools with a large student body, K.U.H.S utilized the homeroom system. During the first period of the day the roll was taken, the Pledge of Allegiance was recited, and school announcements were read.

Homerooms at K.U.H.S were organized by grade level and the students' last names. Inez went by the last name of Dutton, which placed her in Room 215 with Mrs. Rachel Good and all the other students with the surnames starting with D through F. Inez's first-period homeroom established an important haven for camaraderie and gave her significance as an underclassman. The group remained large, sometimes forty-five students. Strong friendships formed as this solid core of students continued together all four years of school.

Curriculum for Inez's first year of high school consisted of some required courses: English, history, and physical education. Freshmen were placed in split semester courses, with Personal Adjustment for the first semester and then health for the second. Inez opted not to take algebra. She stayed clear of anything mathematical because of her struggles during grammar school. Spanish I, drama, and study hall rounded out the rest of Inez's freshmen courses.

The freshmen Personal Adjustment class proved to be one of Inez's favorite high school courses. Boys and girls were in separate classes. Taught by Mrs. Blanche Waters, the course assisted secondary students as they matured into young adults. Students' adjustment and growth in their physical, social, and emotional, as well as scholastic areas, were all addressed.

The special emphasis on etiquette and manners benefited Inez the most. She learned such details as the correct way to answer a telephone and how to set a table for a formal dinner party. Inez recalled the merits of knowing how to make introductions of one person to another.

Mrs. Waters also suggested the girls hold their hands cupped together in front of their abdomens when standing to make a presentation. That way the arms did not hang down in a gawky, unpolished manner. Whatever manners and etiquette Inez learned, she taught to her mother. With these basic principles, both mother and daughter acquired social confidence.

Why did Inez take Spanish I? She never expected to attend college, so it was not to fill a college preparation requirement. The reasons she found herself in the Spanish class remain unknown after all these years.

Both Inez and her brother spoke French when they were young. However, when their mother remarried, the family no longer spoke French at home, since their new stepfather spoke only English.

Henry chose to take two years of French when he was in high school. He excelled in the course. Perhaps Mrs. Blanche Waters, who taught French as well as Inez's Personal Adjustment class, remembered Henry as one of her pupils, for she attempted to convince Inez to study French instead of Spanish.

Mrs. Waters continued to hold great allegiance to her French class when she wrote in Inez's freshmen yearbook, "Inez, with your French ancestry you should be one of my French pupils."

Nevertheless, Inez enjoyed her Spanish class, and she did well in it. Memorizing and conversation came easy for her. The next year

Inez extended her studies by taking Spanish II. She remembered the rote Spanish phrases from class throughout her lifetime. However, much to Inez's regret, she lost her ability to speak French by the time she had her own children.

A Little Drama

Mom, do you remember your first kiss?"

"That was a long time ago," replied my mother, Inez.

"Oh, you remember," I encouraged.

A smile lingered on Mother's lips, "Well, maybe I remember a little something."

Inez waited in the stage wings of the high school auditorium. Sweaty from nerves, she feared she would pass out. *Oh, why did the teacher think I could do this?*

Enrolling in the K.U.H.S. drama class as a freshman seemed a grand idea. Performing became one of Inez's interests after her experience the previous year in the Altamont Junior High production of *Carmen*. It surprised her to find she was one of the few underclassmen taking the course. What fun to be in the same class with older students. It gave Inez the chance to observe the numerous matured Pep Peppers and football players. And daydream about them she did—especially about Frank Hasy, the object of her infatuation. She was smitten with him. Of course, the upperclassmen kept to themselves and never seemed to pay much attention to a lowly freshman like Inez.

That was, until the drama class's production of *The Black Flamingo* in the autumn of 1940. The performance proved to be a colorful, costumed drama set at a notorious inn during the French Revolution.

The movable background and scenery enhanced the play's elements of suspense.

The play's dramatic climax hinged on a hysterical, onstage laugh and the person chosen to deliver it was Inez.

Dressed in a dark, flowing costume, Inez trembled with almost overwhelming stage fright as she waited for her signal. The backdrop loomed in front of her, daunting and ominous. Her dry throat tightened. The drama teacher, Mrs. Bloomquist, nodded her head and pointed to Inez.

It's my turn. I think I'm going to throw up. Inez swallowed her fear, moved to the side of the stage and delivered her suspense-filled, sadistic laugh, on cue.

"MWAHAHA, MWAHAHA, MWAHAHA"

I did it! thought Inez. Just then she miss-stepped and bumped into one of the towering panels of scenery. The looming structure wobbled to-and-fro, threatening to fall. *Oh, no. Not the scenery!*

Putting her two arms up against the scenery, as if being frisked, Inez looked over her shoulder with a pantomimed facial expression of horror and shock which the audience interpreted as the look of a crazed, demented person. The crowd roared their approval and a thunderous applause ensued. Within seconds the panel stabilized. Inez exited the stage.

Drama classmates patted her back, congratulating her for the successful scene. Mrs. Bloomquist approached Inez, all in smiles, and said, "Inez, I'm so proud of you. You were marvelous."

The next day, Inez was amazed at how many compliments she received for her laughter scene. Much to her disdain, she received less desirable attention as she left the drama classroom and approached her locker. Bill Christiansen, one of the over-confident football players from drama, placed his arm around Inez's shoulder. He said in a whisper, "I sure would like to kiss you."

This scared the wits out of Inez. She pulled away from his embrace as his attempted kiss grazed her check and resulted in a mouthful of her hair. Inez stormed down the hall to her next class, leaving Bill stunned.

Even though this boy was a popular athlete, Inez was put off by his arrogance and felt uncomfortable around him. He never attempted another kiss, but always lurked about. Bill even wrote in Inez's yearbook at the end of the year: "You sure are cute, boy would I like to go out with you."

It might have been a different story—if she had liked him.

It was December 31, 1940 and the New Year's celebration was in full swing at the Klamath Falls Armory. All the Army vehicles and equipment had been moved from the building. The place had been set up to host a dance for the locals and influx of military personnel from Camp White, near Medford, and Camp Tule Lake.

The Armory hosted dances most every Wednesday and Saturday night, as well as on special occasions like New Year's Eve. Dances like these helped folks forget the worries of the Depression. A live band played dance music. Locals provided plenty of food for the usual potluck dinner during the dance. Alcoholic drinks were not allowed in the Armory, but punch and soft drinks were plentiful.

Inez stood in a small crowd among other young girls when the Master of Ceremony's countdown to the New Year began. "Ten, nine, eight, seven, six, five, four, three, two, one—HAPPY NEW YEAR!" It was 12:00, midnight. The band and noise makers welcomed the New Year, 1941."

Suddenly, out of nowhere a group of four upperclassmen filtered through a cluster of girls where Inez found herself standing. One of the older boys from the drama class appeared in front of her. But Frank Hasy was not just any upperclassman. He was the tall, good-looking boy she had a crush on.

Frank said, "Hey, I know you—you're in my drama class." With that he gave Inez a big, sweet Happy New Year's kiss.

That was not only Inez's first kiss, but she confessed it was the best one, too.

Did it really happen? Or did Inez dream it? Frank Hasy never gave any indication of their New Year's encounter in the days that followed. Inez's acting career ended with her famed laugh. She never took any more drama classes or participated in other plays. And Bill Christiansen never got anything more than a kiss full of hair.

The Untimely Valentine

Charlie sniffed, then wiped his cold, red nose with the back of his hand. The chilly bite of the wind forecasted an end to the Indian summer. Even so, he made his morning rounds before heading off to work. He viewed with interest the new gridirons at the foot of the bridge. *Gosh those city boys sure worked slow. . . . Guess it took a while to figure out which end of a shovel to use. . . . Have to admit though—they did a fair job of it.*

For two weeks, a crew of a dozen young men from the Civilian Conservation Corps (CCC) installed gridiron cattle guards along the diversion canal near the Dutton farm. Used as an alternative to gates and fences, the transverse grids of metal bars prevented hoofed animals, such as cattle, from wandering beyond designated areas. The new structure allowed foot traffic or vehicles to cross the bridge without the need to open or close a gate with each pass.

Charlie thought as he opened the gate near the house, *Roosevelt believes this civilian "tree army" of his will create work for the jobless and keep youth off the city street corners. Well, more power to him.*

The Depression brought widespread unemployment for even skilled and experienced men. Many families required the help of public assistance to survive. The national CCC work-relief program began during the first one hundred days of President Franklin D. Roosevelt's administration. The program, with its focus on the conservation of natural resources, became one of the most successful of all the president's New Deal initiatives.

The CCC provided unskilled, manual labor positions for unemployed, unmarried men, ages eighteen through twenty-five from all over the United States. Shelter, food, and clothing were provided, in addition to a modest wage of $30 a month. All but $5 of the $30 had to be sent home to the men's families.

"Hey, what's this?" Charlie could not believe his eyes. A trinket decorated the fencepost in the promise of the morning—there hung a heart-shaped piece of white shale with a thin wire threaded through a hole near the top.

"Well I'll be darned," he said, as he gently plucked the heart from its perch atop the post and hurried into the kitchen where his stepdaughter Inez sat eating her breakfast of toast and strawberry jam.

Charlie presented the heart to her and said in a hushed voice, "Here, I think this was meant for you."

Shocked, Inez hesitated before she accepted the untimely valentine. Closer examination revealed a smooth, ashen piece of clay whittled into a delicate 3x4-inch heart. A message carved on the front side said, "If you want to write, you are welcome." Additional carvings on the other side disclosed a name and address: Tanis LeLeux, Route 1 Box 293, Welsh, Louisiana. Without further delay, Inez left the kitchen in search of her mother.

"Mama, look what someone left." Inez showed the clay heart to her mother.

Smiling, Leona examined the heart and said, "It looks like you attracted an admirer."

"I didn't speak with any of those CCC men, but I did feel them looking at me when I tended the garden and shelled peas on the porch. What do you think I should do?"

Leona hesitated, then said with a chuckle, "I believe Tanis is of Cajun descent and comes from the Bayou area of Louisiana. I think it would be okay to write to him. But beware, *LeLeux* means *Wolf* in French."

Inez did write and received a return letter from Tanis soon afterwards. The installation of cattle guards in Oregon had been his first assignment with the CCC. He wrote interesting letters describing his work, travel. and his everyday activities. From further writings, Inez learned he came from a broken home life and was eight years older than she.

Tanis enlisted in the United States Marine Corps after the attack on Pearl Harbor. While stationed at Camp Lejeune in South Carolina for his basic training, he sent photos that depicted camp life, such as the long lines required to get into the mess hall and to see a movie. More appealing for Inez was her first view, per snapshot, of Tanis—a slim, dark haired, and attractive marine posed leaning against the camp flagpole. Inez placed the photographs in her scrapbook.

Inez never met Tanis in person, even though he suggested it once. She continued to write to him every couple of weeks, throughout the war. Tanis fought in the South Pacific Theater and later told Inez he carried her picture with him during the battle in Guadalcanal. The correspondence between the two lasted six years and ended in June of 1946, when Inez wrote to tell Tanis she was engaged and planned to marry.

She never heard from Tanis again.

~

Snaggled Teeth, 1941

With a sigh, Inez leaned towards a small wall mirror nailed over the dressing table. Close examination of her appearance elicited the same daily observation: *Snaggled teeth—that's the only name for them.*

Crooked teeth were a source of embarrassment throughout Inez's life. Her teeth appeared white and healthy, but her mouth did not have room for them. Growing up, she was a "smiley" child. When her permanent teeth grew in, they crowded into wherever there was a hint of space. Where two teeth had been, one large tooth came in. Like parking a Cadillac in Volkswagen space—something had to give. Her brother had a mouth full of perfect, small teeth, like their father. Therefore, Henry felt justified in spitefully calling Inez, "Horse Tooth."

Her canine teeth were the most obvious. She felt they presented as "tusks." These eye teeth perched in Inez's gum line bilaterally, as they wedged on top of, and between, the lateral incisors and first premolars. Once they grew in, Inez was so self-conscious that she stopped smiling.

It was not uncommon to have crooked teeth, and many of her acquaintances did as well. Her friend Alice had her own canine tusks. Braces were a rarity while Inez grew up. The cost of orthodontics was beyond most families' means. Nevertheless, perfect smiles were seen on movie stars. Those ideal choppers resulted from movie studios paying for teeth to be capped with dental crowns.

The misalignment of Inez's teeth was not her imagination; their appearance disturbed her mother as well. Leona implored Charlie to take Inez to a Portland dentist who specialized in orthodontics. Charlie would have none of it. For him, this was an outlandish request. A journey to Portland would be long and difficult, with weather conditions unpredictable. Neither Leona nor Charlie could take time from work to make such a drive. But the bottom line for Charlie was he did not want to spend the money.

The family dentist was consulted, but he would do nothing. Leona was then put in touch with another, older local dentist who gladly agreed to extract the canine teeth. This questionable procedure was done during summer break before Inez entered the 10th grade.

Afterward, Inez returned to her mirror to admire herself—again and again.

Without her eye teeth, Inez smiled once more. Her brother, Henry, still lived at home, but worked two jobs to save for schooling and a car. Therefore, his work schedule kept him away much of the time. Less Henry meant fewer brotherly put-downs, spiteful teasing, and ridicule. Inez developed self-confidence as she came into her own.

As mother-daughter sessions increased, an even closer bond developed between Leona and Inez. Leona served as an excellent model for how to make oneself presentable. She took care with her hair, clothing, and make-up, and paid special attention to protect and moisturize her skin. She believed a person should try her best with what God gave her. Leona's extra effort served her well—her skin was lovely.

A new morning routine accompanied Inez's return for her sophomore year of high school. She washed her face and brushed her teeth. She combed out her hair from the nightly pin-curl setting that had become her habit. Inez placed a dab of Vaseline on her eyelashes and crimped them with an eyelash curler. After counting to 20, she repeated the procedure on the next eye. The Vaseline enhanced the natural darkness of her lashes and helped set the curl.

A bit of creamed rouge went on the apple of her cheeks. A light touch of pressed facial powder and carefully applied pinkish-red lipstick finished her makeup routine. Stepping back Inez thought—*If not a beautiful swan, at least not an ugly duckling any longer.*

Building Up for War

Talk of possible war buzzed everywhere in 1941. Despite its declared neutrality, the United States trained soldiers, sailors, marines, and airmen throughout Oregon. Tangible proof of war preparations appeared as roadways filled with two-and-a-half-ton military trucks, known as deuce-and-a-halves, transporting soldiers to training maneuvers. The mobilization of personnel and equipment influenced everyday life for Inez and her friends.

During this time, Inez enjoyed staying overnight with a bus-mate and friend, Lillian Badorek. Years later, Inez remembered two details about these visits. The first was that Lillian's mother had burn scars on her face and upper body sustained during the 1906 San Francisco earthquake and fire.

However more relevant for the young girls, Lillian's house was situated on Highway 97, the main thoroughfare for military units traveling through Klamath Falls. Lillian and Inez were thrilled to discover a pleasurable pastime. They could wave to the soldiers as the convoys passed by the house on their way to bivouac in the Klamath Falls hills. The multitude of uniformed men was daunting, but what a delight for a teenage girl. Some of the soldiers even whistled and waved back.

Klamath Falls Street Dance, Summer of 1941

In truth, Inez had many friendly acquaintances, but she never had a closer friend than Genevieve Peters. Their sister-like relationship from elementary school remained solid and flourished through the first years of high school. Perhaps, the one-year age difference made the connection significant for Inez.

The reliability of the friendship helped develop Inez's self-assurance in high school, as well as in the rest of her life. The Peters were a stable family unit for Inez. Their home provided her shelter during the stormy winter months—as well as a place where she could be herself with Genevieve, any time of the year.

Mr. Peters knocked on the door frame before leaning in to say, "Gen, a street dance is forming on Main Street. Do you and Inez want to go?"

The girls looked up from reading their magazines. Genevieve turned to Inez who, with a slight smile, gave an eager nod. The girls, 15 and 16 years old, scrambled to change into sundresses, comb their hair, and put on lipstick.

When Army units bivouacked in the nearby hills, the community came together to support the young GIs with an impromptu street dance. This was Inez's chance to meet, up close and personal, some of the soldiers on maneuvers. It proved to be a memorable evening that evoked romance—not directly for Inez but vicariously through Genevieve and her dance partner.

Mr. Peters dropped the girls off in the late afternoon, with instructions to be ready when he returned for them at six o'clock. A portion of the Klamath Falls main streets had been roped off for dancing. Radio music drifted from a store's open door. The large crowd consisted of two distinct groups—locals and soldiers. The soldiers were somewhat intimidating as dance partners since they wore fatigues and clumsy military combat boots.

The two separate groups blended as the area filled with dancers. Both Genevieve and Inez were asked to dance. Later, during a lull in the music, the girls found themselves beyond the actual dance area. They decided to wait for Genevieve's father on the fringe of the crowd.

"Would you like to dance?" A young soldier addressed his request to Genevieve. He appeared to be in his early twenties. He sported a fresh GI haircut like all the other soldiers. Little distinguished him from any other.

Genevieve looked around at the crowd as she said, "Not in front of all these people."

The soldier smiled and replied, "When the music starts, we will have to go down to the street . . . if you want to dance." And that is what they did.

The soldier's name was Bill McNay. After a while, Mr. Peters arrived, and Bill approached him to ask if he could take Genevieve to a movie.

Mr. Peters replied, "Not unless Inez goes too" and he then added, "and I'll pick up the girls, when the movie is over."

Bill agreed to the stipulations and hailed a taxi to take both girls to the movies. As they entered the taxi, Inez found herself poised to sit between Bill and Genevieve. Inez relinquished the place in the middle to Bill, per his request.

As the taxi took off for the movies, Mr. Peters, a World War I veteran, leaned into the car window and said, "Take care of my girls. . . . Remember they're not dry behind the ears."

The two girls learned Bill's family owned walnut groves in the affluent Hillsboro area, 292 miles north from Klamath Falls. Bill had been drafted into the U. S. Army and conscripted for a one-year service obligation. He was what would later be labeled as a "pre–Pearl Harbor peace time draftee." Bill served as the unit cook and had several more months before his service requirements would be fulfilled.

The trio had a pleasant evening at the movies. Inez was fascinated by this soldier; Genevieve was aloof and vague. Goodbyes were said after Bill and Genevieve exchanged addresses. Bill's army unit continued maneuvers the next day and left the Klamath Falls foothills.

In October, Bill McNay returned as a civilian driving a brand-new Chrysler automobile. At the time, it was almost impossible to buy such a vehicle. But there he was. And boy, oh boy, he looked GOOD. No longer a dog-face soldier. He appeared very different with light brown, curly hair, grown out from his GI haircut. He was as Irish-looking as his name implied. Impeccably dressed, Bill carried his tall, well-built frame with dignity and self-confidence. Unforgettable for Inez was his nice-smelling scent of Bill's Gray Flannel after-shave. It was enough to make a fifteen-year-old's heart to go pitter-patter.

On his first visit back, Bill examined Inez's schoolwork and complimented her on her near-perfect typing. She was just learning to type in high school and his positive comments and encouragement meant a lot to her.

Over the next several months, Bill made frequent visits to Klamath Falls to date Genevieve. Her parents liked and trusted Bill. Even though the young couple were not required to take Inez on their dates, the pattern for her to accompany them had been set.

Gen told Inez, "Bill is the one who says, 'Let's go and get Inez.'" The couple drove to the country to pick her up. At other times, they just sat on the Duttons' couch and visited. Bill must have realized the important bond between Inez and Genevieve. Inez believed the couple felt sorry for her living on the farm, in the isolated country conditions.

At 11:00 a.m. PST, on the first Sunday of December, Inez heard the radio broadcast of the surprise Japanese attack that brought war to American soil. Like most Americans of the time, she and her family were stunned. And like many people, Inez did not even know the location of Pearl Harbor.

The next day, Inez's high-school student body gathered in the auditorium for an assembly to hear President Franklin D. Roosevelt make his declaration of war over the radio.

> *"Yesterday, December 7, 1941—a date which will live in infamy—the United States of America was suddenly and deliberately attacked by naval and air forces of the Empire of Japan. . . ."*

FDR's "Infamy Speech" was brief, running just a little over seven minutes. After that, events moved quickly. Germany declared war on the United States on December 11th. The US reciprocated by declaring war on Nazi Germany the same day. With those declarations of war, Inez's life, and the life of every other American, changed.

When war was declared, Bill McNay was called back into the Army. He returned to active duty in February of 1942, with orders to be stationed in Australia.

Before he deployed, Bill and Genevieve came out to the farm to see Inez. When Bill and Inez were alone on the patio, he asked if she would write to him. Bill gave Inez a big hug and kiss when she told him, "Of course I'll write to you, Bill."

It was obvious to Inez that Bill liked Genevieve a great deal. Gen remained noncommittal. Inez believed that was just Gen—a reserved, quiet blonde who wore a perpetual dream-like expression. Someone who showed little of her true feelings in any situation.

Yet, Inez did not understand how Genevieve could seem so blasé and uncaring when Bill left for war. The only emotion she expressed was laughter when the contents of Inez's purse spilled all over the floor, as Bill and Inez hugged goodbye for the last time. Genevieve thought it was the funniest thing she had ever seen.

Where Genevieve was passive about Bill McNay, she was crazy about a guy from high school. His name was also Bill, but he went by Billy. He was a wild teenager who drove a souped-up hot rod. Inez called it half a car because it was missing the entire top. Billy was a reckless driver, and Genevieve loved the thrill of the speed. One evening, Inez feared for her life when she rode with Billy.

Mr. Peters did not like this Billy and told his daughter, "Genevieve, I don't want that guy hanging around."

Genevieve was devastated. She broke up with Billy, the hotrodder, but not before a lot of heartfelt discussions with Inez.

Endings

As Inez's sophomore school year came to an end, students in possession of the 1942 yearbooks were pleased to have them. It had been announced the next year's annuals would be casualties of the times. Paper, ink, and manpower needed to be diverted for the war effort.

Genevieve wrote the following in Inez's yearbook at the end of that 1942 school year:

Dearest Inez

Someday we will look back at this book and think how good it was to have such friends and honestly, Inez you're the bestest "sister" I have ever had. When everyone else was tired of listening to me talk of a certain person you'd listen. Remember all the dances we attended and the Fourth of July in our outfits. Remember when Bill left, and you dropped your purse. Remember when we slept on the cot and you took all the bed, and I took all the blankets. They were happy moments, weren't they? Anyway honey, I'm certainly going to miss you when I move but you'll write, I hope. Remember me once in a while when I'm gone, and I'll never forget you. You're cute hon & you'll go far.

All my Love—Genevieve

In another three weeks, John, Cassie, and Genevieve Peters left Klamath Falls to move to Bremerton, Washington. John returned to his previously held position at the Puget Sound Navy Yard (PSNY), to do his part and help the war effort.

To keep in touch, written correspondence became the new phase of Inez and Genevieve's friendship. Soon Genevieve wrote to tell of her new boyfriend.

Inez had the sad task of writing to Gen of the death of Billy the teenager in a car accident. He had lost control of his vehicle—Mr. Peter's disapproval of the hotrodder seemed prophetic.

Meanwhile, Inez kept to herself the frequent thoughts of Bill McNay. The fragrance of his after-shave lingered for weeks among her couch pillows, where Bill last rested his head.

~

Pep Peppers and School Pride

"Inez Dutton" announced the girl from the K.U.H.S. podium.

Not believing her ears, Inez made her way through the aisles to receive a fragrant white carnation, a symbol of her new honor. During the last assembly of the school year, she had just been named to the elite group of school supporters known as the Klamath Union Pep Peppers.

Nothing could have excited Inez more. She never expected to be invited to join this important school pep squad. For years she admired the older girls who represented the pep for all K.U.H.S. teams. She saw them dressed in their red-and-white outfits on her bus, around town, and in Henry's yearbooks. Once she attended high school herself, Inez was even more impressed by the group of 50 junior and senior girls.

The Pep Pepper organization served as a cheering section, providing the heartiest of support for the mighty K.U.H.S. Pelicans. The girls demonstrated a united team spirit as they performed precision-type drill formations at Modoc Field on the school grounds, during basketball games, and in local parades. Boosting school spirit came in other ways, too. The Pep Peppers assisted in selling season tickets for football and basketball games and sold white chrysanthemums with a central "K" made from red pipe cleaners, to raise money for the teams.

With the world at war and restrictions imposed on the young people of the country, it was reassuring that certain aspects of school activities continued. For a time, the young people could lose themselves in competition against a rival school, rather than in the uncertainty of war. Team sports and organizations such as Pep Peppers promoted school pride and helped develop honor of country.

During the summer, several girls came out to the country to measure Inez before ordering her uniform. Such measurements were required because it was essential each Pep Pepper's skirt hem be the exact same distance from the ground, no matter what the height of the girl. In this way the skirts would be consistent and standardized as the group marched.

The Pep Pepper uniform consisted of a white pullover sweater with a large red and white letter K on the front. The red flannel skirt, flared with gored pleats, proved to be a flattering style for Inez. Red socks and saddle shoes completed the outfit. The girls' attire complimented the Klamath football team uniform. The boys wore jerseys of solid red, with red and white striped arms, and leather helmets for protection.

Inez's friend, Alice Fitzsimmons, not chosen as a Pep Pepper, was quite envious over Inez's good fortune. And Henry, in his typical big-brother response, attempted to deflate the honor by saying, "They must be letting everyone in there now."

Yet, Inez was not discouraged. She cherished her association with the Pep Peppers. The sweet scent of the white carnation lasted a long time. Her selection as a Pep Pepper was the best tribute and validation she'd received in all of her sixteen years.

While growing up, I noticed similarities between my mother's high school and mine. My father, Ted, and all three of us children also graduated from a K.U.H.S.; not from Klamath Union High School, but rather from a small school in California's San Joaquin Valley—Kerman Union High School. Our school colors were also red and white.

However, our mascot was a daunting, fearsome lion—not a mere bird. Much to our amusement we joked, without mercy, about Klamath's chosen mascot, Pelican Pete. What would Pete do to his opponents? Poop on them? We laughed and made comments about the mighty and ferocious "Pelicans"—all the time picturing a Disney-inspired caricature of a lone pelican scarfing up little fish.

Mom, schooled in pride and enthusiasm for her Klamath Union High School and the beloved Pelican Pete, told of how her school's mascot honored the American White Pelicans. I respected her loyalty and always wondered about the unique and honored mascot.

The American white pelican, one of the largest flying birds found in the western hemisphere has a nine-foot wingspan that rivals that of the California condor. Yet, these pelicans are cooperative foraging water birds. They swim in rows, on top of the water, flapping their wings as they herd their prey towards the shore. Perhaps, their group cooperation served as an example of supportive unity and spirit for the Klamath Falls teams.

My mother was adamant that the white pelican was selected as Klamath's mascot because of the birds' history of nesting only in the Upper Klamath Lake region of Oregon. Possibly, the Klamath location was the exclusive nesting area for these pelicans during the 1930s and 40s, while Mom was growing up. However, it is probable that the work of the Water Reclamation Act in the late 1920s which salvaged land for farming may also have disrupted their breeding and nesting in the area. The pelicans now tend to breed in isolated areas of Manitoba, Canada, and Minnesota.

In the past, even though they seldom preyed on the same fish sought by people, American white pelicans were persecuted because they were perceived as competitors. People shot pelicans, clubbed their young, and broke their eggs. The species, classified as endangered in the 1970s due to habitat loss and disturbance to the colonies, is now considered recovered.

With greater esteem for Mom's worthy school mascot and her passion for her much-loved Klamath Union High School—flamed by her participation as a Pep Pepper—I offer an enthusiastic:

"GO PELICANS!"

~

H-E-N-R-Y

"My name is spelled, H-E-N-R-Y," said Inez's brother in a matter-of-fact way, without pretenses, arrogance, or anger.

He continued, "H-E-N-E-R-Y spells hennery, which is where hens are raised." This was almost true, except that a hennery is spelled with two "N's."

Inez admired Henry's character, his competence and intellect (if not his spelling). Even as the caricature of a typical older brother, Henry still held his sister's high regard, love, and devotion. Perhaps calling Inez Horse Tooth, saying she stunk or that she was ugly was Henry's way of expressing jealousy of his younger sister. As an older sibling, he often picked on Inez for sheer entertainment. If anyone else tried the same offense, he would stand up against them.

Henry could have become a rebellious youth with a chip on his shoulder. He had lost his real father and had been dumped into a foundling home at the age of eight. When reunited with his mother, he had to deal with a new stepfather. Henry could have succumbed to the influences of Orin, his worldly stepbrother, who had a propensity to find and fall into trouble. Even his mother's indiscretions could have pushed Henry to noncompliance.

Resilient and cut from the fabric of the greatest generation, Henry was not negatively affected by any of these factors. His initial resentment of a new stepfather was replaced by respect and love.

He accepted Charlie as his father and learned from the older man's wisdom. Charlie taught Henry what he could not teach his own son, Orin: to farm, hunt, fish, and become a responsible man.

Charlie's full-time job at the Lumber Company made him rely on Henry for farm chores and milking. The young man simply did what needed to be done. That also meant studying for school and working odd jobs to earn extra money.

Resourcefulness was another one of Henry's qualities. Years later, he told Inez how he learned to swim at the age of twelve. Despite their parents' admonishment to keep away from the nearby diversion canal, it served as the site for the boy's swimming practice.

Henry tied a rope around his waist, then anchored the other end to the cement bridge piling. With flailing arms and legs, he "swam" out to the full length of the rope. He then pulled himself back to the bridge—just to repeat the procedure over and over in the cold and swift-running water until he taught himself to swim.

Animals fascinated the young Henry. He studied the animals around him. He even performed a caesarean section on a pregnant ground squirrel. The duties of castrating the farm animals fell to Henry. Charlie made a mess of the procedure, whereas Henry's work was neat and bloodless. With this proficiency, Henry altered the male farm animals one and all. If the calves, sheep, pigs, or cats had testicles, Henry removed them.

Dogs were kept on the farm as pets, but they were also used to herd the cattle. Because Henry loved animals so much, the ridiculous way his parents dealt with their dogs greatly disturbed him. At the drop of a hat, his folks dumped their dogs. Just when the kids started getting attached to a dog, it was not there any longer. Plenty of excuses were given when the dogs came up missing. The dog barked too much, it could not be trained, it was no good, the coyotes got it, or the dog just ran off—all of these were reasons used to explain the exiled canines.

One day the dog would be part of the family then, after a few weeks, the animal was gone. Henry calculated his folks got rid of nine dogs in three years. He surmised each dog was sold, traded, or dumped somewhere. Inez remembered visions of Charlie driving away from the farm with the hay trailer stacked full of hay bales and the current dog perched high on the hayrack. Neither hay nor dog returned.

After graduating from high school, Henry obtained a light-blond-colored dog with pale blue eyes. The neighbor found it with several other pups in a badger hole. It was believed to be an Australian shepherd and coyote mix. However, no Australian shepherd had been seen or known to be in those parts. The dog, named Sammy, was so high-strung that he could not tolerate being scolded. He took off in a flash, running across country, at the first words of a rebuke. Sammy did not bark, he yipped in a high, whiny pitch.

At the same time, the farm had an older bitch dog named Hulde, a mixed German shepherd breed. The cattle were herded by both dogs, but the pleading of Sammy's high-pitched yipping was ignored by the livestock. Not until Hulde, the better working dog, slowly gave one deep, throaty bark did the cattle respond, straight away. However, Sammy developed a nipping, instead of yipping, style of herding. He nibbled at the cattle's hooves to herd them to and from the pasture.

Henry loved his Sammy. It broke his heart when he returned from war to discover his pet had been given away. Later, Inez and Henry laughed in agreement that it was a surprise they were never given away like the dogs.

The irony of the joke came too close to the truth.

~

Schooling and Employment

With his intelligence and work ethic, Henry earned good grades in school. Even though he could not afford college and had little hope of attending, he took the college preparation courses such as trigonometry and physics. He excelled in mathematics with his trusty slide rule always close at hand. Fellow students, including Inez, knew not to mess with this calculating device. For if they did, Henry's wrath would come down upon them.

Throughout his teen years, Inez's brother worked odd jobs for his expenses and education. After graduating from high school, Henry found a job sorting out rotten potatoes at R.E. Bailey's Potato Cellar. It was dirty, smelly work with a distinctive rancid odor like human vomit that permeated a worker's nose, hair, and clothing—but it did pay 75 cents an hour. Frugal with his money, Henry bought a used black 1935 Dodge coupe for $50. It became his pride and joy.

Somehow money was found for Henry to enroll in a yearlong Los Angeles technical school. He and his high school friend, Marvin, were roommates as they attended the school together. Marvin studied technical engineering, while Henry studied electrical engineering.

During his time in the Los Angeles area, Henry became reacquainted with his father's branch of the family, the Davids—Uncle Leon, Aunt Ella, and the cousins. They lived in Tujunga Hills, California, just outside of Pasadena. These relationships remained strong for the rest of Henry's life.

The attack on Pearl Harbor occurred halfway into Henry's electrician program. On completion of his schooling, he returned to Klamath Falls and passed the required examination to earn a journeyman electrician certification. However, the 20-year-old could not find work as an electrician. Instead, he took a job at Conifers, the local lumberyard. He had the dangerous job, called "takeoff," that involved unloading the freshly hewed wood planks from the saw blade platform. Henry worked there only a few months before he became ill.

Inez described that time:

> *"The winter before Henry went into the service, he came down with pneumonia. Boy what a sick guy he was. He sat in a lounge chair, all winter and coughed and spit into a coffee can. He was so ill—but that was before antibiotics were available. Finally, after perhaps six weeks he started feeling a little better, so he carried a small wooden three-legged milking stool and walked a few feet and then sit down. He was still so weak.*
>
> *Eventually he regained some strength, but he was too thin for his height to get into the Air Corps. The doctor told him to go out and eat and eat and eat and he finally weighed in, barely over the limit. He was pretty close to 6'1" and only weighed 130 lbs."*

~

Army Air Corps, Fall 1942

"Willy Dinglar got me drunk!" Henry exclaimed, making his confession to Inez at the Armory dance in the fall of 1942. He stood shaking his head back and forth as he attempted to clear away the foggy thoughts. His statement and behavior surprised Inez, for she never knew her brother to indulge in liquor.

After months of recuperation from a lung infection, the diligent 21-year-old built his strength up to enter the military. Once fit for duty, he took a final step before volunteering for the Army Air Corps. Henry had never flown before and did not want any airborne surprises. In a very Henry-like approach, he hired a pilot from the nearby airport to fly him around the Klamath area. It was love at first flight.

The young man's life hung on the cusp of change. Henry's pie-eyed condition at the dance coincided with his upcoming induction into the U.S. Army Air Corps. He answered the call to serve his country in war—and his friends talked him into celebrating.

The next day, still somewhat green from overindulgence, Henry boarded the train bound for basic training at Santa Ana Army Air Base in Southern California. The young man had a lot to learn in the upcoming months, but perhaps the best lessons were taught while partying the night before: think for yourself and don't let anyone talk you into something not in your best interest.

Henry benefited from the military's need for more commissioned officers. Instead of the traditional process of completing an ROTC program or securing a four-year college degree, he was enrolled in a twelve-week Officer Candidate School (OCS) course. Called "ninety-day wonders," Henry and other servicemen graduated with commissions as second lieutenants in the United States Army Air Corps.

Many of the cadets entering the Army Air Corps wanted to be pilots. Tests at basic training determined whether a cadet would be trained as a pilot, a bombardier, navigator, mechanic, and so forth. Because of his aptitude and reflex-test results, Henry qualified to train as a pilot. He also possessed the useful and sought-after trait of being ambidextrous. To have the ability to use both the right and left hand with equal skill was a desirable feature for a pilot.

Even though Henry loved the feeling of flying, he was adamant against becoming an actual pilot. He could take off and fly the plane beautifully, but he could not overcome his fear of getting the plane to the ground. He said he was "scared shitless when it came time to land the aircraft."

Fortunately, Henry also exhibited the psychomotor skills needed to succeed as a bombardier. At Deming, New Mexico, he trained with a bomber crew for this position. His responsibilities focused on targeting and releasing aerial bombs to detonate on specific sites. Training also included learning the navigator's functions. At the conclusion of the course, Henry received his bombardier silver wings.

At Pueblo, Colorado, Henry received further bombardier-navigator training required to lead B-29 aircraft in medium bomber missions. While attending a United Service Organization (USO) dance, Henry met a young college freshman, Patricia Thomas.

Henry had never dated before. Some say, "the uniform makes the man." Others say, "the man makes the uniform." Whatever the case, Pat liked what she saw in Henry, and that was that. Soon Leona and Inez were receiving cards, letters, and pictures from Pat. Inez was happy that Henry had someone special in his life. But she could not help feeling a bit jealous, for Pat and Inez were the same age.

~

Boarding with the Carters, Junior Year 1942–43

"I have a late meeting at the school tonight, and I won't be home for dinner. Could you cook the meal for yourself and the men?" said Mrs. Carter as she took her coat from the hall closet.

"Ah, sure," came Inez's timid reply. Inwardly her heart stopped: *She expects me to cook?*

For the previous two winters, Inez had stayed with Genevieve during the harshest weather. Once the Peters moved to Bremerton, that was no longer an option. During the winter months of her junior year, the school district again funded Inez's room and board. This time she lived with the Carter family. Mr. Carter owned a grocery store, Mrs. Carter was Inez's former junior high teacher, and their only son was a college student.

Per their agreement, Inez helped Mrs. Carter with light housework, such as dusting, making beds, and washing the dishes. For this work, Mrs. Carter paid Inez $3 a week. However, this was the first time Mrs. Carter had requested the girl to cook dinner. Her own mother never asked Inez to cook at home. Self-doubt and anxiety rose at the thought of preparing the main meal.

The menu, determined by Mrs. Carter, consisted of a beef roast, potatoes, and parsnips. Fixing the potatoes was not a problem. As for the parsnips, Inez was not familiar with the vegetable. They looked like white carrots to her, so she planned to boil them in some salted water.

She followed the instructions Mrs. Carter left for the oven temperature setting and the timing to cook the roast. Inez cleaned up the kitchen and set the table as the meat cooked. When the timer rang, she turned off the oven and set the meat to rest while she prepared the vegetables.

Inez began to slice the beef but stood back in devastation. She was accustomed to meat being cooked—until it was leather-like. This was firm on the outside but had a soft, pink-to-red juicy center. *Oh, how can I expect to serve this raw meat?*

Much to her surprise, the two men assured her the beef was perfect. In fact, they said everything was just like they wanted. They not only took second helpings, but they also had thirds. What a great relief to Inez when she realized the dinner had come together by her own doing, despite her trepidation.

As for wintering in town, Inez found the season's hazards still lurked around the corner. The Carters lived close to the high school, but on a steep hill. Rushing in the cold one morning, Inez slipped and fell on the icy path as she made her way to school. She skinned both knees and arrived at school with blood running down to her ankles.

~

Rationing

On a WWII Wartime Poster:

Use it up,
Wear it out,
Make it do,
Or do without.

The U.S. economy shifted overnight into war production. Military products took priority over consumer goods. Citizens were asked to "do with less so they [the fighting force] would have enough."

The advancing Japanese forces disrupted production and availability of rubber, gasoline, and certain foods such as sugar, coffee, and spices. Conserving crucial supplies led to rationing of these necessities. A government-issued coupon system was established to discourage hoarding and to make sure everyone received their fair share of food and other commodities.

By sacrificing on the home front, people like Inez and her family better understood the sacrifices of the fighting men and women. Therefore, rationing became the new normal. Short supplies of items challenged the American public. Recycling drives took place for scrap rubber and metals, such as tin, steel, and aluminum.

As a large portion of the nation's food staples were sent to the troops, families adjusted their recipes to work with rationed sugar, cooking oil, and meats. Homemakers experimented with substitutions that sometimes went wrong.

One evening prior to a dance, Inez ate a salad that used mineral oil as the substitute for salad dressing. She danced with abandonment until a girl told Inez she had something orange colored on her backside. What an embarrassment. When Inez went into the bathroom, she found the orange stain originated in her underpants. The mineral oil had seeped through her bowels. The incident did not put Inez off dancing, but it sure did put her off salads with mineral oil dressing.

Shortly after the United States entered the war, the government and businesses urged people to make gardening a family and community effort. These communal plots of land, called "Victory Gardens," not only helped to make the rations go further, but it also allowed children to be part of the war effort. Inez and Leona had kept a sizable garden for years. Now they enlarged that garden and continued to can even more of their fruits and vegetables.

Because the Duttons lived on a farm, they had adequate poultry, meats, milk, and butter. Oleomargarine, made from vegetable oil, became a popular substitute for butter during the wartime dairy shortages. Inez experienced this butter alternative when eating away from home.

Alice said, "Pass the butter please."

Inez looked around the table.

Alice attempted her request again. "The butter, please," and pointed to an unappetizing cube that had the appearance of lard.

Inez said, "This?" as she picked up the plate with the white cube on it.

"Yah, that's oleomargarine, or it's called oleo. It's used instead of butter, because of the war effort. You know the dairy and butter goes for the troops. Besides, Ma said there's lots of oleo at the store and it's cheaper than butter."

"Oh," said Inez as she bypassed the oleo and instead spread strawberry jam on her toast.

It took forethought and imagination to deal with common personal items suddenly unavailable at any price. The dilemma required finding a workable substitution from what was already on hand or still obtainable.

Being stylish was a high priority for Inez and her mother. The custom of curling their eyelashes was a must for the two. However, replacements for the curlers were no longer available. When the rubber on the eyelash curlers became frayed and beyond use, they resorted to finding rubber around their home to fit the curler. Experimenting, they discovered that a piece cut from the edge of a water bag, such as a hot-water bag or douche bag, fit perfectly in the curler crevice. After all, a gal couldn't leave the house without curled eyelashes.

The scarcity of silk or nylon stockings also became an issue. Both materials possessed the qualities needed for military parachutes—of being light in weight, yet strong. Resourceful women came up with the solution of painting liquid leg makeup, like that used on the face, on those shapely gams. Inez remembered the better-quality makeup blended more easily, without the streaking, compared to the thinner, cheaper liquid makeup.

For the substitution to look realistic, a line was drawn on the back calf of the leg with an eyebrow pencil. It gave the illusion of a seam on the nylon stocking. In the1940s, women's stockings always had such a seam.

Against the backdrop of rationing, occasional splurging occurred. Certain shoes fell into this category. All the high-school girls were wearing them—white rubber boots. This popular item took up Inez's shoe ration allotment for the year. She wore them day in and day out.

However, the boots needed to be wiped frequently, or washed several times a day. Fortunately, Mrs. Shoemayer, the nice elderly neighbor by the bus stop, provided a place for Inez to rinse off her mucky boots before catching the bus.

Inez wore the boots so much that she formed obvious calluses on the back of her legs where the boot top rubbed. When she wore dresses or skirts with regular shoes, the marks were quite noticeable. It was not much of a worry for Inez, because all the other girls had leg calluses from their boots too.

~

Pen Pals

With the advent of war, young girls everywhere were writing letters to servicemen. Inez already wrote to Tanis LeLeux, Bill McNay, and her brother Henry. Sometimes, girls met the men at dances and exchanged addresses. Other times, the girls were given names and addresses of complete strangers by an intermediary.

One friend, Donna Rae Crump, received the name of a serviceman from a mutual friend. The pair wrote to each other throughout the war but never met until it ended. When Donna's pen pal returned to the States, they married and moved to Texas.

Alice Fitzsimmons wrote to a serviceman without ever meeting him. Not only did she have the serviceman as a pen pal, but he sent her a lovely gold stretch bracelet with a heart on it. A matching necklace with a heart-shaped locket necklace was also included. All the girls were jealous of these gifts, especially Inez.

Young people were reaching out to make connections during those uncertain times. Inez met one good-looking serviceman at a dance, and they exchanged addresses. He scared her when he wrote ten letters in five days.

When the possibility came for Inez to write to an unknown serviceman stationed in Hawaii, she jumped at the chance. Instead of jewelry or even a friendly letter, she received a correspondence that reflected an egotistical attitude. Inez never wrote back to him, but his picture ended up in her photo album. Later, Inez wrote to another pen pal whom she never met, Bill Skyes. His picture also went into her photo album.

~

Portland, 1943

One afternoon, Leona said, in matter-of-fact manner, "Inès, I've got to go to Portland tomorrow and I'm taking you with me."

Inez nodded her head in compliance. She thought, *I guess I'll be missing a couple days of school.*

Just before the end of her high school junior year, Inez and her mother boarded a train for the unexpected trip north. Inez did not think too much about the timing or the purpose of the journey. But soon she discovered it was not a pleasure trip. The daughter accompanied the mother as moral support. The United States Immigration Department had summoned Leona as part of an investigation.

Inez waited alone in a shabby hotel room near the government building. She finished her English assignment, before killing time by flipping through one of her mother's magazines. Inez watched the flow of the traffic build at the end of the day.

When Leona came into the room, she was pale and exhausted.

"Mom, what's happening?" asked Inez.

Leona sat stooped at the edge of the bed. "According to Department of Records, I was born in Canada but failed to comply with the procedure of reporting every year as a foreign national. Since the United States is in the middle of a war, this is a very serious violation—Inès, can you get me a glass of water?"

Inez went to the sink, filled a glass with water, and handed it to her mother. Leona took a deep drink before continuing. "When my father obtained his naturalized US citizenship, we were told the law made all of his underage Canadian-born children US citizens too."

"You always vote in all the elections," said Inez.

With a wistful sigh Leona proceeded. "Yes, I believed myself to be a true United States citizen. But these men are saying since I married your father, who was not a citizen, then I forfeited my own citizenship. This sounds untrue, but that's what I understand I'm being told."

Inez waited in the hotel room while her mother suffered through two more days of harsh interrogation. Leona returned at the end of each day shaken and ill with severe migraine headaches.

Leona related discussions held about her first husband, Henri, who had twice formally stated his intention to become a U.S. citizen. The first time occurred when he registered for the draft during the First World War. He formally declared his intention again in 1925. In these and other instances, his hospitalizations for lung infections prevented him from accomplishing citizenship. However, Henri's father and several of his brothers became documented U.S. citizens.

Had Leona come to the Immigration Department's attention due to her recent practice of proudly displaying her son's bombardier wings on her coat, and someone complained? Perhaps, Henry was being considered for special military undercover service. Or maybe all of it was just a case of mistaken identity.

When the Immigration Department finished their grilling, Leona was seemingly dismissed without any explanation or apology. Tight-lipped about the actual proceedings, Leona indicated she was cleared of wrongdoing. The mother and daughter returned home to Klamath Falls and never discussed the incident again.

In 1946, Leona received her naturalized United States citizenship.

~

Accidents Happen

When Inez returned from Portland, she found her high school focused on the end of the school year and graduation. On a Friday after lunch, the senior class displayed its bravado and staged a skip-day event. Inez and Alice, though juniors, were unaware of the yearly practice or of the plans. However, many others came to school dressed down for the occasion. Some even dressed as hobos and carried hobo bags and cans.

The seniors congregated on the grassy area of the school grounds, then strolled toward town as a group. With abandonment, the entire student body, including Inez and Alice, joined the group to walk the mile to downtown Klamath Falls. At the end of the day, the wayward students returned to school to pick up their books and, like Inez, boarded buses home.

Alice lived in town, so she did not ride a bus. She entered the near-deserted school building to retrieve items from her locker. Trash, not yet collected from the day's activities, lay in piles in the hall. At the precise moment that Alice rounded the hall corner, a boy, exuberant from the day's events, kicked at a discarded coffee can. The can rocketed towards the unsuspecting girl, and its sharp edge cut deep to the bone in her plump lower shin.

The wound, a horizontal slice about 3½ inches long, required many stitches to close and left an unsightly scar. Alice, unable to walk or return to her classes, missed the rest of the school year. When she transitioned from bed rest, she required the aid of crutches to move about. What upset Alice the most was the restrictions to her dancing.

~

Bremerton, Summer of 1943

Inez tells more of her story:

"After the end of my junior year, Mom and I took a trip to Bremerton, Washington to visit the Peters family.

Cassie and John Peters met when he was hospitalized during the First World War. They were familiar with Bremerton, because they lived and worked there for about fifteen years before moving to Klamath Falls in the mid-1930s.

John moved his family back to Bremerton to resume wartime employment at what was then called the Navy Yard Puget Sound (NYPS). Later, in 1945, the name changed to the Puget Sound Naval Shipyard (PSNS).

I was at Bremerton nearly three months. What started as a personal visit extended into employment for the two of us. Bremerton, after all, was a hub of wartime activity. With John's help, I got a job at the Supply Department at the Navy Yard Puget Sound (NYPS), a seven-story complex on the base. Mom got a temporary job waiting tables at the Navy Officer's Club where Genevieve worked."

~

American Gumption

Inez shaded her eyes with her hand. Something on the water caught her attention. She continued to watch with interest. The year was 1943 as Inez observed history in the making.

Just a short while before, Inez had stepped onto the beach to enjoy the sunny summer day. It was a welcoming, pleasant afternoon, without the usual Bremerton rain. The pebbled beach could have yawned with sleepiness, it was that quiet.

No one else seemed to be around. However, in the distance, on the horizon of the Sound, Inez could see a flurry of activity. A swarm of small tugboats labored to bring a towering, damaged vessel into one of the Navy Yard's dry-docks on the Puget Sound.

People appeared out of nowhere, as they abandoned their tasks and gathered to watch with Inez. They too were fascinated by the scene. The tugboats, tiny but mighty, continued their work at a snail's pace. The smaller crafts maneuvered the ship around the crooks and bends of the bay. It was an important effort. The battleship had an appointment for restoration; the tugs were hell bent on getting her there.

Someone in the crowd exclaimed in awe, "Why, that's the battleship, the U.S.S. *West Virginia*."

Everyone on the beach knew why the United States was at war. On December 7, 1941, the Japanese army had launched a surprise air attack on the U. S. Pacific Fleet. That morning the U.S.S. *West Virginia,* moored at Pearl Harbor on "Battleship Row," was the first of eight battleships to be strafed, bombed, and torpedoed during an air assault that left the ships crippled and in flames.

The *West Virginia,* the third—and most severely damagedbattleship to be salvaged from Pearl Harbor was patched just enough to restore her to watertight integrity and put her afloat. The battleship left Pearl Harbor on May 7th. This was "Wee Vee's" memorable arrival at the NYPS on June 9th, 1943. All the spectators on the shore clapped and cheered.

A lump formed in Inez's throat as she witnessed this dramatic scene from the beach that day. The image of the disabled battleship being ushered in for repairs while the entire crew, dressed in white uniforms, stood on deck at parade rest, would be remembered by Inez for the rest of her life. The destruction and loss of life from twenty months before brought a sad note to the viewing. However, there existed great anticipation and pride of American gumption—the will to fight back from devastation.

~

Bremerton Adjustments

When the United States entered the Second World War, Bremerton and the Navy Yard Puget Sound (NYPS) experienced an overnight boom. The shipyard, with seven dry docks, served as the only battleship repair yard on the West Coast. The NYPS's mission became to repair the battle-damaged ships of the U.S. Pacific Fleet and those of its allies.

American warships were either towed to the NYPS or limped under their diminished power to be repaired. During the war, the naval yard restored 18 aircraft carriers, 13 cruisers, and 79 destroyers. Also rebuilt were 26 battleships, including the U.S.S. *West Virginia*—some of them more than once.

The 32,000 shipyard workers built 53 new vessels, including 5 aircraft carriers, 13 destroyers, and 8 destroyer escorts. In addition, they overhauled, repaired, or fitted out another 400 warships. To accomplish this mission, the NYPS operated 24 hours a day.

Bremerton's population ballooned from 10,170, according to the 1930 census to over 80,000. This sudden increase caused a housing shortage in Bremerton and the surrounding Kitsap County. Shipyard workers were often forced to find housing in nearby Seattle. With gasoline rationed and automobiles hard to come by, thousands of workers and naval personnel commuted by ferry to Bremerton.

When the time came for Leona to return to Klamath Falls, the Peters helped Inez find a room to rent for the rest of the summer. Even with the housing shortage in the Bremerton area, she found a place with the Basalt family. The best part was that the room was located just two houses away from the Peters.

Compared to the Peters' cramped, basic house, the Basalt home seemed like a grand beach house—open, airy, and spacious. The feeling of staying so close to the water was a novelty for Inez. Both houses were built on stilts over the rock-filled beach, although Inez never saw the bay water come up to or under the houses.

The Basalt family consisted of the husband, his wife, and their three sons. Unfortunately, the two older boys were shy, quiet, and homely. It was the youngest son who caught Inez's interest. Although only 13 or 14 years old, he was quite attractive with his sun-bleached hair and tanned athletic body. The young boy spent his summer days alone, out on the bay waters, sailing his small dinghy. Inez enjoyed watching his craft glide along the bay.

It was from the Basalt brothers that Inez learned card games such as Gin Rummy, Hearts, Poker, and Solitaire. The foursome filled many summer hours playing cards.

Before coming to Bremerton, Inez had taken high school business classes, along with typing and shorthand. Because of these classes and her strong typing skills, she qualified to work in one of the offices of the NYPS Supply Department. No doubt, John Peters used his influence to secure the important sounding position of Junior Clerk Typist for Inez.

Inez's typist position marked a significant transition in her life, and it served as a rite of passage. However, since Inez was not yet 17 years old, Leona became concerned for her daughter when she heard the supply department employees were expected to rotate to night shifts.

Regardless, John Peters was adamant Inez would not work any swing or graveyard shifts. Aware of the influx of civilians and military personnel coming into the Puget Sound area, he understood how vulnerable a young girl might be if placed in a compromising situation. John had already arranged to have his own daughter, Genevieve, escorted home after her evening shifts as an Officers' Club waitress, and he was no less protective of Inez.

Inez did not expect the climate to differ much between Klamath Falls, Oregon, and Bremerton, Washington, but it did. At home in Klamath Falls, precipitation fell in the form of snow rather than rain. So even though it snowed heavily in the Klamath region, actual rainfall was slight during the summer months.

By contrast, Inez found it usually rained every day in the Bremerton area. She could easily get drenched as she walked to and from the bus stop. To deal with the area's wetter climate, Inez purchased an umbrella—the first umbrella she had ever owned . . . or even used. In addition, she picked out a stylish trench coat to protect her clothing from the deluges.

Other adjustments to the new job were harder to accept than the umbrella. With this first employment, Inez was required to change her official identity to her legal name. To get her work permit, she had to use her real father's last name of David. It seemed strange to be called Inez David. She had gone by Dutton, her stepfather's last name, from the time she was five years old, all through her school years. Inez thought of herself as being a Dutton, because in her way of thinking, Charlie was her father.

~

NYPS Orientation

Every new job requires an orientation, and Inez's position at NYPS was no exception. Her orientation included a tour of the supply department and the shipyard. In truth, only a few points of the tour drew Inez's interest from her daydreams. One such moment came when each new employee was asked to wear a gas mask during the tour. Perhaps this was to acquaint the new staff with the feeling of the mask's confinement for the wearer. It may also have been intended to serve as a reminder of how crucial this wartime device could be for survival, as well as how to put it on and wear it properly.

At the end of the tour, the group members were instructed to remove their masks, thus exposing them to a small amount of tear gas. The demonstration made its point with Inez. Without the mask, she experienced the gas burning her throat and producing tears that stung her eyes.

Another part of the tour showcased the Navy Shipyard's purpose. The group viewed the huge, impressive, hole of a dry dock. Ships were placed in the waterless area during construction, for maintenance, or for repairs. The dry dock could also be flooded so the ship might be drifted into place. The space was drained to allow the watercraft to come to rest on a dry platform, and then the work could begin.

The orientation concluded with a brief, yet specific, warning for the women to be aware of secluded, wooded areas. It was suggested that whenever a woman found herself walking near a thicket, she should move to the middle of the road so as not to be surprised by an attacker.

~

Employment at the NYPS Supply Department

The Supply Department maintained lists of the supplies needed for the ships dry-docked at the NYPS. Numbers of specific types of bolts, nuts, and nails were compiled on these supply lists. Many of the lists were for repairs of supplies for ships damaged or sunk at Pearl Harbor. Inez did some filing, but mostly she typed invoices of Landing Ships and Tanks, known as LSTs. Carbon paper was not used, so often she retyped the same long lists, over and over. It could be boring work but when she completed the final section, she felt a sense of accomplishment.

Much of what Inez worked on during her earlier days at the Supply Department was the inventory of The *USS West Virginia*—the same battleship she witnessed being maneuvered into the dry dock by the tugboats.

Her work might have been routine, but Inez came across an unusual incident when she entered the women's bathroom near her department. She smelled the pungent odor of a distinctive smoke. The aroma reeked somewhere between skunk and burnt popcorn. She knew immediately that was not the smell of regular tobacco. It was unlike any cigarette or tobacco smoke she had ever known. Inez encountered the odor several more times before she discovered it came from a fellow worker who routinely smoked during her break.

The girl stated she had bad sinus troubles and explained the smoke eased her symptoms. This most certainly was marijuana, only it was twenty years before the hippie revolution of the 1960s and seventy years before the use of medicinal marijuana.

One day, much to Inez's surprise, the actor Henry Fonda appeared at the Supply Department. Dressed in the uniform of an enlisted sailor, he walked alongside and behind Inez's desk. She could not believe her eyes. Inez later learned Fonda, at that time, was assigned as quartermaster, third class on the U.S.S. *Satterlee*, a destroyer docked in Seattle.

The military career of Henry Fonda was unusual for a movie star. He enlisted into the Navy at the age of 37, as a seaman and not as an officer. Typically, movie stars obtained officer status as they could wear a uniform while staying out of the fighting. Often, they made propaganda films, toured with the USO, or hosted bond rallies at the Hollywood Canteen.

Fonda was given an ultimatum to report to Naval Headquarters in New York for reassignment to an officer training program. He was commissioned as Lieutenant, junior grade on September 15, 1943, with the expectation that he would use his new commission to make training films for the War Office.

However, Fonda had other plans. He preferred to work in the newly established Air Combat Intelligence, assigned to the Central area of the South Pacific Theater. There his work resulted in a Bronze Star and the Navy Presidential Unit Citation.

Inez did not have a chance to meet Henry Fonda or even exchange "hellos" with him. However, with the brief glance, Inez was amazed at his similarities to her own brother, Henry.

~

Angel to the Rescue

My mother, Inez, and I were discussing one of my friend's accounts of how she sensed the presence of an angel at the time of a car accident. When I asked if Mom ever felt she had met an angel, she quietly nodded her head.

She then said, "I certainly did . . . that was an angel that helped me, in Bremerton."

Inez smelled the whiff of an acrid, just-lit cigarette at the same time she spied a trace of orange that glowed in the darkness. Was her imagination playing tricks on her? She strained to see if a shadowy figure was ahead. The possibility she was not alone on the path startled her. *Certainly, that is a man on the trail.*

Every woman has felt the terror of being in a situation with the possible threat of being overpowered by a man. Just as other women in such circumstances, Inez asked in silence: *Oh, why did I let myself get in this trouble?*

The city bus had just dropped her off from an evening at the movies with a co-worker. Within seconds the clamoring bus raced to its next destination, leaving Inez in the seemingly deserted wooded area. From the bus stop, Inez crossed over the paved road and entered the lane that led down towards the bay and to the Basalt's beach house. The route was a rolling, block-long incline, that was more dirt and gravel than road.

The daily rain encouraged the vegetation to flourish, lush and abundant. The growth encroached onto the road and formed a foliage tunnel, a little larger than a car's width. Inez walked in the middle of the lane as recommended in her shipyard orientation. Besides, she did not want the outstretched, threatening branches to snag her clothes.

Inez was familiar with this area; this was the path she took every day since starting work at the shipyard. But things felt and looked different in the dark—especially intimidating when a girl was by herself.

The lonely sound of the foghorn registered in the distance. Some evening rain had fallen, but it had passed. The wind dropped to almost nothing, just as the thicket closed in on Inez. The mugginess of the air made her skin sticky and hot while she made her way through half of the distance to her lodging.

That was when she noticed the figure and the glow of a cigarette. The background noise of insects and birds ceased. She attempted to step softly. However, the snapping of a twig beneath her foot sounded as loud as a shot in that hushed night.

The bright tip bounced and jerked as it proceeded closer and closer to Inez. She stood paralyzed. The orange glow fell to the ground. There was the scuffing of leather on gravel as the phantom snuffed out the cigarette.

What now? thought Inez. All the warnings from her orientation and from John Peters flooded back to her. Any second the man was going to come through the night mist. *Will he do something terrible to me?*

"Would you like a ride?" came the question from a woman's voice. Inez turned to see a lady in a car behind her. Inez, so intent with what was in front of her, had not heard the approaching car.

"I have a daughter your age and I see that man ahead of you," said the woman.

In a flash, Inez scrambled to the passenger seat. As the car picked up speed, the form on the lane must have dissolved into the thicket, for no one was on the road.

The lady drove right to the Basalt's doorsteps. She did not discuss why she was out driving that night. After offering the woman her thanks, Inez entered the beach house visibly shaken. She remained chilled by the scary memory of the stranger in the dark, but she was grateful for the lady angel—whether human or celestial—that came to her rescue.

And neither the lady nor her car was ever seen again.

~

Fear

Inez and Genevieve stepped out from the movie theater. Something big and gray drifting in the sky caught Inez's attention. "What's that? It looks like the *Hindenburg*."

"No silly, that's a barrage balloon. Remember, I told you my boyfriend, Cliff, was assigned to the battalion here in Bremerton." When Gen spoke Cliff's name, a dreamy smile floated across on her face.

Her friend's reaction made Inez smile, until she noticed numerous barrage balloons hovering about the sky. Inez rubbed the goose bumps on her arms.

She said, "It gives me an eerie feeling seeing those silent balloons suspended like that—I don't think I'll ever get used to the need for them."

Americans were vulnerable. The security they once relied upon was gone. After the bombing of Pearl Harbor, rumors spread of Japanese patrol planes flying over San Francisco and of enemy warships off the Washington coast. In addition, newspapers reported warnings from Canadian and U.S. officials of possible Japanese marauder attacks on coastal towns. Feeling unstable and anxious, communities experienced a lump-in-the-throat fear, as they asked the question, "Are we prepared?"

The Seattle-Bremerton area scrambled to compensate for its questionable security against the threat of air attacks. Anti-aircraft guns were installed to protect the Northwest from the Pacific Ocean access. Camouflage was used to mask the Boeing plant and other important buildings. In addition, barrage balloons soon dotted the view of the horizon. Even though their use was extensive in other parts of the world during WWII, barrage balloons were unknown to most Americans.

In the early days of the war, these floating aircraft quelled fears by providing a sense of security and protection to the residents of the West Coast. They were neither festive, party balloons, nor the powered and steerable aircraft called "blimps." Metal cables, handled by teams of five or six men, tethered the 50 x 32-foot crafts over military production sites in the districts of the Boeing plant at Seattle, and the Bremerton Puget Sound Naval Shipyard.

The locations and altitudes of the crafts were changed every few hours. When all the balloons were in the air with their cables tied to the ground, a type of netting was formed. Such an obstacle course made it more difficult for attackers to approach key defense targets.

However, the system was not designed to snare aircraft as unsuspecting flies in a spider web. The real objective of the barrage balloon was to keep enemy planes from flying at low altitude over targets. A mere touch of a wing to the metal cable would damage the enemy planes. If shot, the balloon would explode taking the aircraft with it. All these factors forced enemy planes to fly higher, which made them less accurate and brought them within range of intense anti-aircraft firepower.

Barrage balloons were as much a psychological weapon as anything, but the crafts did deter enemy aircraft from flying low at night over targets in London, England. In truth, as a defensive measure for the Pacific Northwest area of Washington State, balloons were never put to the test. Of course, no Japanese plane ever made it to Seattle to be shot down by anti-aircraft guns or foiled by barrage balloons. But the threat and the fear were both very real.

For Inez, it was more than being aware of the barrage balloons in the area. Barrage balloons became personal to her. Inez explained the nature of her interest:

> *"Genevieve met a soldier, Cliff Kiel, who was stationed on a barrage balloon site in the hills above the bay. An attraction developed and they became engaged. She just finished her senior year of high school.*
>
> *In August, he got his orders to be transferred from Bremerton, so they immediately arranged to get married. I understand the reason for the quick transfer was because the previous threat of the enemy launching an attack from the Aleutian Islands had ended, and the barrage balloons were no longer needed in the Washington area."*

From Cliff Kiel's transfer, Inez learned that other vulnerabilities had existed all along, to the Puget Sound area and to the country. Six months after the Pearl Harbor attack, the Japanese targeted the American-owned chain of over 150 volcanic islands, extending 1,200 miles westward from the Alaska Peninsula. The enemy troops established military bases on the islands of Kiska and Attu. The Japanese launched air strikes from captured Dutch Harbor to support their offensives in the Aleutians and to the Battle of Midway, in the central Pacific Ocean.

The Americans broke the JN-25 code used by the Japanese Naval Command. By deciphering the code, the Americans were able to prepare for the attack on Midway. A decisive naval battle of World War II resulted.

With the use of that same code, the U.S. determined the enemy was ill prepared to initiate an invasion on the West Coast of North

America. Thus, in August 1943, the recapture of the remote islands of Kiska and Atta led to the removal of the only Japanese foothold in the Aleutian territory. Inez's uncle, Eugene Doyon, served in the Aleutians as an Army Signal Corps Officer, after the U.S. base was re-established.

As water ripples in a pond form rings from a tossed pebble, global events influenced the lives of a young couple in love, like Genevieve and Cliff, but also affected friends and family.

What became important to Inez was the marriage of her closest friend. Genevieve's friendship had been better than a sister relationship. For years, the two girls shared their thoughts and dreams, their goals, and desires with each other. Now, at eighteen years old, Genevieve's dreams of marriage were coming true.

All the wedding arrangements were done in such a hurry it was hard for Inez to remember much of it. She felt sad that Genevieve wore a royal blue velvet dress with heavy, dark brown walking shoes for her summer wedding. Style sense took a backseat to the war.

With Gen's marriage came the end of the girlhood camaraderie. Friendship with Bill McNay, the street dance soldier, also ended. Bill stopped writing to both girls when he heard of Gen's engagement and wedding plans. However, Genevieve continued to correspond and exchange Christmas cards with Bill's mother for many years.

Inez wrote about her friend:

> *"Genevieve was a very close friend and I was sad to see her leave. The man she married, Cliff Kiel, was from New York, so when he was discharged from the Army they moved back there. They bought a home in Levittown, New York. At that time, it*

was a building complex of thousands of houses, basically all alike, built after the war to house new young families.

Cliff and Genevieve had four children—two older and then came two little girls. Shortly after, they found Genevieve had cancer of the cervix and died when her two little girls were six and eight. She was in her forties; her mother, Cassie, also died young from cancer. About two years later, Cliff died of cancer, too. How sad for the family. I never saw her again after their August 1943 wedding."

I never realized the importance Genevieve and her family played in my mother's life until she explained it to me many years later. Of course, I did not live in Mom's circumstances or have the relationship of such a sister-friend as Genevieve.

The two friends kept in touch by exchanging Christmas letters each year. I do not even recall when Genevieve died. Her death just seemed to have been mentioned in passing. I believe I was newly married and involved in my new life. I did not realize the impact of losing such a close friend.

Genevieve's father, John Peters, remarried shortly after Genevieve's mother, Cassie, died. His second wife, Myrna, was ever so sweet and faithful to continue to correspond about the Peters family to Inez in yearly Christmas cards.

Inez remembered the pleasant smell of talcum powder with all of Myrna's correspondence.

~

Trip Home

Inez returned home at the end of summer. However, she found wartime travel chaotic and antiquated. Trains and railroad equipment, well past their prime, were taken from storage and put to use. Many soldiers and mothers with children, desperate to get where they were headed, crammed the old train compartments.

The train ride from Seattle to Klamath Falls proved to be a rough journey. Much jerking and shaking ensued as the train progressed down the tracks. Inside, the train compartment grew so uncomfortably warm and stuffy that windows were left open. Soot blew in and settled everywhere. Grime and ashes covered faces and clothes, reminiscent of train travel standards in a previous era. Yet, the relic trains were still greatly needed to supplement the war effort.

When the train came into the Oregon station of Eugene, the announcement surprised a young mother. Flustered, she grabbed her toddler with one hand and gathered her possessions with the other. Her swift exit from the train left her newborn still sleeping on the train seat. The porter realized her mistake. He scooped up the baby to intercept the mother before the train departed from the station. When handed the baby, the shocked mother burst out in tears.

The forgotten baby incident left Inez disturbed and shaken. She attempted, instead, to think of her three months in Bremerton and all she experienced during the past summer.

Darkness had fallen when Inez's train pulled into the Klamath Falls station. Through the window she saw Charlie waiting on the platform for her. Retrieving her bags, Inez disembarked as the drier, hot Oregon air welcomed her home to her final year of high school.

~

The War Continued

In 1932, to comfort a frightened nation, President Franklin D. Roosevelt started his radio Fireside Chats. People perceived FDR as a caring uncle, one who spoke directly to them. Thus, the chats reassured people through the dark economic times of the Great Depression.

FDR continued with the same Fireside Chat format of reassurance and encouragement as he discussed the war. He also challenged Americans to help in the struggle. The radio talks stimulated the Allied morale as it boosted domestic efforts throughout the war years.

Civilians were kept abreast of the war news by radio, theater newscast, and newspapers. As Inez entered her senior year, in the fall of 1943, the airways were filled with talk of fighting in many unfamiliar locations.

In European operations, Allied bombing attacks on Germany continued. The Russians slowly forced back the Germans from Stalingrad as the Allies invaded Italy from Africa. The Pacific campaigns in the faraway Solomon Islands and Tarawa in the Gilbert Islands—places once considered as exotic havens—now represented death and destruction for both Americans and Japanese.

Inez remembered daily newspaper and radio reports of destroyed or damaged Allied ships or aircraft. The names and numbers of the units accompanied the types of lost crafts, such as Marauders, B-17s, etc. Lists of servicemen killed in action also appeared in the Klamath Falls newspaper, *The Herald and News.* Saddened, Inez read the name of Harold Darrah, whom she dated several times, listed in such a newspaper article. He was a submarine sailor, the son of a co-worker of Leona's at the airfield diner.

Final School Days

Had all her experiences in Bremerton been just a dream? When Inez returned to Klamath Union High, she felt a strangeness as she walked the school halls. Nothing had changed, yet everything felt different. Perhaps a maturity from her employment as a Junior Clerk Typist at the Naval Supply Department gave Inez a realist's view of life beyond K Falls and high school.

Inez approached her education in a new way. Instead of succumbing to senioritis, she developed a vigor towards her remaining classes. Her main subjects for her last year included office machines, English, and biology.

Preparations for office work took on new meaning for Inez. She hoped to be employed as a secretary once she graduated. Mastery of the Comptometer and the Marchant calculating machines were required by the school's business curriculum.

The Comptometer, a type of electro-mechanical device, performed addition by simply pressing the keys. It functioned faster than an electronic calculator and performed subtraction, division, and multiplication, as well. The Comptometer remained in use for specialist applications for fifty more years, until it was replaced by computer software.

As for the Marchant, it was dubbed America's first calculator and was known as the typewriter's ugly cousin. It specifically added and calculated for a payroll. Even though it was light in weight, the Marchant remained a complicated machine with complex instructions.

Inez did alright with the Comptometer and the Marchant calculating machines, but they were not her strong suit. She found them to be too complicated for her liking and never felt comfortable in operating them. The school owned only a few machines and offered limited time to practice.

Her teacher for the advanced business courses was Mrs. Shannon. However, it was Mr. Palmer, the head of the Business Studies Department whom Inez associated most with her business courses. He was a pleasant looking man of average build in his mid-thirties. Mr. Palmer served as Inez's teacher when she was a fledgling typist. He continued to encourage, inspire, and support Inez and her fellow business students throughout their high school years.

The required courses of biology and senior English had to be fitted into Inez's final year's class schedule. Although they were quite different from each other, Inez enjoyed both subjects.

Biology was the first step towards understanding science. It aligned with nursing and the study of medicine. Even though Inez had little hope of entering the medical field herself, she still was fascinated by science.

Senior English included the study of literature and compound sentence structure. The English teacher, Mrs. O'Neil, had the reputation of being a strict tyrant. However, Inez knew her brother Henry had high regards for this teacher. Mrs. O'Neal mentioned that she remembered Henry from four years previously, and even seemed kind and encouraging to Inez. It was Mrs. O'Neal who pointed out that the class of 1944 could always remember they graduated in a leap year. Though the class was challenging, Inez applied herself and thus did well.

To Inez, her English teacher was always "old Mrs. O'Neal." She appeared to the teenager as a little old lady with gray hair, who wore glasses she removed when addressing the class. In reality, she was in her early forties.

Inez's senior English class served her well. Whatever she learned enhanced her writing abilities with the many correspondences she maintained through the years. Inez never had the chance for higher education or college. Yet, what she took away from her own high school English class helped her proofread many assignments and research papers for her three children. It did not matter if the written papers were for high school or college, Inez gave each task a polished finish.

As for science, Inez passed that fascination on to all three of her children. They all graduated from college with medical-related degrees. Inez's passion fueled their passions. Her desires became their livelihood.

~

Roland "Tony" Tonick

Reading at her desk, Mrs. O'Neal, the 12th grade English teacher, looked up as an office messenger entered the room. The courier carried a folded piece of paper that she handed to the teacher before hurrying out of the classroom.

The teacher scanned the message with concentration. Clearing her throat, she said, "Inez Dutton, please proceed to the office."

Alice turned to her friend, her eyes large with questioning. Inez responded with a slight shoulder shrug. She felt the burning curiosity of her classmates while she took her blue sweater from the back of the chair, slipped her arms through the sleeves, and lifted out a section of her hair caught in the collar.

Inez gathered the nearby schoolbooks and her brown leather purse before approaching the teacher's desk for the hall pass. Finished with the dismissal, Mrs. O'Neal returned to her reading.

Once outside the classroom Inez shivered. Was it due to the chilly autumn day or anticipation of the unexpected? The empty hall echoed her footsteps. Passing by the cafeteria, she heard the clinking of dishes and silverware as kitchen workers readied for lunch. The aroma of franks and beans filled the air.

Inez hesitated at the office door. She gulped a breath of resolve and entered.

"Excuse me. I'm Inez Dutton. I was told to come to the office."

The lady behind the counter smiled and pointed to the waiting seats on the left. Inez turned to see a young man in an Army uniform standing, grinning at her.

Surprised, Inez realized the stocky, fair-haired sergeant in his mid-twenties was Ronald Tonick. "Tony," as everyone called him, stepped forward in exuberance and stood next to her.

Grabbing her hand, Tony said, "My unit has received orders for overseas. Your mother gave permission for you to leave school with me. I have a taxi waiting."

Inez could hardly understand what was happening. "Well, if Mom thinks it's okay, then it must be alright."

Inez and Tony stopped at her hall locker on the way out to put away her books.

Tony said, "Are you hungry? I'm starved. Let's go and get some lunch."

They stepped through the school doors towards the taxi. Inez mused to herself, *And here I thought I was going to have franks and beans today.*

It had been an unlikely beginning for a relationship. It occurred the year earlier, on Columbus Day, October 12th, 1942. Oliver, the man-friend of Alice Fitzsimons' mother, dropped off Alice and Inez at their first and only dance at Klamath Falls Moose Lodge. Oliver and Alice's mother planned to pick up the girls, juniors in high school, from the dance at a pre-arranged time.

Inez and Sergeant "Tony" Tonick made it through only a portion of a dance before it was time for the girls to leave. He did ask for her address. However, in the rush Inez doubted he even heard her name. And he could not write down her address because neither of them had paper nor pen. To Inez's astonishment, Tony wrote a letter to her straightaway. And he continued to write to her regularly.

Inez learned much about Tony through their letter writing. He was proud of the three chevron stripes he wore on his Army uniform. He had worked hard to become a "buck" sergeant. He explained his assignment as a training sergeant while stationed in Medford, Oregon at Camp White. The flat terrain of the area helped make it one of the major training centers for the U.S. military.

Tony told of being raised on a farming ranch near Killeen, Texas. Unfortunately, his family's property had been commandeered under eminent domain for the newly constructed Camp Hood. It was said that Tony's uncle was so distraught about the takeover of his family land that he committed suicide.

The properties of many central Texas families made up the 108,000 acres that transformed rural farming land into Camp Hood. In early 1942, Fort Hood became known as the U.S. Army's Tank Destroyer Tactical and Firing Center.

The phrase "If you can't beat 'em, join 'em" perhaps described Tony and his four brothers. The fact that all five of the men served in the U.S. military gave the family local recognition. Their story was featured in the Killeen newspaper. Tony sent Inez the newspaper clipping, even though he was not in the picture.

The two young people wrote through the school year and continued their correspondence while Inez worked in Bremerton. But it was still a shock to have this young soldier come to take her out of school.

After eating a sandwich at a nearby lunch counter, Tony spied a photography studio next door. He said to Inez. "Say, my folks have never seen me in my uniform. Since I'm all dressed up, do you mind if we stop and take a picture for them?"

The idea was agreeable with Inez. She had to admit, Tony cut a fine figure in his army uniform of olive-drab trousers and jacket decorated with three stripes of a sergeant's rank. A matching saucer hat topped off the outfit. Olive drab was anything but dull and dreary on Tony—with his broad shoulders and blond hair.

When the photo session was completed, Tony handed a large portrait of himself to Inez. He said with a smile, "Here's something to remember me by." And he gave Inez a juicy kiss. Then hailing yet another taxi, Tony said, "Let's go see your farm."

Inez's mother, Leona, invited Tony to stay for dinner. When she asked about his nationality, Tony answered, "Probably a Nazi." This meant he was of German descent. Perhaps the answer showed a bit of defensiveness—whether a joke or a source of shame —of his blond, stocky appearance.

Nevertheless, Tony impressed Leona as a good match for Inez. Leona told him she could only offer him the living room couch to sleep on, but he was welcome to stay at the farm until his leave was over. Tony quickly accepted.

Inez and Tony spent the next several days together walking around the farm, exploring Miller Hill and talking by the diversion canal. She enjoyed being with him, especially since they shared only a few minutes together in a dance, the year before. Tony seemed to really like Inez—he certainly kissed her a lot.

After two nights at the farm, Leona drove Tony to the Klamath Falls station where he boarded a train to make connections with his army unit before deploying overseas.

While Tony was in harm's way, Inez waited anxiously for word from him. It was over six weeks until she received his correspondence via the patriotic Victory Mail, or V-mail. The combined letter-envelope reduced the weight and bulk of mail, thus furthering the war effort. This standardized form became the main way to correspond to a soldier stationed abroad.

Inez knew mail censors blackened any sensitive information that might compromise military security from all V-mail. Prior to forwarding, every letter's content was photographed onto microfilm. The thumb size film negatives were forwarded and reproduced to 60% of the original size when they arrived at their destination. This made a secure and efficient way to manage mail in combat zones. The technique blocked espionage communications as well. Invisible ink, microdots, and micro printing would not be reproduced in a photocopy.

In his first letter to Inez, Tony mentioned that he had been in Australia. He conveyed, "I can't tell you where I am now. The natives are black as tar, but they have red hair." When Inez mentioned this to some servicemen, they said, "Your fella must be in New Caledonia."

Even though Inez did not know the location of New Caledonia, she repeated her discovery when she wrote back to Tony. His answer could only be limited to, "Yes." In truth, any confirmation or discussion of his whereabouts was a security risk.

For Inez, the idea of red-haired natives left an indelible association to New Caledonia. The explanation of the hair color remained a mystery. Was red hair the result of recessive genes from sailors that visited the island long ago? Or perhaps the iron oxide of soil built up on the scalp and hair. Did the people originate from the Solomon Islands or some Australian aborigines that are naturally blond or red haired? The question remained unanswered.

A million American soldiers and sailors passed through New Caledonia. The island was transformed from the picturesque "Paris of the Pacific" paradise into the largest forward Allied base in the Pacific theater. An assignment to New Caledonia usually allowed for repairing equipment and ships, and as a time for rest and war operations training. Preparation to confront Japanese forces also included the challenges of humidity, heat, snakes, and insects—especially the ever-present mosquitoes. After New Caledonia, Tony's Army unit went on to other South Pacific islands, such as the Gilbert Islands and then the Marshall Islands. Inez was not sure where else Tony traveled, because correspondence slowed between them.

Boarding at the Conradys

As the winter of Inez's senior year settled in, she roomed in town with an Italian couple, the Conradys. This home was a large two-story house with at least three bedrooms rented out in a boarding-house fashion. The boarders shared an upstairs bathroom.

The Conradys had a pet Pomeranian dog they greatly loved and indulged. This was the first time Inez had seen such a breed. Cocky and animated, the pint-size animal served as an entertaining companion for the couple. Perhaps, since the Conradys were childless, they treated the dog like his name—Baby. However, it shocked Inez to see the dog brought up to the dinner table and fed with a fork.

One morning Inez went down to the Conradys' kitchen to make herself toast for breakfast. As she entered the deserted room, she found Baby lying abandoned, dead on the kitchen sink. It gave Inez quite a start to see the dog, so active the evening before, now lifeless in the kitchen. She never discovered whether the dog's demise resulted from some sort of accident or poisoning, or if the death was caused by a heart attack from too much rich food.

Sometimes living in a boarding house setting could be intimate—a little too intimate. Inez heard banging upstairs when she was seated in the downstairs parlor. It did not take long to link the upstairs pounding to the lovemaking of the newlywed couple boarding in one of the rooms in the house. What Inez found comical was that within minutes of the obvious lovemaking session, the young wife would burst from her bedroom, heading towards the common bathroom. Dressed in her bathrobe, with a determined look on her face, she carried her trusty douche bag in her hand.

Perhaps sexuality was in the air. Walking to her room one day, Inez spied a pile of magazines by the door of the man who lived across the hall from her. With some curiosity, and because she was nosy, Inez glanced to see if the magazines were of any interest.

What she saw was eye-popping. Piled next to the wall were adult magazines that showed naked men and women in posed group pictures, advertising nudist camps. These photographed naked people in action poses while in recreational settings, such as beaches and mountains. *Oh, my goodness!* Inez hurried away as fast as she could.

Inez managed to stay clear of the owner of the nudist magazines until one evening when she was downstairs in the parlor, dressed up for a special occasion. With her hands behind her neck, she struggled to close the clasp of her chain necklace. Out of nowhere this gangly, middle-aged neighbor-man came from behind the seventeen-year-old Inez and gave her a prolonged bear hug.

Inez froze, mute and terrified, but he left the room without saying a word. That night, and many nights afterwards, Inez found herself afraid to go to sleep. No locks secured any of the bedroom doors.

~

Christmas

When Christmas 1943 came around, Henry, away at bombardier training, sent money to Inez and their mother for Christmas gifts. Leona jumped at the chance to put her Christmas money towards a gray fur coat. It was not a fox, squirrel, or mink coat. Marten fur made up the coat.

Inez questioned her mother about martens. She was told the small animals, found in forests and wooded areas across the northern hemisphere, were valued by fur traders for their bushy tails. Martens, related to badgers, ferrets, and wolverines, had scent glands used for sexual signaling and marking territory.

Leona had long desired to own a fur coat. Unfortunately, the one she chose ended up having a smell that could only be described as skunk-like. When Leona left the room, Charlie joked with Inez, "A marten is just another name for a skunk."

As for Inez, she shopped until she found just the right gift—a delicate silver identification bracelet. Inez wanted such a bracelet for a long time, and she had given up the hope such a gift would come from one of her pen pals.

The clerk at the jewelry store said, "Little lady, that looks perfect on your small wrist."

To make it more special, Inez had the name "David" engraved onto the small identification section provided. When she returned to school, after the Christmas break, many girls noticed her new bracelet and questioned her about her new boyfriend, David. Of course, her explanation of being her legal last name was not as titillating as receiving a gift from a new love.

~

Waiting

In general, those high school years were a waiting time for Inez: Waiting on the war. Waiting to grow up. Waiting for someone special to love. Waiting for the next note to be played, so she could continue with her song of life.

Inez waited on the war with its uncertainties and tensions. Classmates and local boys left home. This included her own brother, Henry. The war changed everything and everybody.

She waited for the end of her childhood, to complete high school and to go on to the next phase of life. Inez tasted independence while she worked in Bremerton during the previous summer. She assumed she would become a secretary or clerk, since her high school curriculum had been mostly business prep classes. Even though she fantasized about joining the Nurse Cadet Corps, she couldn't see that happening. Other than her two aunts who were nurses, Inez did not have other female role models. Her own mother had minimal training as a beautician but ended up working at a lunch counter.

Finally, Inez waited to find her Mr. Right. Many local girls married right out of high school. Even her best friend, Genevieve, married shortly after her own graduation. Inez's mother and grandmother both wed when they were seventeen. Tony was special to Inez, but there had not been any commitments. So, Inez waited.

Then, before Inez realized, her high school days and senior year came to an end. Because resources were diverted for the war effort, the usual yearbooks were not published during those years. No annuals were available to the underclassmen during Inez's junior year.

However, a special edition of the *El Rodeo* yearbook—more like the napkin edition—was printed with minimal pages, placed in a thin, red cardboard cover, and distributed to the senior class of 1944.

For the yearbook, each senior listed his or her hobby and ambition. Inez's entry said her hobby was writing to the "One Over There," (i.e., Tony Tonick) and her ambition was to become a Cadet Nurse. Also listed was her nickname, "Inie," but she never remembered anyone calling her by that name.

When the yearbooks were distributed, people congratulated Inez. She had been named the senior class "Best Female Pal." What a pleasant shock for her, but she wondered about the validity of the named positions. Inez did not remember voting for any such honors. Stranger still and laughable, she did not even know the guy, Mike McAdams, who was voted the "Best Male Pal." The twelve couples "voted" for special categories were honored by having their enlarged senior pictures displayed on separate pages from the other graduating seniors. Quite a tribute, considering the size of the yearbook.

Inez was so glad to have the keepsake of her senior yearbook. She perused it so often that the small, ring plastic spine cracked and broke away—she simply wore it out.

Graduation

"Anticlimactic" could describe Inez's graduation. The commencement, held at the school during the day, was not attended by either of her parents. Almost three hundred students earned their high school diploma. About one-third of the senior boys had chosen to serve in the military before graduation. With so many key males gone, the ceremony was somewhat flat.

However, a graduation was a milestone and celebratory gifts were in order. Mrs. Conrady of the rooming house fame gave Inez several graduation gifts. One of these was a *Better Homes and Gardens Cookbook* that served as a trusty guide for Inez through fifty-plus years of marriage. The other gifts were two pieces of painted Italian pottery—a small pitcher and saucer. It always seemed meaningful to Inez that the pottery pieces were Italian, just like the Conradys.

Inez never had a wristwatch and she wanted one. Several girls at school had "Mickey Mouse" watches but that was not her family's style. The long-awaited gift of jewelry came from her parents in the form of a gold-colored Helbros watch with a metal clasp band. The anticipation to show off and wear her new timepiece to school the next day, kept her from sleeping. Inez was so excited she continued to glance at the new watch throughout the night.

She came to wear the Helbros watch on her left wrist while she wore her David bracelet on her right wrist. The two pieces became Inez's standard jewelry. Even though the watch was inexpensive, she wore it for the next ten years.

About the time of graduation, Inez came into the possession of a Multnomah steamer trunk, made by the Portland Oregon Multnomah Baggageman Company. Inez was not sure if it was an actual graduation gift or if it was handed down from her mother.

The trunk was not made of leather but appeared to be some sort of pressed cardboard. Advertisements touted the construction of three-ply fir wood veneer that made the wardrobe trunk "man-proof" and able to withstand rough handling. That proved to be true because the sturdy trunk stood up to Inez's multiple travels and moves over the years.

One more graduation gift appeared. To Inez's surprise, she received a check for a stunning sum—$100—from Tony.

On the heels of Inez's graduation came the Invasion of France. On D-Day, June 6, 1944, the military offensive established a solid beachhead into Europe; within weeks, a million allied troops were on French soil. Much was also happening in the Pacific Theater. By mid-summer, the arm of American troops advanced on Saipan and Guam in the Mariana Islands. This brought Tokyo to within range for land-based Army Air Force bombers.

Back in Oregon, brother Henry returned home from six months in England. During that period, he had flown thirty-five B-17 and B-24 Liberator flights. However, Henry did not spend all his leave in

Klamath Falls. Before long, he was on his way to Colorado with an engagement ring for his sweetheart, Patricia.

~

The Marines

Mrs. Conrady entered the backyard. "There you are. I have someone for you to meet." Inez looked up, squinting into the sun. She finished pinning her printed, black and white blouse on the clothesline and stepped over to Mrs. Conrady. As they walked to the front yard, Inez smoothed down her hair and wondered: *Who can this person possibly be?*

Next to a dark blue car parked at the curb stood a group of several girls and three Marines. Inez recognized the girls from school. The young Marines appeared bashful and awkward, yet happy to be talking with the young women. Even though the men joked among themselves, an anxious, edgy tension existed. One Marine nibbled constantly at his fingernails.

A friend of Mrs. Conrady, Mrs. Grafton, also stood by the car. She managed the Klamath Commandos, a military support organization similar to the United Service Organization (USO), where soldiers congregated for coffee, donuts, sandwiches, and music. The group provided hospitality and entertainment activities, helping meet the social needs of servicemen.

Mrs. Grafton said: "We've just picked up these fine Marines from the train station. They arrived from San Francisco and are assigned to the Klamath Falls Marine Barracks. . . . Inez David, I would like you to meet Corporal Robert Dewey."

The sallow, blond Marine reached to shake Inez's hand. "Call me Bob."

Inez learned Bob was from Chicago, Illinois, and 22 years old. Thin and haggard in appearance, Bob did not make much eye contact. When he did, his light blue eyes told of strain and worry. In truth, Bob looked like he had been fighting in the jungle for months.

After an awkward silence, Bob asked Inez, "What do you do on weekends?"

"Oh, I usually go to the movies or local dances with my girlfriends."

Bob looked up from staring at his feet. "If I found a date for your friend, would you like to go to the movies with me . . . tomorrow?"

"Sure, that would be fun," said Inez but she wondered: *Why did I agree? He looks beaten down and so sad, that's why.* She glanced at him again. *It's his eyes.*

Bob broke the silence between them. "When are the dances held?"

"Mostly on Saturday nights at the local Armory Hall," said Inez.

Mrs. Grafton stepped forward. "Well, it's time to get these Marines settled in their barracks." Mrs. Grafton, the girls, and the Marines loaded into the car and drove off.

Mrs. Conrady turned to Inez, "Those poor Marines. No more than boys. They've seen combat for 28 months straight in the South Pacific: Going from Guadalcanal, to Tarawa, to the Marshall Islands, and then the Gilbert Islands. . . . Coming to the Marine Barracks here in Klamath Falls is their first time back to the States."

Inez said. "I've heard of the Marine Barracks, but I don't know anything about it."

Mrs. Conrady explained, "A Marine general saw his South Pacific troops suffering from tropical diseases. He asked Washington to build a treatment and recuperation center on 800 acres, four miles from downtown Klamath Falls. The first Marines and Navy personnel arrived in April."

"Why did they put it here at Klamath Falls?"

"Because of our higher altitude. . . . It's believed the cooler weather prevents activating the malarial symptoms."

"Malaria? Is that when a person gets shakes and chills?"

"Yes. War is about more than bombs and bullets. These men are suffering from a variety of fly-and-mosquito-borne tropical diseases. The worst one might be filariasis, which is sometime called elephantiasis. . . . Did you see how sickly and edgy the Marines appeared? It's no wonder—war is hard on people. I saw it after the Great War. They called it shell shock. But now the term is combat or battle fatigue."

Inez thought of her brother, Henry, in England—*I'm sure glad he wasn't in the Pacific.*

Then she realized it was getting late. "Excuse me, Mrs. Conrady, I need to get ready for tonight's dance."

Later that evening Inez arrived at the Armory Hall ready to dance. Bewildered, she found Bob waiting for her. To her dismay, the night dragged on as the couple sat and watched others dance. Bob and Inez never danced themselves. However, Bob, attentive to Inez, indicated an interest in her.

When the dance was over, Bob took Inez back to the Conrady's house by taxi. He stopped Inez on the porch. "Will you wear my ring?" Bob presented his gold signet ring with his initials on a ruby stone."

At first Inez refused the ring. "You don't want to give me your ring." *Egads,* she thought. *This is only the second time I've seen you.*

Yet, Bob persisted as he said, "I like you and I really want you to wear it."

Inez wondered, *What does this ring have to do with me?*

She did not know how to turn down his offer. Finally, Inez took the ring when she realized how important it was to him, but the responsibility worried her. The huge ring dwarfed her small hand and the possibility of its loss concerned Inez. *I guess I can try wrapping some string around it to make it tighter.*

❁ ❁ ❁

The next day, Sunday, Bob called to finalize arrangements for their movie double date. Bob planned to bring another Marine, Otto. Inez would bring along her girlfriend, Alice.

But first Bob had a question to ask. "What does Alice look like?"

Inez answered, "She looks something like me . . . only heavier."

"How fat is she?" was the quick response from the other end of the phone.

"Well not really heavy but sturdier than me," Inez replied.

The Marines decided to take a chance and agreed to meet that afternoon in front of the Commando Center, since Bob knew the location.

Before Bob hung up the telephone, he made a point. "Remember Inez, you are my date. No doubt you will want to be with Otto—he's a good-looking guy. But you are my date."

When the time came to meet, the girls waited for a long time in front of the Commando Center. Unbeknown to the girls, the Marines were across the street checking them out before jaywalking over to greet them.

A tall, dreamy Nordic-looking Marine with green eyes came right over to Inez to introduce himself, "I'm Otto Mansker. It's nice to meet you, Alice."

Bob immediately stepped in. He pointed to Alice and said, "No, this here is Alice—Inez is my date." Perhaps this was the only time Inez wished she was Alice.

Over the next several weeks, the foursome of Inez, Bob, Alice, and Otto went to the movies together. Several times they visited the ice cream parlor afterwards. Otto proved to be the life of any party. He was a pleasant, fun-loving fellow from St. Louis—and acted like a big kid.

A definite contrast existed between Bob and Otto. Bob remained reserved, quiet, and moody. At times he exhibited shaking spells and, though tall, he was thin and hunched over. Otto seemed to be the picture of health.

When Bob came by himself to see Inez at her rooming house, they sat outside on the front porch. Inez showed Bob some snapshots of her and her friends. After he left, she noticed one of the recent pictures of her was missing.

One day Otto approached Inez with a question, "Why are you dating that kike, Bob Dewey?

Inez looked at Otto in confusion, he continued, "You know he's a Jew, don't you?"

Surprised by Otto's venom, Inez did not even know what being a "Jew" meant. At the time, she thought it was another type of Christian denomination, not an entirely different kind of religion. However, she noticed Jewish people rarely mixed or married outside their group.

Perhaps, when she was introduced to Bob as "Inez David," he assumed she was Jewish. Likely, Mrs. Grafton and Mrs. Conrady thought she was of Jewish descent too. Inez had never run into the situation before because she went by "Inez Dutton" until required to use her legal name when she started working in Bremerton.

Inez did not have any special feelings for Bob. He was just a guy that seemed to like her. She enjoyed double dating when Otto was present. She could tell Otto liked her too. He had privately told her he wanted her to be his date when they first met in front of the Commando Center. But a relationship could not develop between Inez and Otto. Inez could not cross her friend, for she knew Alice had fallen hard for Otto.

Time came for Bob's scheduled six-week furloughed home visit to Chicago. Before he left, he visited the boarding house with a purpose. Without a change in his demeanor he said, "I would like my ring back."

"Certainly," said Inez. Relieved to give back the ring she never wanted; Inez retrieved the ring from her purse where it was held for safekeeping. None of her attempts to make the finger hole of the ring smaller worked. He must have noticed she did not wear the ring. Maybe, Bob asked for his ring back once he realized Inez was not Jewish.

She handed Bob his signet ring, he nodded, turned, and left the porch. Inez assumed Bob went on furlough the next day.

With Bob gone, another Marine, also from the rehabilitation center, started to be included in the group. Herb was a sweet, blond guy, just about 5' 5"—Inez's height.

One afternoon, Otto wanted to go horseback riding. He proved to be comfortable on a horse, but not poor Herb. A city kid from Springfield, Illinois, he was afraid to be on the mount. No matter what, Herb's horse hung back from the rest and ended up facing the wrong way. As the group rode, they kept looking back and asked, "Where is Herb?"

Finally, Otto came up behind Herb and in a loud voice, yelled "Hey." The horse jumped and took off running, with the unfortunate Herb holding on for dear life. Otto was able to catch the runaway horse before any harm came to either the animal or to the city-slicker Marine.

As the group joked and kidded, Otto razzed Alice with comments of her being heavy. Inez remembered Otto telling Alice, "I love every bone in your fat, sassy body." Alice did not care much for the "fat comments" but she was in heaven with Otto's attention. Perhaps, Alice took the statements for meaning more than fun joking, for she fell hard in love with Otto. She clung to him, but Otto was not interested in making a commitment to her. They soon broke up.

The time came for both Herb and Otto to leave on their allotted furloughs. Inez knew Herb was serious about his girlfriend back home. Therefore, she was not surprised when she heard Herb married while home on leave.

During another Armory dance, Herb eagerly showed Inez a picture of his new wife. She saw a very young girl looking out from the photograph. Inez did not have contact with Herb again until he called to ask if she wanted to have lunch with him. She knew he was lonely, but Herb was a married man.

Inez told him, "That's not a good idea and I'm not comfortable with that." Later, she met Herb's young wife when she joined him in Klamath Falls. Inez thought they made a cute couple.

From the earliest of times in history, malaria went hand and hand with war; this continued to be true of the twentieth century. Sometimes, malaria became a catchall term for tropical diseases susceptible to humans. Such diseases posed an important health hazard to troops in the South Pacific during World War II. More than just chills, fever, and fatigue, these diseases resulted in liver involvement, affected the brain with seizures and coma, or even caused death. The significant loss of manpower and money compromised America's fighting ability.

Many of the men at the Klamath Falls Marine Barracks were in treatment for elephantiasis. Inez knew this condition as filariasis. The infection spread to the Marines from bites of mosquitoes and black flies carrying parasitic and microscopic roundworms. The condition was characterized by gross enlargement of body parts, particularly the limbs. Unfortunately, commonly affected areas also included the external genitals, such as swelling of the scrotum. Because of this, filariasis was one of the most feared diseases since it was believed to cause sterility and was irreversible.

At the Klamath Falls Marine Barracks, which the locals referred to as the rehabilitation center, the treatment focused on eating large, healthy meals, exercise, and continuing a Marine lifestyle. Preventive psychiatric treatment was provided for the crisis of the body's self-image and battle fatigue.

Within a year of its opening, treatments proved that malaria and filariasis, believed to be incurable diseases, could be successfully treated. When birth rates doubled the national average, the psychological fears of sterility disappeared for married Marines in treatment. Twenty-two months after its opening, the Marine Barracks/rehabilitation center was no longer needed.

~

Working Girl

Reminders of war crept into Inez's life. A soldier engaged to one of Inez's neighbors died when he parachuted into Normandy on the first day of D-day, June 6th, 1944.

With high school completed, Inez concerned herself with obtaining a job. She did not have to search far. Her landlady, Mrs. Conrady, knew a Certified Public Accountant (CPA) friend in need of a secretary. In her opinion, Inez would be perfect for the job. The CPA hired Inez because of his friend's enthusiastic recommendation.

The transition to the new job required Inez to move from the Conrady's rooming house to another rented room in a different part of Klamath Falls. This room, unlike her previous one, had a lock on the door and no creepy neighbors to worry about.

Inez soon discovered that her new boss ran a large, thriving accounting business. Besides his main office in Klamath Falls, the CPA also maintained offices in San Francisco and Portland.

She found that her basic high school education and business courses were not enough for this office. Being ill-prepared to cope with the pace and demands of the position made Inez mismatched from the beginning. Good grades in shorthand classes could not overcome the problem of a frozen, blank mind whenever she attempted to take dictation from the CPA. Frustration and humiliation caused even more embarrassment.

The older sister of a friend, Fran Gillcrest, worked at the Klamath Falls office as a certified secretary and an administrative professional. This co-worker attempted to help Inez as much as she could, but unfortunately, Inez did not improve quickly enough. The CPA understood the problem, but Inez was gently dismissed after only several weeks on the job.

Despite the reasons, the job loss devastated Inez. Perhaps, she and her family were lulled by the ease with which Inez had obtained her summer job in Bremerton, which John Peters arranged for her. Inez could have trained to advance her career and enhance her expertise in the business field, but that was not the case. She felt pressured to find another job right away to pay for her room and board. Her mother and stepfather had separated once again.

Klamath Falls Telephone Company, 1944

"Mom, did you have a telephone while growing up?"

"No, the farm was never wired with telephone lines," answered my mother, Inez.

"How about the places in town—in Klamath Falls? Did they have phones?

"Oh, they did . . . but I kept my distance. I never touched them."

"Yet, you went to work at the Klamath Falls Pacific Telephone Company?"

"Yes, I needed a job. Alice already had a day shift job at the telephone company, so I thought 'How bad can it be? If Alice can do it, so can I.'"

Inez's mother was disheartened and upset when told of her daughter's plan to work for the telephone company. Assigned to the second shift, Inez would work until late in the evening and be dismissed after 11:00 PM—not the best or safest situation for a young female. Leona viewed the position as undesirable for a young woman such as Inez. In 1944, operators received meager pay for stressful, demanding labor. Leona told Inez, "I had higher expectations for my daughter than the telephone company."

A few days later, while shopping at Woolworth's drugstore, Inez bumped into her high school business teacher and mentor, Mr. Palmer.

"Inez Dutton, or should I say Inez David? How are you? I've been anxious to hear how you are doing in your position with the CPA office." Mr. Palmer was all grins as he greeted Inez.

His enthusiastic inquiry about her job prospects turned to a frown when he noticed Inez near tears.

"Oh Mr. Palmer! I'm sorry to tell you I was let go after only a couple of weeks. It was so overwhelming . . . I couldn't keep up with my shorthand . . . it was awful."

The teacher worried his lip with concern and sympathy. "I am sorry to hear this . . . I was afraid you were not sufficiently prepared for such a demanding position. But you must not give up."

Inez sighed with resignation, "My friend Alice Fitsimmons works as a telephone operator, and I've decided to be one also."

"Truly you can do better than working at the telephone company. You were one of my best business students and you have excellent organization skills." Mr. Palmer's disappointment showed as his words echoed Leona's sentiments.

Inez rushed her response, "Well I better be going. It's nice seeing you." She knew Mr. Palmer cared about her and respected her work in school, but she had made up her mind about the telephone company.

"I wish you the best and let me reiterate, you were not prepared for such a difficult position . . . Being a telephone operator is okay for Alice, but you must strive for better."

Nevertheless, Inez entered the world of communications. She found herself seated in front of a bank of switchboards, with rows of flashing button-lights and extendable cords. *The cockpit of a B-17 could not be more intimidating,* thought Inez as she sat at the switch board.

Each operator had a large, heavy, horn-shaped mouthpiece microphone that hung around her neck as she spoke into it. The headphone sets had one hard, round receiver, for listening. To avoid the one ear from becoming irritated or sore, the operator would have to switch the receiver from side to side as often as possible.

"Ladies, let us review." The matron supervisor truly enjoyed her authority.

"A light on the switchboard will appear with each telephone call. It is your task to respond to the call light as soon as possible. Out of twenty-five operators, the light will be answered within . . ." the matron points her bony index finger to a shy mousy blonde sitting in the front.

"Ahh, within ten seconds, Ma'am?" The supervisor gave a slight nod and turned to pace the other way.

"By hand-connecting each call, the operator will plug one of the . . ." the matron pulled a cord from her pocket and stared at Inez.

Inez answered, "The operator plugs in the 'answering cords' into the jack and switches her headset into the circuit to ask for the desired number by saying, 'Number, please.' "

The supervisor plugged the cord into the jack on the switchboard. "Go on, Miss David. And do speak up."

With more force Inez said, "The operator will then plug the other 'ringing cord' into the local jack of Klamath Falls or plug into the trunk line circuit to start a long-distance call to talk to other operators in distant cities."

After demonstrating, the matron continued with her review. "To handle distance calls, to the major cities such as Portland or San Francisco, the operator will need to know which routing is to be used."

With hands clasped behind her back, the woman paced back and forth as she spoke. "Expect at least a twenty to thirty-minute wait to put these calls through to the desired destination. Often the long-distance calls are made from a pay phone. The length of the call will determine the cost of the call."

Brushing imaginary lint from her skirt, the supervisor continued. "You, as the operator, must be aware of how long the call was active. You must give the price still owed before the call is disconnected. Unfortunately, much of the collection for a call depends upon the honor of the caller."

With a gloating look she said, "Ladies, you can be assured I will be ever present, roving behind you . . . catching your mistakes . . . pointing out unanswered call lights."

Inez had a difficult adjustment to the demands of the job. The constant background chatter of the operators while confined to one of eight stations, in a room without windows, proved to be harder than she had imagined. The two-month training period was relentless. Memories of flashing lights haunted her when she attempted to close her eyes to sleep at night. Of the handful of girls that started the orientation with Inez, only half completed the training. The rest could not handle the complex system and washed out.

Getting off work after 11 p.m. did have a silver lining for Inez. Alice's ex-boyfriend, Otto Mansker, reassigned as a military policeman (MP), made it a point to wait outside the telephone company when Inez's evening shift ended. Every night, he escorted her home to the boarding house.

Inez said she could have "gone" for Otto with his fun-loving spirit, his good looks, and those big green eyes. But it just would not have been right with Alice still pining away for him.

When Inez heard an interesting rumor about Otto, she confronted him on their next after-work walk. "Otto, what's this I hear about you getting married?"

He replied. "I thought I should stop the scuttlebutt." Inez did not say anything about the conversation to Alice. Inez asked around, but nobody seemed to know exactly what Otto meant.

Later, Inez wondered, *Otto, did you get a girl pregnant?*

Nothing more was discussed about Otto's marriage, even though he continued to walk Inez home most nights after the end of her shift. She worked for the telephone company for a total of six months. Inez's career as a telephone operator came to an end when her mother decided that they would travel to Tujunga Hill, California (outside of Pasadena) for a Christmas visit with Uncle Leon, Aunt Ella, and the cousins.

Inez didn't remember even telling Otto good-bye.

Part Six

Southern California

1945–1946

~

A Visit with the Davids

During the 1944 Christmas holiday, Inez and her mother traveled by train to Southern California to visit her Uncle Leon and Aunt Ella. Inez last saw her "David side" of the family thirteen years before, just prior to journeying with her brother from Montana to Oregon. Henry renewed ties with the family first while he attended trade school, and then during flight training in the Los Angeles area.

Besides her aunt and uncle, Inez met her cousins, Bea and Leo, with their respective spouses and children. Her younger cousin, Kenneth, was in the eighth grade; his older brother Art served in the Navy.

For the first time, Inez met her attractive Aunt Marthe, the youngest of her father's sisters. She and her son, Warren, came from Washington to join the Christmas celebrations. Cousin Warren, several years older than Inez, always wanted to dance with her. A jukebox on the patio, jimmied with a slug instead of a coin, provided all the current dance tunes.

At the time of the visit, Uncle Leon owned and operated a liquor-beverage store in the Tujunga–Sunland area. Inez could see her uncle enjoyed being a businessman. It was hard for her to believe he was once a farmer. He had an air of sophistication and class. Like Inez's father, Uncle Leon preferred starched, white dress shirts for work.

But the two visitors were not prepared for a shocking discovery: Uncle Leon had a remarkable resemblance to President Franklin Delano Roosevelt. The two men had the same hair coloring and both wore pince-nez eyeglasses. Combine those with similar long narrow facial features, small, close-set eyes, and prominent chins—add a toothy grin—and Leon was the spitting image of FDR. Thus, Leona and Inez joked during the visit, with the punchline, "Ha, ha . . . but Aunt Ella doesn't look anything like Eleanor Roosevelt."

Aunt Ella had an imposing, heavyset figure. Her round, meaty face and straight salt-and-pepper hair might have indicated American Indian heritage. She maintained her status as a great cook and a meticulous housekeeper; in addition, Aunt Ella laundered all the dress shirts for the family's three working men: Uncle Leon, her married son, Leo, and her son-in-law, Don. Leo held a civil-service position at a government facility nearby, while Don was an undertaker. To whiten their dress shirts, Aunt Ella washed them with hydrogen peroxide instead of bleach. Heavy starch came next before the shirts were ironed to stiff perfection. It was assumed that Aunt Ella enjoyed all the work generated by such an extended family. The three families lived in the same house or nearby. Inez's mother said, "they lived like Indians."

This kind of talk, and its casual tone of discrimination was not uncommon during the 1930s and '40s. Every ethnic group seemed to want to put themselves above another ethnic group. But in this instance, Leona was jealous and somewhat resentful of Ella from their days together in Montana.

The subject of Inez being Jewish came up again. Uncle Leon laughed as he told of how many of the Jewish liquor dealers gave him special deals and lower prices because they believed the last name David meant he was Jewish also. But in fact, Leon and Ella were devout Roman Catholics.

~

Staying in Southern California

Once Inez and her mother arrived in Southern California, they agreed the trip could be more than just a holiday visit. The excitement of staying in the Los Angeles area captivated the two. Leona did not want Inez to stay alone, and they decided to find work at one of the area's military facilities, as they had done in Bremerton.

After the New Year they searched for a place of their own, and found a small, temporary apartment in the Sunland area. The room came furnished with a youth-size bed that mother and daughter opted to share. They slept fitted together like spoons in a drawer with choreographed sleeping throughout the night. When one wanted to change positions, that person would say, "Turn" and the two would turn in tandem. This continued until Leona became disillusioned with the LA area and decided to return to Oregon. Perhaps, the nocturnal routine hastened Leona's departure for Klamath Falls.

Before she left, Leona wanted Inez established in a better living situation. Yet, searching for a job and a place to live proved more difficult than either of them expected. They found a room that seemed full of promise. But when the prospective landlord went on about having only a devout Christian girl living at the house, Leona became offended. She chose to walk away from the room and lost the $30 deposit.

Just as time came for Leona to return to Klamath Falls, Inez found a room to rent in the Glendale home of a nice elderly couple. Inez made a good impression on them and they frequently invited her to dinner with them.

Besides defense work, Inez placed applications for different types of positions. A job opportunity came up at a dry cleaner in Glendale. Hired to do some pressing and ironing, Inez primarily ended up accepting the dirty clothes when customers dropped off their cleaning.

Inez's mother was not happy to hear of her daughter's new job. Leona worried that it was unsanitary and just too dirty of a job for a young girl. After all, she might be exposed unknowingly to other people's excrement. The message to Inez was to ditch the cleaners and find another job.

In the meantime, Inez found the train systems in the Los Angeles area easy to maneuver. She felt safe traveling to wherever she wanted to go. At first, Inez returned on weekends to stay with her aunt and uncle in Tujunga Hills. It was fun to be around the David family as she got to know them even better.

Her cousin Bea's husband, Don, related stories of being shot down behind enemy lines in France. The Free French Forces kept him hidden in haystacks and such as he worked his way back to England. He returned to his family's funeral-home business after being discharged from the military. Inez remembered Don's amusing, off-the-wall comments on ways to relax and position a corpse in the coffin for burial.

On these weekend visits, Aunt Ella included Inez in grocery shopping trips. Inez could see why Aunt Ella had her heavyset figure. Each time, they stopped at See's Candies, a California candy store, to buy foot-long pecan rolls and large boxes of peanut brittle.

Inez found her Aunt Ella was very devoted to her faith. She decided that Inez needed to know and say the whole rosary for herself, which included ten sets of "Hail Mary." In addition to this, Ella expected Inez to attend Catholic Mass during her weekend visits. This was very foreign to Inez, and she soon found other activities to fill her weekends.

During this time, Inez discovered ways to try out new experiences. On one of her days off, she went with friends to the Long

Beach amusement park, called "The Pike." The Cyclone Racer, built along the shoreline on pilings over the water, became Inez's first roller coaster ride. Afterwards, she learned the ride was the largest wooden dual-track roller coaster in the country. Not liking the dropping feeling, Inez determined that since she had done the roller coaster ride once, she did not need to do it again—ever.

L.A. and Alice Too

Inez exited the streetcar from Glendale at the Los Angeles Train station. She checked the arrival time for the train from Klamath Falls and waited expectantly. It was early spring in sunny California, with green foliage and blooming flowers everywhere. The previous, colder weather was only a memory. Still, Inez could not believe people complained about how it was "so cold." She thought, *What's wrong with these people? If they lived in Oregon, they would really know cold weather.*

However, the day was cheery and sunny— a perfect welcome for Inez's friend, Alice Fitzsimmons. In a letter, Alice had mentioned how nice it would be if she could join Inez in California. Never believing in a million years that Alice's mother would allow her daughter to move so far away from home, Inez wrote that "Yes, it would be nice." She did not offer an invitation to join her, but Alice took it that way. What a surprise when Alice relayed her arrival date and time.

Inez enjoyed being on her own during the past few months. She had mixed feelings about sharing her new life with Alice.

When Alice stepped off the train, she looked especially attractive and stylish. She wore a flattering wide, red headband that contrasted with her dark hair. Alice squealed and hugged Inez with glee. It had been almost four months since they had last seen each other, and the two had a lot of catching up to do. It was like old times by the time they got back to Glendale. The girls planned to share the room Inez was renting from the nice older couple.

As they unpacked Alice's belongings, Inez noticed a pile of clean white strips of rags that Alice quickly put away. Inez recognized the rags as what Alice and her mother used for their menstrual periods. Alice's mother faithfully tended to the cloth strips, so they could be reused monthly. Before long Inez observed a new box of Kotex sanitary napkins in the cupboard. The cloth rags were never seen again.

With eagerness Alice reported all the Klamath Falls news and gossip. During a lull in the conversation, Inez asked, in a nonchalant way, "And whatever became of Otto Mansker?"

Alice huffed through her nose and looked away. "I don't want to talk about it."

And nothing more was ever said on the subject.

With her mother's continual concerns about the dry cleaners, Inez found another job at Glendale's F.W. Woolworth Company. Usually referred to as Woolworth's, the retail chain store was also called a five-and-dime because it sold many different items priced at five or ten cents.

Inez lacked retail experience, so she was stationed in the notions department, where she sold such items as stationary, pen sets, and picture frames. She never overcame her fear of making change from a purchase. Alice had worked at the Klamath Falls Woolworth's candy counter during high school, so she also found employment at the Glendale Woolworth's. Working at the candy counter had more prestige than working in notions. However, neither girl was paid much.

Both Alice and Inez hoped for better jobs and applied for federal employment. When only one job came available, they agreed to wait until both could be hired at the same time—but that never happened.

Even though their take-home pay was minimal, the girls had a whirlwind time as they made the most of their location. Alice came across discount coupon booklets from many of the well-known tourist stops and sights in the Los Angeles area. Once the girls purchased the booklets, they felt obligated to use whatever was available, to get their money's worth. With a plethora of things to see and do, the two headed out for the sights—after all this was L.A!

Their first stop was the nearby Forest Lawn Cemetery in Glendale. where many Hollywood stars were buried. The girls at first questioned the idea of viewing a cemetery for pleasure. However, Forest Lawn presented an impressive landscape of rolling hills, extensive lawns, and splashing fountains. More than the run-of-the-mill cemetery or memorial park, it offered a museum, an art gallery, an architectural showcase, and a Hollywood tourist trap, all rolled into one.

~

Who Wears Short Shorts?

The next Sunday, Inez and Alice planned to travel just a little ways away from Glendale to Griffith Park, at the eastern end of the Santa Monica Mountains. Alice decided to take advantage of California's reputation for nice weather, so she put on white shorts. She convinced Inez that she should wear shorts as well.

However, when their landlady spied the girls' attire and exposed legs, she demanded, "You girls must change out of those shorts immediately." She continued, "I don't want you two parading around in front of my husband like that."

Inez turned towards her room to change her clothes when she heard Alice become defiant. "Oh yah? You have no right to tell us what to wear. . . . Your old husband can just look the other way."

The older woman pointed to Alice. "I won't tolerate a sassy mouth. I want you out of my home." A stunned Inez groaned to herself. *I knew Alice would cause trouble. Now what am I going to do?*

She sighed and rushed to catch up with Alice who headed towards the streetcar stop. They went to the park wearing their shorts and put off worrying about the consequences until later.

Alice read aloud from the brochure, "The municipal Griffith Park covers 4,310 acres of land along the Los Angeles River. It's the second largest urban park in North America."

Inez said. "Alice, what are we going to do about our rooming situation?"

Ignoring the question, Alice continued, "Griffith Park was donated to the City of Los Angeles as a Christmas gift in 1896 by a successful mining investor, Griffith J. Griffith. Later he willed money to build the Greek Theatre and Griffith Observatory. . . ." Skimming ahead, she exclaimed, "Oh, the 'Hollywoodland' sign is located on the southern side of Mount Lee."

"ALICE!"

Alice looked up and sighed. "I'm sorry, but that place was too small for us anyway. I'm scheduled off tomorrow and I'll find us a much better place. . . . In the meantime, can't we stay at your aunt and uncle's?"

"I suppose," said Inez.

Alice smiled. "Okay. Don't be a wet blanket. Let's enjoy the day."

The Griffith Observatory—the jewel of Griffith Park—sparkled as Southern California's gateway to the cosmos. The girls found the observatory on the south-facing slope of Mount Hollywood, where they enjoyed a stunning view of the Los Angeles Basin. The Basin included downtown Los Angeles to the southeast, Hollywood to the south, and the Pacific Ocean to the southwest.

Alice pointed, "There's the Hollywoodland sign. I never thought I would see it for myself."

The girls explored the space- and science-related exhibits, looked through telescopes, and viewed the live show in the Samuel Oschin Planetarium. They learned that the observatory's benefactor, Mr. Griffith, opposed building it on a remote mountaintop, or to giving access only to scientists. He wanted to make astronomy available to the public, for people like Inez and Alice—all without a charge.

Dazzled by what she saw, Inez said, "I never noticed the stars and planets like this in Klamath Falls."

On their walk about Griffith Park, Inez and Alice saw more than planets and stars. They noticed several men bicycling in the area. One guy rode his bike wearing just a jock strap; another rode by with nothing but a big grin. In fact, the shocked girls discovered all the grinning people standing about were also nude.

Somehow the girls had wandered into a nudist camp—on visitor's day!

~

The Saropians

The problem of their rooming situation remained. Inez went to work the next day, while Alice searched the classifieds for a place to live. She found a listed room with a bath in an established residential area in East Hollywood, within the city limits of Los Angeles. The home, located close to shopping and transportation, was on a lovely, tree-lined street in what was called "Little Armenia." Alice put down a deposit to hold the room.

Alice took Inez to the home the next day to sign a rental contract, and the girls started moving immediately. They did not have much to move; however, Inez did have her Multnomah Baggageman. Without means to transport it, she had the trunk shipped to the new location.

The home belonged to an Armenian family—Mr. and Mrs. Saropian, their four children, and a grandmother. The huge residence seemed to have an endless number of rooms with elegant features, such as glass doors that opened into the dining room. The family all slept in downstairs bedrooms, while Alice and Inez shared one of the upstairs rooms.

Born in Greece, Mr. Saropian had met and married Mrs. Saropian in New York before moving to Los Angeles for employment with California Shipbuilding Corporation, known as Calship. Tall and lanky, he tended to be overbearing towards his wife who was petite and much younger than he. Perhaps, in reaction to his domineering traits, Mrs. Saropian was mild-mannered and meek.

Mrs. Saropian told Inez that her husband bought her many nice things. She often spoke of living in New York and seemed to miss her life there. She told of how New Yorkers dressed up and wore gloves for simple, everyday shopping. Mrs. Saropian kept busy cleaning or working in the house. Inez never saw her get dressed up or even leave the house.

Mr. Saropian exhibited a gruff exterior, but Inez sensed a kind heart, for he was generous and loving to his kids. The four Saropian children— three cute daughters and a three-year-old son—were tended with care and always smartly dressed. However, the boy, a large toddler, was the pride of the family, and was spoiled by them. He did not need to walk, for the rest of the family carried him everywhere.

Even though the girls' rooming contract did not include meals, they were frequently invited to dinner to sample some of Mrs. Saropian's Armenian dishes. Inez had little knowledge of the location of Armenia or what the food was like there, but she loved her first serving of rice pilaf.

One weekend, the Saropian family included Inez and Alice in a trip to the beach. The eight people piled into a spacious late-model sedan that looked ancient but was well maintained. Inez was not sure where they went that day, but Mr. Saropian first drove into the foothills to visit a friend. When he returned to the car, he carried some homemade soft cheese. He urged Inez to try some because he thought it was so delicious. Inez, reluctant to take a taste, wondered; *Was this safely prepared?* Mr. Saropian continued to offer the cheese until Inez gave it a little taste: *Gee Whiz, what's the deal? I don't think this is anything special.* She had never tasted soft brie cheese before.

Conditions appeared perfect when the group arrived at the unidentified beach. Inez thought to herself, *Another beautiful California day. . . . I'm surprised we are the only people here. Perhaps this is a private beach . . . I don't see any signs posted, like on a public beach.*

Blankets and towels were set up for sunning and preparations made for swimming. The three little girls joined hands with Inez and Alice as they all stepped through the sand towards the water. *What fun!*

However, after venturing into the shallow water, only several feet from the shore, Inez found herself being pulled down into the ocean by the extreme force of a strong riptide. The girls were all drawn into the current as their arms and legs struggled to keep their heads above water. Inez panicked for both herself and the others. After what seemed like an eternity, the group made it back to the sandy beach, sputtering and coughing up sea water. Neither Inez nor Alice knew how to swim and the experience re-enforced Inez's fear of water—especially of the ocean.

Smoking

The Saropian grandmother tended to be a bit of a hermit. She stayed in her downstairs bedroom near the kitchen, but never seemed to eat. Inez only noticed the small, withered woman when she scurried into the kitchen to light her cigarette. She held the cigarette in her mouth while leaning over the stove top to reach the flame of the burner's pilot light. Inez worried every time she saw Grandma doing this. *How does she keep from catching herself on fire?*

Smoking was not a new concept to Inez. Her maternal grandfather, Louis Doyon, had a favorite saying: "If a man doesn't smoke, he has much worse habits instead."

Her mother, Leona, smoked cigarettes on and off through the years. Medical advice of the times recommended smoking for lung problems. Therefore, Inez's own father smoked a pipe with Copenhagen tobacco. Both Inez and her brother loved the aroma of Copenhagen and associated the scent with fond memories of their father, even many years after his death.

Smoking as a habit took root during World War I. Tobacco companies touted a smoke break as a way for soldiers to mentally escape from their grim circumstances, thus boosting overall troop morale. Believed to lighten the hardships of war, smoking cigarettes often became the last and only solace of the wounded.

With the rise of World War II, tobacco companies continued to foster this culture of wartime smoking. Free cigarettes were sent to the troops. Brands, such as Chesterfields, Camels, Old Gold, Lucky Strikes—were part of the GIs' C-rations, right alongside the more obvious staples of meat, vegetables, and starches. Cigarettes became such a part of battlefield life that these symbols of pleasure and comfort were also used as currency.

During wartime in the 1940s, people smoked cigarettes everywhere. Movie screens showed actors lighting up. Every soldier, sailor, and marine on the street was smoking. Inez's brother Henry returned from the war smoking a pipe—and yes, even Grandma Saropian smoked as well.

Often when a soldier or sailor met a girl like Inez or Alice, he acted the gentleman and offered her a cigarette. If she said, "No thanks, I don't smoke," the refusal became the butt of a joke or condemnation. The girl was considered downright unsophisticated, a goody-two-shoes, thinking herself too high and mighty to partake in a smoke. Such became the issue with Inez and Alice. They decided they might as well learn how to smoke, like everyone else.

Their opportunity came when Alice read an announcement in the newspaper that cigarettes would be available for ration coupons at a certain time and place. When the two arrived at the location, they found hundreds of people lined up waiting, as if for a popular movie. After they stood for a long time, each girl received one pack of off-brand cigarettes. They raced home to try their treasures.

What came next was nausea for Inez. Alice turned green and vomited as she said, "Ohhh, I'm so sick."

After this experience, Inez threw her pack of cigarettes away, but Alice continued to smoke hers to the point that they became a habit. Alice liked the way the cigarettes curbed her appetite and helped keep her weight down. After seventeen years of smoking, Alice finally kicked her addiction and threw away her cigarettes.

And Grandma Saropian continued lighting her cigarette from the flame of the burner.

~

Hollywood Boulevard

In 1910, a portion of the major east–west street in Los Angeles, California was renamed from Prospect Avenue to the more elegant-sounding title of Hollywood Boulevard. This thoroughfare began as a winding residential street at Sunset Plaza Drive in the Hollywood Hills West district. Crossing Laurel Canyon Boulevard, it proceeded east, through Hollywood's Little Armenia, to become a major access street to Vermont Avenue.

Hollywood Boulevard sparked the interest of both Inez and Alice, as they ventured out from their rented room in Little Armenia. During this time, Inez developed her favorite hobby and pastime—shopping. Compared to Klamath Falls, Los Angeles offered greater selections in clothing and other items. Even though Inez did not have much money, she enjoyed window shopping. Besides, it was a lot more fun to shop in the California sunshine than in the freezing Oregon weather.

However, the girls had to overcome a few rough spots. The two seemed to have similar taste in clothing. Many times, when shopping separately, they found each had purchased the same shoes or outfit. Usually, it could be sorted out between them. However, in one instance when both girls brought back the same pair of shoes, neither would give up her treasure: a pair of black suede platform sandals with ankle straps, bought on sale.

Such a find did not come around every day.

~

The Owl Drugstore

The sun-drenched weather provided opportunities to visit the public beaches of Venice and Santa Monica. The Owl drugstore on Hollywood and Vine became an important destination for the girls after they had spent too much time at the beach on an overcast day.

Alice, with her fair skin, suffered such a severe sunburn that blisters formed on the back of her neck, back, thighs, and calves. She cried with pain as the two girls tried to decide what to do. Alice would not go to a doctor, perhaps because it was late in the weekend or because she did not have the money.

Finally, Inez convinced her to consult with a pharmacist at the Owl drugstore. He suggested diluted tannic acid in water but warned too much tannin could have an adverse effect on one's internal organs, such as the liver. He instructed Inez to dunk a cloth into the mixture, dab the medicine on the sunburn, and leave it on overnight. The girls were grateful when the morning brought a substantial improvement in Alice's sunburn.

One afternoon, Inez and Alice exited that same Owl drugstore as a man entered. Inez and the man exchanged friendly smiles when recognition dawned on the two. It was Bob Dewey, the marine from the rehabilitation center in Klamath Falls whom Inez had dated. Bob seemed pleased to see her. In fact, he grabbed Inez off her feet and swung her around.

Bob looked like a different person in civilian clothing. Inez enjoyed seeing the "new Bob," healthy and strong, as he held himself upright and confident. Talkative and enthusiastic, he asked for her phone number to arrange a get-together.

Alice was not pleased to see Bob. She appeared indignant as she stood with her arms crossed and had a sour scowl on her face. It did not matter. Bob never made further contact—or perhaps, Alice never gave Inez the message if he did call.

~

Sentimental Journey

With hopes of a victory in Europe, families anticipated the homecoming of their loved ones. However, not all soldiers would return home unharmed and not every casualty occurred on the battlefield.

One evening proved to be an unexpected traumatic experience. The two roommates were on their way to a dance at the Hollywood Palladium. They had attended several previous dances there. However, this time, as Inez watched the flow of traffic from her streetcar window seat, her pleasant ride turned to horror when she witnessed a dreadful accident.

A yellow taxicab barreled into the intersection as a group of marines walked across Hollywood Boulevard and Vine. The vehicle rammed into one of them. knocking him off his feet. Flung into the air, he landed on the taxi's hood and smashed against its windshield.

The shocking sight left Inez shaken and distraught. What a helpless feeling to have seen this tragedy unfold. Inez 's thoughts repeated the incident over in her mind. Yet, the unaffected streetcar continued with its usual routine, as if nothing had happened.

When the girls arrived at the Palladium, their festive mood was greatly dampened by what they had just witnessed. Nevertheless, the tragic event helped solidify memories of that night, setting it apart from previous Palladium dances they attended. Featured with Les Brown and his Band of Renown was a cute, young female singer with a great voice. At the time, Inez did not know the singer, but soon everyone would recognize Doris Day.

In 1945, the Band of Renown released its recording of "Sentimental Journey." During the same period, the Allies achieved a victory in the Battle of the Bulge (also known as the Ardennes Counteroffensive). This European battle was to be the last major German offensive campaign on the Western Front.

Since the song's debut coincided with the conclusion of the war in Europe, it became the unofficial homecoming theme for thousands of returning veterans, bringing Doris Day new prominence. She became the most popular female band singer of 1945. With her striking good looks and bubbly personality, she was sought out by the movie industry Soon she became a mega movie star, as well as a singer.

For Inez and Alice, the famous Hollywood Palladium was the ultimate jewel that exemplified Hollywood's reputation as "Tinsel Town." Located on Sunset Boulevard, between Gower and Vine Streets, the Palladium opened in October of 1940 and soon grew to be a lively Hollywood nightclub. Although classified as a theater, the Palladium became Hollywood's largest entertainment center for dance, live music, and special events.

The Hollywood Palladium featured an unique type of curved and modernized Art Deco architecture, known as Streamline Moderne. The automobile entrance and rounded columns conveyed glamour. Once inside, patrons were greeted with chandeliers, chrome work, and a color scheme of silver and pearly gray satin-walls with coral accents. Colorful bursts of lighting came from impressive technological wonders.

However, the Palladium was all about dancing. The iconic, springy 11,200 square foot kidney-shaped maplewood dance floor could accommodate up to 4,000 dancers. The dining area around the dance floor seated an additional 1,000 people—but the floor itself offered standing or dancing room only.

Inez knew she was not dancing at the Klamath Falls Grange or Armory Hall whenever she visited the Hollywood Palladium. The atmosphere felt like New Year's Eve every night. She remembered the Palladium dance floor packed so tight she could not turn around, much less dance. Inez later heard that between 1940 and 1961, over 22 million people had danced on the giant maple dance floor.

~

Relationships

The next time the girls had a chance to go dancing at the Palladium, Alice begged off at the last minute. Angry at her roommate, Inez boarded the streetcar and proceeded alone to the club. That night, Inez met a Seabee stationed at San Clemente. After the dance, he escorted her back to her place by way of the streetcar. He was the first and only serviceman to do this from any Los Angeles dances. The Seabee was a perfect gentleman; however, Inez realized this action was too bold. She never again went alone to a dance or allow a stranger to escort her home.

Inez did not see the Seabee again, but she did correspond with him several times. She continued her other wartime correspondences as well, writing to both Tanis and Tony. Tony's letters became fewer and farther between. After some time, he wrote to say that he was being shipped back to the States and would write when he had a stateside address to give her.

During a previous outing at Griffith Park, Inez and Alice met two sailors who happened to be from their high school graduating class, Bill Long and Fonzi Parish. Fonzi had been named the Best Male Dancer of KUHS Class of 1944.

Later, Fonzi connected Alice with one of his soldier friends from Klamath Falls. The soldier and Alice really hit it off. She became serious about him, but a problem developed—they were first cousins.

Inez thought this guy was sleazy and he gave her the creeps. She discouraged Alice from continuing the relationship, but Alice was smitten.

Alice spent all her free time with this new boyfriend. Perhaps this was the reason she hadn't gone to the Palladium with Inez. When Alice's mother learned of the relationship, she demanded the cousins stop dating. Her divorced mother was convinced that nothing good could come from the father's "Fitzsimmons side" of the family. Finally, a broken-hearted Alice complied with her mother's wishes.

~

The Death of FDR

On April 12th, 1945, while Inez worked in the Woolworth's Notions Department, word came of the death of President Franklin Delano Roosevelt. Roosevelt, elected in 1932 as the 32nd President of the United States, had been President for thirteen of Inez's eighteen years of life. Even though her parents never voted for FDR, the words "president" and "Roosevelt" had become interchangeable to her.

Inez, along with the stunned American public, was unable to adjust her mind to the tragic news of the president's death. The sense of loss could not be expressed. Businesses and bars suddenly fell silent. Men and women wandered aimlessly out of their homes onto the streets.

People credited FDR with easing the pain of the Great Depression. They felt he knew their hurts and cared about their troubles. It seemed inconceivable that anyone else could be the papa-father that FDR represented to them. Still in the middle of a world war, Americans now fought a sense of loss and apathy without their Commander-in-Chief.

Citizens looked to Roosevelt as one of their family members—in fact, many displayed pictures of FDR in their homes. Previously, companies took advantage of the president's popularity by selling framed pictures of him. Therefore, when the announcement came of FDR's death, people flocked to Woolworth's and Inez's notions department to snatch up any such framed photographs.

The store's inventory sold out fast; its manager searched the store basement for any FDR photos in picture frames. None were to be found. Many disappointed people left Woolworth's without their desired memorials.

~

V-E Day

In less than a month, Germany's leader was also dead. The Allies kept their battle resolve, even with the death of FDR. By contrast, when Adolf Hitler committed suicide on April 30th his successor, Reichspräsident Karl Dönitz authorized Germany's surrender.

The eighth of May 1945 marked the day German troops finally laid down their arms throughout Europe. With the groan of sustained effort . . . and then a sigh, the war in Europe had ended. The Allied armed forces celebrated the absolute and total submission of Germany. The Nazi war machine had been defeated.

From that day forward, Victory in Europe Day, generally known as V-E Day, was marked as a day of remembrance of the formal acceptance of an unconditional surrender. With much reason to rejoice, cities in Great Britain, the United States, and formerly occupied Western Europe displayed flags and banners of victory.

The war and threat of war that had been in the forefront of most of Inez's life was no more. This brought great joy but tentative celebration to Inez, Alice, and the rest of America. They knew more struggles and fighting remained with the Japanese forces. Therefore, men and women in military uniforms continued to be a strong and highly visible presence in Inez's daily life.

~

Grauman's Chinese Theatre

As the streetcar passed by, buildings along Hollywood Boulevard blended into a mass of concrete and color. One of Southern California's most recognizable sights came into view. Inez smiled and stretched her neck a bit to see her favorite L.A. landmark: Grauman's Chinese Theatre. The name elicited both the real and the make-believe Hollywood essence of 1930s and '40s. She thought, *I can't imagine Hollywood without it . . . I'm lucky to live close by.*

Often referred to as "The Chinese" by locals, Inez loved the building's design. It resembled a giant red Chinese pagoda. Constructed in the form of a tower several stories tall, each spire tapered slightly toward the top with an upward curving roof. The front of the building featured a huge Chinese dragon with two genuine Ming Dynasty lion-dogs, called "heavenly dogs," that guarded the main entrance. Tiny dragon figures wrapped up and down the sides of the copper roof.

Soon after moving to Los Angeles, Inez and Alice explored the theater's famous courtyard. Aside from the unusual architecture, the girls were drawn to the site's famous tradition: a display of the handprints, footprints, and signatures of Hollywood's biggest stars captured in the cement sidewalk.

The girls learned that this practice was said to have started with three movie stars, who were also investors—Mary Pickford, Douglas Fairbanks, and Norma Talmadge. This set a precedent as prints and famous signatures in concrete continued to be immortalized from the late 1920s onward. Alice and Inez discovered signed concrete blocks in the forecourt representing many of their favorite movie stars.

Alice, excited at her find, said. "Look—Mary Pickford's tiny handprints."

"Yes, there's Greer Garson and Gary Cooper."

"Here's Judy Garland and Micky Rooney. Fred Astaire and Ginger Rogers are over there. Oh, and Clark Gable . . ."

Inez said, "Here's my favorite one—Shirley Temple. Hmmmmm, it was done in 1935. That made her seven years old. Look how sweet . . . she has written 'Love to you ALL,' with her handprints on one side of the ALL and her footprints on the other. Her name is printed in capital letters that take up more than half the cement square.

"Gosh, this is wonderful, and so much better than seeing it in a movie newsreel."

Inez knew that Grauman's Chinese Theatre was well-known for its gala Hollywood movie premiers. But it was also equipped for live theater as well as for cinema. The Theatre became the place for first public performances of plays, musicals, and movies. Fans flocked to these events to see the celebrities as they arrived and walked the red carpet into the theatre. In 1944, glitz and glamour came full force to Grauman's Chinese Theatre when it was chosen to host the film industry's Academy Awards.

The next year, Grauman's Theatre hosted the 17th Annual Academy Awards. Inez and Alice listened, along with the Saropian family, to the presentations as the program was covered for the first time by the ABC radio network. Broadcast nationally, it was also transmitted overseas to American GIs. Bob Hope hosted as Master of Ceremonies as the movie *Going My Way* was named Best Picture. Awards for the year's best actors went to Ingrid Bergman for *Gaslight* and Bing Crosby for *Going My Way*.

With a jolt, Inez realized she had been daydreaming and soon her stop would be coming up. She looked forward to her plans for the evening. The girls held tickets for an advertised promotion for war bonds that night. This would be their opportunity to attend their own live performance at the Grauman's Chinese Theatre. *Will I really sit where the audience of movie stars sat during the Academy Awards?*

Once back in her room, Inez freshened up and slipped into her chosen outfit: a dark blue dress with a fitted waist and bell skirt. Her platform shoes went nicely with the dress. She completed the final touches to her hair and the roommates left to catch a streetcar to the Theatre.

Arriving at the Theatre, they found an exciting atmosphere with eager crowds and the bright lights of a movie premiere. Inez and Alice passed through the exterior grandeur of Chinese ornamentation to a plush interior lit by chandeliers. The ornate main lobby featured elaborate wall murals illustrating life in the Orient. The splendid auditorium displayed bold red and gold columns and a formidable Wurlitzer pipe organ. The setting delighted the girls.

As advertised, the evening encouraged the purchase of war bonds. The program included the upcoming drummer, Gene Krupa, and his orchestra. But the Andrews Sisters were the main attraction of the night.

Patty, Maxene, and LaVerne Andrews were considered America's favorite singing sisters. Starting as children, the sisters developed the close harmony sound of the swing and boogie-woogie music popular during the 1930s and 1940s. While teenagers jitterbugged, and young men enlisted into the military, the singing team formed the most profitable stage attraction in the entire nation.

"Boogie Woogie Bugle Boy," "Ac-Cent-Tchu-Ate the Positive" and "I'll Be with You in Apple Blossom Time" were just a few of their musical hits. The Andrews Sisters found themselves in high demand as singers, radio personalities, and celebrities. They appeared in seventeen Hollywood movies.

Nevertheless, the group believed it was their patriotic duty to give back to the soldiers who fought and sacrificed so much for their country. The Andrews remained active in wartime entertainment by singing, dancing, and signing autographs as they volunteered their free time to entertain thousands of enlisted and wounded servicemen. In addition, they participated in an eight-week USO tour where they entertained and visited bases, war zones, hospitals, and munitions factories. All the while they encouraged U.S. citizens to purchase war bonds with their rendition of Irving Berlin's song "Any Bonds Today?"

What a night to remember! Being fans of the trio, Inez and Alice had followed the sisters' music on records or by radio and later watched them in movies and newsreels. The roommates could not believe their good fortune to be viewing such icons of the era— the Andrews Sisters— performing right in front of them.

~

War Bonds

War equipment and military operations were costly. The U.S. Congress and President Roosevelt helped finance these expenses through war bond drives. Large scale campaigns were launched to sell war bonds at rallies, schools, and places of employment. The nation now asked every citizen, such as Inez and her family, to participate in this war effort. As a student, Inez purchased 10-cent war bond stamps, one at a time, to collect in a $10 booklet.

Sometimes sporting events and movie theaters, such as Grauman's Chinese, offered free admission with the purchase of a war bond. Inez's attendance at Grauman's was not her first experience with events promoting war bonds. Patriotism paired with America's fascination with movie superstars and personalities, such as the Andrews Sisters, Bob Hope, and even "dat silly rabbit" Bugs Bunny to generate needed money.

While Inez worked at the Navy Yard Puget Sound (NYPS) in Bremerton, many celebrities and Hollywood stars appeared at sponsored war bond rallies. At an early rally, she saw First Lady Eleanor Roosevelt. Inez remembered the movie star Ginger Rogers because she wore what appeared to be a real mink coat in the muggy Washington weather.

Across the country, factories and other workplaces joined in, for it was a way for every person to share in the endeavor. Inez participated with fellow NYPS workers when challenged to put at least 10 percent of every paycheck into the promoted loyalty bonds.

Individual bonds varied between $10 to $10,000 and matured at the end of a ten-year term. The buyer paid 75 percent of face value. Thus, a $25 bond would cost $18.75. Many people viewed bonds as a loan to the government. Citizens agreed to purchase war bonds and save them until maturity. After the war, bonds could then be redeemed to purchase houses, cars, and appliances.

In Los Angeles on June 9, 1945, Inez and Alice attended one last war-bond rally. Even though it had been a month since the Allied victory in Europe, fighting continued in the Pacific. The U.S. government, still in need of money for the war effort, hoped citizens could support this last push to raise funds. The goal for such a tour was not only financial but also to spur on the resolve of a war-weary nation. Thus, a 30-day tour featuring victory parades, as well as sale of war bonds, was scheduled for Boston, Denver, Los Angeles, and Washington D.C.

A group of 47 military heroes, including two generals from Southern California, participated in the war bond parade. Both Lieutenant General James H. "Jimmy" Doolittle and General George S. Patton, Jr. played vital roles in winning the war.They were now expected to use their popularity to help win the financial war.

A welcoming crowd of hundreds of thousands viewed the parade as it proceeded along Hollywood Boulevard, through downtown Los Angeles, to a packed Los Angeles Memorial Coliseum. Inez and Alice were unable to get close to the actual parade, because of the large crowds.

That evening the Memorial Coliseum held a crowd of 100,002 people— for Inez and Alice were in attendance. The girls did not want to miss history so close to where they lived. They made it a point to be at the rally to purchase war bonds and to do what every other person in the crowd came to do: honor and welcome the generals and the rest of the group as proven leaders in battle, and true red, white, and blue heroes.

The official aim of the tour was achieved. Generals Doolittle and Patton helped sell millions of war bonds.

Ice Skating, Anyone?

The girls lived near Hollywood and Beverly Hills, but Inez did not tour any of the actual movie studios. Nevertheless, celebrity sightings were possible and always a treat.

Once Inez found herself standing in a crowd, behind a corded-off area. Hollywood celebrities and movie stars, dressed in suits, furs, and glittering gowns, disembarked from their limousines to attend an extravaganza—featuring an ice show.

Due to the influence and performances of Sonja Henie, Ice Follies, Ice Revues, and Ice-Capade movies with an ice-skating theme became popular in Los Angeles during 1945. Henie reigned as the queen of figure skating with her ten World Championships, six European Championships, and three Olympic gold medals. With her glamorous demeanor and innovative techniques, Henie permanently transformed the sport of ice skating. First to wear the costume of a short skirt and white boots, she also made use of dance choreography that enhanced her skating routine. With her fame, ice skating evolved into an accepted and legitimate Winter Olympics sport.

Perhaps, the event which Inez observed that night was the premier of the 1945 movie *It's a Pleasure,* starring the figure skating champion and Olympic medalist herself. The film showcased the peppy little blonde with her photogenic face and athletic abilities as she performed amazing feats in an elaborate ice show. This was Sonja Henie's thirteenth movie, but the first to be filmed in the vivid motion picture color process, Technicolor.

That night, Inez spotted another champion athlete-turned-movie-star, Esther Williams as she walked into the theater. What Henie did for ice skating, Williams did for swimming. She starred in movies as well. Several of her movies co-starred with the popular heartthrob and leading man Van Johnson.

However, Inez saw it was Sonja Henie whom Van Johnson escorted that night on the red carpet. Rumors at the time suggested a Henie/Johnson romance. Possibly, the romance was invented for publicity, but Inez had to admit that the two blond celebrities made an exceptionally cute couple.

With all the buzz about ice skating, Inez decided to get back into the sport. She, along with her brother Henry and stepbrother Orin, had enjoyed ice skating during the winters at their Oregon farm. The pond by the diversion canal froze to a good skating surface.

Even though she had her own pair of white ice skates, Inez was told she must rent a pair from the indoor ice rink. The skates offered were brown, ill-fitted, and very uncomfortable.

Inez stepped onto the ice with weak ankles and wobbly legs. She did not expect so many people would be on the ice. Waiting for a crowd of skaters to pass by, she tentatively glided out on the ice with one stride, then another. Boom—someone slammed into her from behind. Inez tumbled. She found herself engulfed in a tunnel of skates and legs, stepping over her.

Crawling on hands and knees, Inez hastened to exit the rink. Once safely away from the chaos, she decided to forget about skating. She turned in her rented skates with a wistful thought: *Next time I'll let Sonja do the skating and I'll just watch.*

~

The Hollywood Bowl

Inez and Alice participated in more than viewing Hollywood movie stars and celebrities. On a lovely summer evening, the two attended an open-air opera in pursuit of some local culture.

The Hollywood Bowl, legendary for outdoor live music performances since 1922, offered a setting of natural acoustics due to the amphitheater being carved into a hollow in the Hollywood Hills. Known for its architectural design, the amphitheater's band shell was designed with a distinctive set of concentric arches, described as circles and spheres of different sizes sharing the same middle point. The clean lines of this design with white, almost-semicircular arches, were admired and copied for music venues throughout the country. However, the famous Hollywoodland sign that Alice was so fond of remained unique to the Hollywood Hills.

The Bowl hosted the Hollywood Bowl Orchestra, the summer home of the 1945 Los Angeles Philharmonic. Years later, Inez easily remembered the program she attended that night at dusk. It was *Carmen* by the French composer George Bizet, which featured the "Toreador Song." This was probably the only opera that would have been familiar to Inez. Her junior high class had staged *Carmen* at school in 1935.

~

The Challenge

Inez could hardly believe what she heard from her roommate, "Alice, you plan to leave Woolworth's candy counter?"

"Yes," said Alice. "I saw a posting today about enrollment for PBX training. With my telephone operator experience in Klamath Falls, I should qualify. Only problem is I'm a little short on cash and the deadline to sign up for the course is on Monday. . . . Do you think you can loan me some money for the PBX course?"

"Well, I guess so," answered Inez.

Inez loaned Alice money for the extensive Private Branch Exchange (PBX) program. However, without Alice's Woolworth's paycheck, their money came up short for the monthly bills. To cover expenses, both girls asked their families for financial help. Inez reluctantly inquired if her mother would send $25 to tide her over until payday. She was shocked and grateful when a larger sum of $50 was cabled instead.

As an experienced telephone operator, Alice adjusted well to the private telephone network. Such networks were set up in companies and hotels. The system used different communication channels to link internal telephones while also connecting calls to the outside public telephone network. Operators manually plugged cords into the switchboard to make the connections.

After Alice finished her training, she landed a plum job as a PBX operator at an exclusive hotel. Located close by in the Bel-Aire district, the job offered a good salary. The only downside was that it had rotating shifts.

Alice's decision to leave Woolworth's challenged Inez. She wanted to find a better job for herself as well. It would also please her mother.

Each of her mother's letters expressed her dissatisfaction with Inez's work situation: "If you can't get a better job than Woolworth's, then you should come home and work at a Five and Dime in Klamath Falls. I expect better for you, Inez. You did so well in your business courses at school. I am sure you could land a better job than at a drugstore, or the telephone company or at a laundry. You need to look a little harder."

Inez heard her mother's disappointment—loud and clear.

Golden State Milk Company

Inez discovered an advertisement for employment in the newspaper help-wanted section. The position, for an assistant clerk-typist at a milk company, was located farther south than her usual Hollywood Boulevard neighborhood. She consulted a map and found the company was situated in the 2.12-square-miles of the Watts area, a neighborhood in South Los Angeles.

On the day of her interview, Inez boarded the streetcar at Washington Boulevard for a twenty-minute trip to the industrial area of Watts. Inez enjoyed venturing into parts of the city she had never seen before. She noticed a prevalence of African American people on the streetcar and along the route. This differed from other routes she traveled.

When Inez entered the milk plant, a pleasant looking, husky blond man in his late thirties appeared from his office and offered his hand in greeting. "Hello. Inez? I'm Clarence, the paymaster of the Golden State Milk Company. Did you have any trouble finding us?"

Inez felt at ease with Clarence and said, "No. The streetcar stop was very close."

"Good. I'd like to take you on tour of our milk company." Clarence smiled and handed Inez a white coat, hair covering and booties, then put on his own.

He ushered Inez through the door and raised his voice to talk above the factory noise. The familiar smell of milk permeated Inez's senses as they passed through the extensive milk bottling plant. All the while Clarence pointed out the different procedures by which the milk was separated, pasteurized, and processed into glass bottles.

Workers dressed in white jumpsuits and white head coverings moved around the machinery.

As Inez watched the milk bottles go down the assembly belt, she read some of the slogans printed on the back of the bottles:

Drink your way to Health with GOLDEN STATE MILK

Healthful Beauty comes from within
DRINK GOLDEN STATE MILK

Don't be old at Forty DRINK MILK

Drink More Milk IT'S GOOD FOR YOU.

She couldn't help but smile.

Mesmerized by glass bottles in continuous motion, Inez got lost in her thoughts: *This milk company is quite impressive, especially compared to our milking barn at home. . . . I've never cared much for drinking milk, but I think I'd really like working here.*

Clarence continued the tour. "Okay, let's go into the creamery." Mechanical paddles stirred the contents of large stainless-steel vats. Inez viewed all stages of making cheese and butter. Somc machines separated curd from whey, while other equipment churned butter. Butter cubes and cheese forms moved along different conveyor belts.

The two left the mechanized area and walked towards the office. Clarence said with pride, "The Golden State Milk Company is one of California's largest milk bottling plants and the leading milk products manufacturer west of the Rockies. We are associated with dairies and creameries throughout the state and handle almost a third of the milk sold. We also have the largest fleet of delivery milk trucks in California."

Inez turned to Clarence and said, "This is very impressive."

Passing by the large offices of the headquarters, Clarence and Inez entered the cramped space that was the payroll office. Part of the office had a tiny room, called the "vault," that could be secured with a lock. It contained five or six sacks of dime-sized compressed wood fiber tokens, known as red points. The tokens were used in the rationing system for meats and dairy items during and after the war.

Clarence pulled out a wooden chair from one of the desks so Inez could sit down. "Now for what we do here . . . This milk-bottling plant also houses the main headquarters for seven Golden State branch locations in the immediate and surrounding areas of Southern Los Angeles. Such a big organization requires a lot of bookkeeping. That means our payroll office services those branches, and we are responsible for tracking all the employees' hours and wages.

"Well Inez, I did a lot of talking but I am impressed with your references. I believe you will blend in nicely with our little family here at Golden State. I am glad to offer you the position of junior clerk-typist."

Inez, thrilled and anxious to start work, accepted the job offer on the spot. Her job at Woolworth's paid the minimum wage of 40 cents per hour. The position of payroll junior clerk-typist paid a salary of $80 per month. The one drawback of the job was that it required Inez to join the union and attend the monthly meetings. She ended up paying a five dollar fine every month because she never went to any of the union meetings.

Inez knew it would be a good place to work when on her first day the other member of the payroll team complained, in a teasing manner, about Clarence's smoking.

"Clarence, what are you smoking?"

"Chesterfields," was Clarence's reply.

"Well, it smells a bit like horse manure to me."

This banter came from Ginny, the company's bookkeeper. Tall, slim, and attractive, she wore her brown hair in a short style. Ginny was only in her late thirties or early forties, but eighteen-year-old Inez remembered her as mature. Most of all, Ginny impressed Inez as a woman of the world. After all, she wore nice clothes, had a well-to-do man-friend, and drank Canadian Club whiskey.

Ginny possessed a wealth of knowledge about bookkeeping and payroll. She obtained experience from her previous position as a bank teller where she developed a good sense with numbers, rapidly made change, and did business transactions without any automated assistance.

As the seasoned bookkeeper, she took Inez under her wing while she oriented and prepared her for the workload. Patient and encouraging whenever Inez made a mistake, Ginny never belittled or intimidated her.

Soon after she started, Inez completed her work early in the shift. Not wanting to appear as a slacker, she said, “Clarence, I’ve finished all my work. If you don’t have something else for me to do, I could go next door to the Headquarters’ office to help them out.”

Clarence’s reaction was to almost lose his temper. He shook his head saying, “No, no, no. That’s a bad idea. You don’t need to do Headquarters’ work for them.” Catching his breath and checking his attitude, he offered up a little smile as he said, “Don’t worry, Inez. Payroll will be plenty busy when the time comes.”

True to his word, when payroll time came around Inez found sufficient work to keep her busy. Even though her job description listed her as a typist, she did no typing. Instead, she kept the milk company’s records and payroll accounts. At first, she tracked all the casual workers’ hours. Golden State hired many servicemen who picked up a day per week or pay period, as their schedules allowed. By midsummer, she was trusted to post all the entries for the seven branches into the payroll book.

Company employees were paid every two weeks. The team of Clarence, Ginny, and Inez logged long hours in preparation for the bimonthly paydays. To get the payroll out in time, the three worked late into the evening—until at least 10 P.M.—as payday approached. Sometimes they did not finish until after midnight.

The area around the plant was isolated and somewhat seedy. To take public transportation home at night, by way of a streetcar or bus, was threatening and considered too dangerous for the women. Fortunately, company policy arranged for one of the reliable workers from the bottling section to drive Ginny and Inez home after these late shifts.

Inez viewed Ginny as a mentor in other areas beyond work. Eager to learn, Inez listened to her advice on social or personal matters and took her suggestions for interesting places to visit. Inez mentioned a commotion in front of the dance she attended the previous Saturday night. When she recounted the heavy presence of squad cars and uniformed policemen arresting people from the dance, Ginny became concerned.

She said, "Oh no, you girls don't want to be there—it's known as a pickup joint for ladies of the night. It would be best if you two stay clear of that place."

Inez answered. "Yes, we've been to some crummy places . . . even entered a nudist camp by mistake. We used coupons from the booklet Alice found."

"I'm aware of those types of booklets. . . . I know of some reputable coupon booklets for you girls featuring local events and tours, rather than the one your friend has."

The girls followed Ginny's recommendations and never had any more trouble—and no more nudists camps either.

Clarence, Ginny, and Inez worked well together as a team with all their desks in the same small office, without partitions. Despite the close quarters, their pleasant camaraderie continued, thanks to

Ginny's dry sense of humor and Clarence's typically good-natured ways. Inez admired the two immensely.

However, circumstances happened that neither Ginny nor Clarence could control. One day Ginny and Inez found a pale and sickly Clarence as he half sat, half laid on the bags of red points in the "vault."

Clarence moaned, "Oh, Ginny, I am so sick."

With concern but attempting to lighten the mood, Ginny said, "Clarence, you just have to stop eating at that greasy spoon across the street."

Too bad it was not the fault of a greasy spoon. Clarence, the married father of a three-year-old—and to Inez's thinking, the nicest man she ever met—was diagnosed with stomach cancer. He would be dead within a year.

~

V-J Day, August 14, 1945

The end of World War II came so unexpectedly, as did the Japanese surrender—or did it? Inez learned from newsreels that in late July 1945 an ultimatum, called the Potsdam Declaration, was signed by the United States, United Kingdom, and the Nationalist Government of China. This document outlined terms for the surrender of the Japanese Empire. Without such a surrender, Japan would face "prompt and utter destruction."

Japanese forces had hunkered down in scattered locations throughout the South Pacific Islands, resolved to remain in the fight. Inez read in the newspaper that when Japan refused to lay down their arms, the United States responded to the standoff by dropping atomic bombs on two Japanese cities. The first warfare atomic bomb was detonated above Hiroshima on August 6th of 1945. The next was released over Nagasaki, three days later. The world was never the same.

Unlike V-E day, the term V-J day or Victory Japan Day applied to several days in 1945. Due to the difference in time zones, August 14th was the date when the surrender was announced in the Eastern Pacific Islands, the United States, and the rest of the Americas. However, U.S. President Harry S. Truman declared September 2nd as the official "Victory Japan Day," since that was the actual date the document of surrender was signed by Japan.

Nevertheless, a victory day was a day worthy of celebration. It has been said August 14th, 1945 was "the day Americans began to smile again." Unconstrained joy was everywhere.

V-J Day, August 14, 1945

⊕ ⊕ ⊕

In Los Angeles, Inez had turned nineteen years old just three days earlier, on August 11th. When word came of the surrender, Alice insisted the two girls join the August 14th victory celebration. The streets were filled with a glorious and joyful party—laughter sounded, car horns honked, loud music played, and church bells rang.

Alice and Inez milled around with the rest of the crowds enjoying a festive mood, like the midway at a carnival. The buzz of excitement for peace was easily caught. Inez wondered if she should pinch herself to see if she was dreaming.

Smells of liquor, car exhaust, and tires wafted in the warm afternoon as convertibles jammed with partygoers continued to honk horns and wave flags. So many people overflowed into the roadways that traffic came to a standstill. Hollywood Boulevard became a parking lot.

Dispersed in the crowd, soldiers and sailors kissed women, just as in the famous New York Times Square photograph. Somehow Inez and Alice missed out on these celebratory kisses.

Nevertheless, as the afternoon became evening, lights throughout the city of Los Angeles and the West coast turned on for the first time in a long time. No more need for blackout drapes. The war was over.

~

Shirley Temple

Inez glued the last of her collected paper cuttings into the scrapbook. Many years before, her mother had suggested she start this pastime. Inez dutifully maintained the scrapbook throughout her formative years. Their friend Mrs. Zetzman supplied her with second-hand *Photoplay* magazines that offered plenty of articles and pictures to cut out. The scrapbook documented neither Inez nor her family but stemmed from a fascination with the most famous celebrity of the 1930s—Shirley Temple, THE child star of all times.

No one compared to Shirley Temple. Her shining, dimpled face and energetic little body projected optimism and enthusiasm when gray news and hopelessness prevailed throughout the Depression days. Audiences could not get enough of her motion pictures. Movie magazines capitalized on the fervor. Therefore, Inez and Leona could not be criticized for their devotion to the tiny youth who was bigger than life.

Inez kept abreast of Shirley Temple's life through *Photoplay* magazines and theater newsreels. In 1943, 15-year-old Shirley met her husband-to-be John Agar. He was seven years older, the brother of one of her classmates, and the son of a Chicago meat-packing family. At the time, Agar was a sergeant and a physical training instructor in the Army Air Corps.

Shirley, the iconic child star touted as all grown up and ready to marry, appeared to guide the way in post-war relationships with her fairytale romance. Great interest followed the couple's courtship and the proceedings that led up to their wedding. As the autumn of 1945 rolled around, the talk of Los Angeles was of the upcoming Temple-Agar wedding. Shirley was 17½, 16 months younger than Inez.

The couple's Episcopal nuptials, held on September 19, 1945, were conducted before five hundred guests at the Los Angeles Wilshire Methodist Church. The wedding reception was celebrated at the bride's home on Rockingham Road.

The newlyweds spent their first honeymoon night at the exclusive and luxurious five-star Hotel Bel-Air, located in Los Angeles on Stone Canyon Road. Nestled in twelve acres of landscaped gardens, the Hotel Bel-Air advertised itself as the most beautiful and romantic hotel in the world. Certainly, it was a peaceful getaway where the rich and famous went to hide. Would anyone expect less for America's sweetheart?

What a surprise for Inez to discover she had a distant connection to Shirley Temple and her honeymoon. The PBX operator manning the Hotel Bel-Air telephones the night of September 19th happened to be Inez's friend and roommate, Alice Fitzsimmons.

Alice was a headphone and phone jack away from the honeymooning couple as she fielded both well wishes and crank calls to the couple's suite. Calls for "Shirley Temple" lit up the hotel switchboard all night. Somehow information leaked to the public as to where the newlyweds were scheduled to spend their honeymoon.

One would like to think that same scrapbook of Shirley Temple magazine clippings remained in a trunk somewhere with Inez's other memorabilia. However, the book was not found. Only a doll replica of Shirley Temple as a child of the 1930s resided in Inez's bedroom. This cherished Christmas gift—from Inez's oldest daughter Lynda—was sweeter and cuter than any old scrapbook.

~

Holidays L.A. Style

Inez became acquainted with two sisters who worked in the Headquarters office portion of the Golden State Milk Company. Inez remembered the two sisters wore their naturally curly hair in a cute, short hairstyle. As the holidays of 1945 approached, Inez and Alice were pleased when they were invited to the sisters' apartment for Thanksgiving dinner.

The siblings enjoyed cooking and it really showed. They presented a feast of all the traditional dishes of turkey, stuffing, mashed potatoes, string beans, cranberries, and desserts. Everything tasted so good to Inez and Alice. Perhaps, this was their first home-cooked meal in a long time. Inez and Alice considered the creamed onion casserole the masterpiece of the meal. Neither girl had tasted anything like it before and they could not stop eating it until the bowl was suddenly empty.

On the Sunday after Thanksgiving, Inez and Alice went to the legendary Hollywood Santa Parade, later called the Hollywood Christmas Parade. In 1929, the business community joined together to transform the stretch of Hollywood Boulevard between Vine and La Brea into a twinkly winter wonderland called "Santa Claus Lane." Even the street signs were temporarily changed to read "Santa Claus Lane."

The event was so successful that it became an annual parade. The parade route expanded to over three miles along Hollywood Boulevard, then back along Sunset Boulevard. Santa Claus himself appeared at the end of every parade.

Each year the parade featured the participation of numerous Hollywood celebrities. The elaborate Yuletide displays with tinsel trumped any other in the country. Perhaps this was how Hollywood received the nickname of "Tinseltown."

The Hollywood Santa Parade had been suspended during the War, from 1942 to 1944. Thus, when Inez and Alice attended the parade in 1945, its triumphal return was greatly anticipated. Record-breaking crowds turned out for the event. The extravagant holiday decorations served as prime background for photo opportunities and publicity as actors and celebrities filed into the VIP grandstand.

The two girls were situated quite close to the viewing grandstand when they noticed the actor Edward G. Robinson approaching the seated area. Robinson, often cast as a movie tough guy, drew a final puff from his cigar and tossed the butt close to Inez's feet. By the time she thought to retrieve the cigar as a souvenir, many other people scuffled to get it themselves. Inez missed out in obtaining a Hollywood treasure— or perhaps not.

During the next year's parade in 1946. The cowboy/singer/actor Gene Autry was riding his horse along the parade route and heard the children yelling excitedly about the coming of Santa Claus. Autry was so inspired by their enthusiasm that he, along with Oakley Haldeman, wrote the song "Here Comes Santa Claus." (You know: "Here Comes Santa Claus... right down Santa Claus Lane.")

Gene Autry became a perennial Grand Marshal of the Hollywood Christmas Parade, in part because he wrote the "Here Comes Santa Claus" song. However, Inez and her family will always remember his contributions to Christmas with other holiday songs he recorded, such as his biggest hit, "Rudolph the Red-Nosed Reindeer," in 1949 and "Frosty the Snowman," in 1950. These three Christmas songs bring out the child in every listener.

The Train to Fresno, 1945

"Mom, tell me about your move to Fresno."

My mother, Inez, replied. "Alice mentioned she didn't know the details of when I left Los Angeles. . . . I don't think I ever told her the whole story. I was so embarrassed—I just wanted to forget it."

"You were embarrassed?" I struggled with what might have caused such shame for my mother.

She said, "I was just so dumb . . . well more ignorant than dumb, I guess."

I can't believe I actually made it. Inez's heart rate slowed to normal as she found herself once again watching scenery go by from the passenger train. The weeks prior to this trip had been a blur as she closed the Los Angeles chapter of her life. She was on her way to the city of Fresno in the San Joaquin Valley of California. Her stomach fluttered in anticipation of the new beginnings set before her. *For good or bad, I'm on my way to Fresno!*

In early autumn, Inez received word from her parents that their Oregon farm had sold at last. Leona and Charlie waited over ten years to be free of farm life. Their first use of this new freedom involved a visit to Charlie's relatives in Sacramento. While traveling through the area, they searched for a new home in Roseville, north of Sacramento. But the area did not suit them, so they continued south through the San Joaquin Valley. The Fresno area felt more to their liking and they purchased a small bungalow on Nevada Street, near downtown.

The Duttons moved into their new residence by the end of October. It had been a year since Inez left Oregon and just knowing her parents were nearby made her homesick. With the upcoming holidays, Inez reasoned she could join them in Fresno.

As much as she liked her job at the Golden State Milk Company, Inez resigned her position. She packed most of her possessions into the Multnomah steamer trunk she brought to Los Angeles. Inez arranged for the trunk to be shipped and purchased a train ticket to Fresno for the morning of Sunday, December 23, 1945.

The day before the scheduled trip, Inez placed her remaining belongings into a suitcase and called to reserve an early morning taxi to take her to the train depot. With all that done, she went to the Golden State Milk Company's Christmas party. The celebration also served as a farewell party for Inez.

Saying goodbye was bittersweet. Inez worked with Ginny and Clarence for six months and became very fond of the two. She took away good memories of that night, with Ginny advising her to stay away from sugary alcoholic drinks: "They tend to catch up with a person." Clarence made the perfect Santa Claus as he dressed the part and handed out presents from his goody bag.

On the morning of the trip, Inez rose early to get ready. It was still dark outside as she finished her packing. Her two coats would not fit into her suitcase. *That's okay, I'll wear the light one and carry the heavier one.*

Inez waited for her expected taxi—and waited. She looked out the window. *Gosh, the rain is really coming down. I better call the taxi company to see what's the delay.*

The telephone rang and rang on the other end. When answered, the gruff voice of the dispatcher came on the line. "Yah?"

Inez cleared her throat and said, "Hello. I called yesterday and made a reservation to be picked up . . ."

"Lady, there ain't no reserved pickups from yesterday. What with it raining cats and dogs and Christmas in a couple of days, we got a lot of calls. It's first-call-first-served. You gotta wait your turn." CLICK.

Whether the call was dropped or if the dispatcher hung up on her, Inez did not know. But when she tried the phone number again, she only got a busy signal. With urgency Inez rushed back to her room and attempted to wake Alice, but to no avail. Her roommate had worked a night shift and would not stir.

Now panicking, Inez put on her lighter coat and gathered up her purse, suitcase and other coat as she hurried down the stairs. None of the members of the Saropian family were in sight. Without further delay and for the last time, Inez left the Los Angeles boarding house.

She headed towards Western Avenue to a familiar streetcar stop. This was several blocks away on one of the busy main streets of the area. The wind and rain fought against her as she held tight to her umbrella. *I thought it wasn't supposed to rain in Southern California. Well it's pouring rain this morning.*

Within minutes of leaving the house, she was drenched. The deep street gutters filled with swift-flowing water, making it difficult to see where the sidewalk ended. Inez realized she could not juggle an umbrella, purse, and suitcase while she continued to carry her extra coat. Therefore, she stopped under a building overhang to put the coat over the one she already wore.

Inez arrived at the boulevard dizzy from exertion. She searched in desperation for a streetcar, a bus, or a taxi—not one could be seen. Panic choked Inez. *Now what? Time is running out. I must not miss my train!*

Desperate times call for extreme actions. In the torrential rain with trucks and automobiles whizzing by, Inez adjusted her awkward load. She edged closer to the street curb and did the unthinkable, something she had been schooled against—she stuck out her thumb to hitchhike.

Motorists rushed by, ignoring Inez. Just when the situation looked hopeless, a middle-aged man in a rusted, beat-up car pulled off the road towards her. He reached to roll down the passenger car window and yelled over the traffic noise, "You don't often see a woman thumbing around here. Is something wrong?"

Inez sputtered the explanation through the water that streamed down her face, "I have a train to catch, but I can't get a taxi or a way to get to the train station in time."

The man hesitated, then smiled. "Little lady, today is your lucky day. I'll get you to the train station. Throw your things in the back and let's go."

Despite the limitations of being bundled in two winter coats, she quickly deposited the suitcase and other items into the back and jumped into the front. Inez dripped onto the seat as the windshield wipers swished away the relentless water streams from the window. The dry oasis of the car became less welcoming when she detected the strong smell of beer and sweat that wafted over from the driver. Furthermore, Inez did not recognize the roads or the watery scenery that passed by. *Oh, what have I done?*

Inez's fears were soon laid to rest. The driver maneuvered like an expert through the traffic to the train station. When Inez mentioned her trouble obtaining a taxi, the man frowned and said, "If you would have told the taxi dispatcher you held a train ticket, you would have received taxi priority."

He also explained, "I work at the train yard. I just finished my shift and was on my way home when I spotted you. . . . Don't worry, little lady. I know a shortcut and I'll get you to your train in a hurry."

True to his word, they soon pulled up right in front of the train depot. After everything was out of the car, Inez thanked the man and offered him the only money she had in her possession—a dollar bill.

He shook his head and smiled, "No, you better keep your money. And good luck to you." With that, he drove off.

Inez entered the station and searched for a woman's restroom to straighten herself up from the ravages of the rain. After drying herself with paper towels, she proceeded to comb her wet hair and re-apply her makeup. The process took longer than she realized.

As she exited the bathroom, she came across a redcap porter. He asked, "May I help you, Miss?"

When Inez showed him her train ticket, the redcap took a quick look at his pocket watch, deposited her suitcase and coats on a push-cart and spoke over his shoulder. "Follow me, you haven't got much time before your train leaves."

People, things, and locations blurred by as they raced through the station, weaving in and out of the crowds and around corners, cutting in front of seated travelers. Disoriented by the activity, Inez kept up with the redcap and his cart the best she could when she heard the tooting of the train. They entered a large cement tunnel and ran towards the train. The redcap directed Inez through the train door and took her directly to her assigned seat.

Once again, out came that lone one-dollar bill from Inez's coat pocket. She meekly offered it to the redcap. "I'm sorry but this is all I have."

The porter nodded and smiled, saying, "That will do just fine, thank you."

Inez settled in from her race to the train and calmed when she found herself seated next to a pleasant middle-aged woman. The two talked about the Glendale area before Inez went in search of the ladies' bathroom. She found the restroom, but she also found the day held more challenges for her.

After using the facilities, Inez powdered her nose and just started to comb her hair when she heard a female voice harshly say, "Give me your comb."

When she connected a face with the voice, Inez saw a disheveled, twenty-something coffee-colored women scowling at her. For the second time that day, liquor fumes drifted in the air.

The woman's friend whispered to Inez, "I'm sorry, she's had too much to drink."

The first woman reiterated, "I said, give me your comb." She crowded into Inez.

Inez did not even share her comb with her roommate, Alice. In a weak voice Inez said, "I don't like to loan out my comb."

The woman raised her voice as she slurred her words, "I'm just as good as you. . . . I'm better. My husband is in the Army, just like yours."

In a hushed voice the companion said, "I told you before, she's had too much to drink. You best leave and get back to your seat."

Still stunned, Inez managed to put one foot in front of the other to return to her seat. She told her seatmate what happened, then added, "You know, I've rarely spoken to people of color, yet three crossed my path today. The drunken woman intimidated me, but her friend tried to shield me. . . . and what would I have done without the helpful redcap? I should be grateful for the two good ones and not dwell on the bad one."

The older woman thought for a moment before saying, "Even though the war has brought about many changes, our country is still learning to deal with a war for racial equality. A lot of emotions and circumstances have to be addressed." She patted Inez's hand. "I'm just relieved you walked away from the confrontation without harm or more trouble." Inez nodded.

While her seatmate dozed, Inez stared out the train window. Yet, her attention was not on the landscape. It had been a stressful day, but it was also a day of growth. She accomplished much by using her wits and learned the travel lesson of flexibility. However, Inez still expected perfection of herself: perfection in punctuality and perfection in preparedness.

She contemplated the happenings of the day and continued to reprimand herself: *How could I have resorted to the unladylike behavior of hitchhiking?* After seven decades, Inez still sensed the recklessness and embarrassment of "thumbing for a ride"

The train slowed. Inez felt her ears pop from the change of barometric pressure. Murmuring increased from people around her. Some passengers stood, while others craned their necks to look out the windows.

"What is it?" asked Inez.

Her awakened seatmate answered, "That's the Tehachapi Loop. The railway descends in a spiraling route. That way it lessens the angle of the grade of going from a mountain range to the valley floor."

Fascinated by their snaking route through the mountain pass, Inez was caught off guard when the train entered the tunnel. However, she saw a sight to behold when they emerged from the darkness. The train passed over itself going around the loop, or as Inez described it: "I saw the tail-end of the train go by, and that wasn't something a person saw every day."

The scenery of barren, lofty peaks and ridges dotted with patches of chaparral and scrub trees changed to pastures and cultivated farmland. After many stops along the San Joaquin Valley, the train arrived at Inez's destination. As she departed from the train, Inez could not help but wonder, *What's in store for me, here in Fresno?*

~

The San Joaquin Abstract and Title Company

The Christmas holiday came and went. Culture shock set in with each passing day of the new year. Inez struggled to reconcile the differences of a city in the valley to Los Angeles. Fresno really did not feel like home to her. Perhaps it would at some time in the future. She did not know anyone except her parents, and they were away at work much of the time. Her mother worked as a waitress in a diner and Charlie worked at a lumber and construction outlet.

Inez had trouble adjusting to the grayness of the San Joaquin Valley. Her sunny Southern California days had been replaced by the hazy skyline of Fresno fog. Even Klamath Falls was known for sunshine most days of the year. Since coming to Fresno, Inez had developed a terrible nasal congestion such as she never experienced before. Whether due to allergies or a sinus infection, she never knew.

With too much time and nothing to do, Inez became bored. She started to think about the Army Sergeant, Tony Tonick. They wrote to each other for almost three years through the war, from her junior year in high school and while she lived in the L.A. area. Tony promised to contact her when he returned to the States. However, Inez had not heard from him since before she left Los Angeles. She wondered if something was wrong.

During a moment of weakness, Inez allowed her mother to read Tony's last letters. Leona gathered up a pencil and paper and handed it to Inez. "I don't believe Tony wants a relationship with you. You need to break up with him first. Now write what I tell you."

Inez, the dutiful daughter, copied the words of the scathing letter and sent it on to Tony. She knew this was the wrong way to deal with the problem. When Valentine's Day came to her attention, she decided to send a simple, non-gushy Valentine card to Tony. On the card Inez wrote: "To a fellow who means a lot to me" and mailed it to Tony's last known overseas APO address.

As if things were not bad enough, employment in Fresno eluded Inez. Her parents could not offer any help. When she could not find a job listed in the want ads in the newspaper, Inez felt compelled to go through an employment agency. Her unemployment frustration became so apparent Leona suggested that perhaps Inez could return to L.A. and get back her old job with Golden State Milk Company.

Just when things seemed the bleakest, Inez received a job offer through the agency. With her previous experience, she qualified as a Bookkeeper Assistant. The business was the San Joaquin Abstract and Title Company located in downtown Fresno on Van Ness Avenue, several miles from her house. Inez could walk from her home on Nevada Street to the bus stop near the Roosevelt High School, on Tulare Street, and take the bus to the title company.

Leona, confused about her daughter's new job asked, "What does a title company do?"

"Well, a title company basically handles any legal documents that affect a property. They make sure the title of the real estate or land is legitimate. Then title insurance is issued for that property. If there is a dispute over the title, the insurance protects the lender and the owner against lawsuits."

"And you work in the bookkeeping department?"

"Yes," said Inez. "The Title Company consists of two departments. The front area houses the rooms where the title officers conduct their business with the clients. My area, the business portion, is in the back."

Inez worked with the company's seasoned bookkeeper, Plesey. An all-business, Armenian lady in her 50s, Plesey did her bookkeeping in an old-fashioned way. However, Plesey was nice to Inez and patiently taught her that style of posting.

Once Inez asked, "What do I do if I make a mistake?"

Plesey answered, "Don't make a mistake. . . . Avoid mistakes so you don't have to go back and redo." Inez heard the message loud and clear. It was good advice.

Since most of the Title Company employees were middle aged, it pleased Inez to meet another young woman near her own age. Claudine, one of the company's five title officers, investigated any irregularities that affected the use or transfer of the properties.

Her fair complexion, along with her blond hair, blue eyes, and sturdy frame, suggested a German heritage. Claudine was outgoing with a hearty laugh. Inez liked her right away. The two young women formed a quick friendship. Unfortunately, Claudine spent the bulk of her time at the courthouse in search of documents and information.

When the girls were able to chat, Inez learned Claudine grew up on a ranch with a vineyard, west of Fresno. She lived in an apartment in town with her sister and a cousin. Claudine had three brothers but spoke with particular pride of her brother who had recently returned from the war in Europe. She kept abreast of the nightspots in town and knew a lot of people. Laughing Claudine said, "Heck, I'm related to half the population of Fresno."

The subject of dancing came up. Since her recent breakup with a boyfriend, Claudine seemed ready to get back into circulation. She suggested the two girls attend the upcoming Valentine's Day Dance held at the Rainbow Ballroom.

Inez agreed and thought, *Dancing is what I've been missing.*

~

Sorry Sister

Inez and Claudine were to attend a mandatory business meeting at the Hotel Californian on evening of the Valentine dance. Inez squeezed in some last-minute errands before the meeting.

When she returned home, the mail on the entry table caught her attention. A letter addressed to "Inez David," showed a San Francisco return address. The already-opened envelope revealed the violation to her privacy: *What's this? Oh Mother! How could you?*

From the one envelope, Inez pulled out another smaller envelope. She discovered the Valentine she had sent to Tony, just the week before.

Inez opened the Valentine intended for Tony. Where she had written, "To a fellow who means a lot to me," her words were crossed out. Written on the edge of the card was another message: "Sorry Sister. Tonick is back and I have him. You should be ashamed, (signed) His wife."

Many people may have received a "Dear John" letter but not many received a "Sorry Sister" one. Leona came up and put her arm around her daughter's shoulder. The mother did not have much to say, except for, "I had a feeling . . ."

Inez did not know whether she felt like laughing or crying. But she thought, *Goodness, that was unexpected. There's no doubt about it now—it's over!*

She did not have time to dwell on what had taken place. Inez would have to rush to catch the bus for her meeting. *I guess I'll have to be like Scarlett O'Hara and think about this tomorrow.*

Night of the Valentine Dance

Inez blocked out thoughts of Tony that night. She concentrated her attention on the grandeur of the Hotel Californian with its Italian Renaissance architecture. At the time, the Californian held the distinction of being the only three-star hotel between San Francisco and Los Angeles. As one of the tallest buildings, the hotel offered a magnificent view of downtown Fresno. However, with the promised evening of dancing ahead, the dinner and quarterly business meeting of the night were easily forgotten.

When the meeting ended, Inez and Claudine found it had turned dark outside. With no time to lose, the high-heeled duo began their trek from the Hotel Californian at Van Ness Avenue and Kern Street towards the Rainbow Ballroom at 1724 Broadway Street. Claudine frequently walked such distances, but not Inez. However, the conversation and camaraderie proved enjoyable as they shared thoughts on fashion, current events, and dancing.

Wanting to know more about where they were going, Inez said, "I'm anxious to see the Rainbow Ballroom. I've heard it started out as an indoor pool."

"That's right," answered Claudine, "It was called the Natatorium. I guess Fresno needed a dance hall, so the building was remodeled. They drained the pool and covered it with a large dance floor and added a bandstand."

"Do you go there often?" Inez's breathing increased with the exertion.

"Oh yes," smiled Claudine. "It's quite the hot spot in town. I've danced there since the beginning of the war." She brushed away a lock of hair from her face, "You know, Fresno is a military town, with the Rainbow as the favorite hangout for servicemen from Hammer Field and Camp Pinedale. Alcohol is restricted, but there is a lot of popular dance music and good clean fun."

Inez said, "It seems that Fresno attracts a lot of top bands."

"We are lucky that we get all the big bands and orchestras—Glenn Miller, Harry James, Woody Herman, Tommy Dorsey. They stop in Fresno while traveling between L.A. and San Francisco. . . . And here we are."

Before Inez realized it, the girls had walked over three-fourths of a mile to the Rainbow Ballroom. Claudine opened the door, and the two young women joined the merriment.

Six months after V-J Day, the Rainbow Ballroom remained as popular as it had during the war. By the time Inez and Claudine arrived for the Valentine Dance on that 1946 February night, the dance floor bustled with lively music. The two wedged themselves into the spirited crowd. Soon a soldier whisked Claudine to the dance floor.

Looking around, Inez noticed the dance area was surrounded by arches inlaid with Spanish-styled tiles. The size of the polished maple dance floor was impressive. Even though it was not the Palladium, she estimated the dance area could accommodate a thousand couples. Consequently, Inez had plenty of subjects to people-watch.

After the dance music faded, a man with a pleasant smile approached Claudine as she returned from the dance floor. Claudine made the introductions, "Inez, I'd like you to meet Ted. This guy is not only my older brother, but he happens to be my favorite dance partner."

With a hardy laugh like Claudine's, yet in a bashful manner, Ted shook Inez's hand and said, "I'm glad to meet you." Inez could tell Ted liked what he saw.

The brother and sister stepped onto the dance floor and melted into the crowd. When the music ended, Ted brought Claudine back to where Inez stood. He asked Inez for the next dance—the last dance of the evening.

That night Inez met someone new and significant in her life. Ted was blond and fair with blue eyes and had a great set of shoulders. He was also a smooth dancer. Ted wore a brown, double-breasted jacket and even though he was not heavy or tall, when Inez glanced at their reflection in the mirrors alongside the dance floor, it confirmed her feeling of dancing with a bear—a gentle Teddy bear, as it turned out.

This was Inez's first dance at the Rainbow; it was also her only dance there. How fitting that Inez met Ted at a dance at the Rainbow Ballroom. An unofficial word-of-mouth survey indicated the majority of the 1940s' married couples of the Fresno area "met at the Rainbow" and romances flourished.

No pot of gold hid at the end of the Rainbow—Ballroom, that is. However, Inez found her treasure—a husband who shared in a stable household for over fifty years. She bloomed to motherhood with three children in six years. But possibly the best bonus came to Inez when she acquired the extended close-knit family and the home of which she always dreamed—a place to belong.

The End of the Beginning — I love you Mom.

Early June Rites Read In South

In a double ring ceremony read on Saturday, June 1 in the Lutheran Congregational church of Biola, Calif., Inez David, daughter of Mrs. Charles Dutton of Fresno, formerly of Klamath Falls, became the bride of Theodore Scheidt of Kerman, Calif.

The Rev. Jonathan Weber read the service.

The bride wore a suit of powder blue for her wedding with pink and black accessories. A white orchid was pinned at her shoulder.

Maid of honor was Claudine Scheidt, sister of the groom. Best man was Gordon Lung. Following the ceremony a reception was held at the home of the groom's parents, Mr. and Mrs. August Scheidt.

Soon after, the couple left on a wedding trip to the bay area and from there motored up the coast route into Oregon stopping in Klamath Falls and in Henley to visit the bride's brother and sister-in-law, Mr. and Mrs. Henry L. David.

Mrs. Scheidt is a graduate of Klamath Union high school with the class of 1944. Last fall she moved from this city to Fresno.

Mr. Scheidt is a native of Fresno and was recently discharged from the army air corps after serving three years.

They will make their home in San Jose until fall when they plan to move to Biola.

WED IN BIOLA, Calif., on Saturday, June 1, were Inez David Dutton, formerly of this city, and Theodore Scheidt of Kerman, Calif. Following a wedding trip on the California and Oregon coasts they are at home in San Jose until fall when they will move to Biola.

~

Directory of Names and Places

Aimee Rose (née Doyon) Jaynes: One of Inez's maternal Doyon aunts. Researched the Doyon trek to Montana. Wrote a small booklet titled *The Doyons*. Was a Navy RN in WWII.

Antoinette (née David) Favre-Veraud: The oldest David sister, who remained in France. Married to Alfred Favre–Veraud.

Alice Fitzsimmons: Inez's high school friend, and her roommate in Southern California.

Alice Louise David Sala (1883 –1953): Older sister of Henri David; married Anton (Tony) Sala.

Bob Dewey: Marine from the Rehabilitation Center / Marine Barracks, 1944. Dated Inez and gave her his signet ring.

Charlie McKinley Dutton (1897–1981): Married Leona in 1931. Stepfather to Inez and Henry. Father of Wana and Orin.

Cora Gray: Charlie's first wife. Mother of Wana and Orin.

Cora May (née Dutton) Farley: Mother to Charlie and Dewey Dutton. Also went by Franklin and Frost.

Chris Kettlehut: Charlie and Dewey Dutton's father. Chris remarried and had 10 more children.

Claudine Scheidt (1924–2008): Inez's friend from the title company; youngest sister of Ted Scheidt.

David Scheidt (Theodore David): Clinical laboratory scientist. Ted and Inez's youngest child and only son.

Délima Rose (née Provost) Turcotte (1864–1913): Married to Evangeliste. Mother of Rose Aimee, grand-mère of Leona, and great-grand-mère of Inez.

Edouard (Edward) Louis David (1888 –1951): The brother of Henri David. Married Jean Halbordier in 1916. No children.

Evangeliste Turcotte (1861–1948): The father of Rose Aimee, grandfather of Leona, and great-grandfather of Inez.

Fred Schwartz: Second husband of Rose Doyon. Fred owned property in Montana as well as in Hereford and Amarillo, Texas.

Herb: A Marine from the Rehabilitation Center / Marine Barracks, 1944.

Henri Auguste David (1891–1930): Married Leona Doyon on August 7, 1920. Their children were Henry Louis David and Inez Rose David.

Henry Louis David (1921–1978): Inez's older brother. Married to Patricia Thomas. One child, Lauraleigh.

Île d'Orléans: An island in the middle of the St. Lawrence River near Quebec City in Canada.

Inez (Inès) Rose David (Dutton): Born August 11, 1926. Daughter of Henri and Leona David; Married June 1,1946 to Theodore (Ted) Scheidt. Children: Lynda Gail (1947), Teresa Ann (1950) and T. David (1952)

Jack Calvin: Purchased the David farm in 1936 but defaulted and walked away in 1939.

Jean Doyon: The Doyon patriarch. He arrived in New France in 1644 as indentured laborer, then became expert pit sawyer and a pillar of the New France community. Inez's 10x grandfather.

Josephine (née Fayard) David (1860–1924): Mother of Henri and grandmother of Inez.

Lea David Griat (1899–1990): Henri David's sister; married Edouard Felix Griat.

Leon Sylvain David (1894–1966): Henri David's brother; married Ella A. (Ruella) Renault in 1917. Children: Beatrice, Leo, Arthur, and Kenneth.

Leona (née Doyon) David Dutton (1903–1997): Mother of Inez and Henry. Eldest daughter of Louis and Rose Doyon.

Lessmister sister: The younger Lessmister sister became Fresno real estate agent Helen Smades. Helen helped Inez sell the Scheidt farm in 2000.

Louis Auguste David (1859–1930): Father of Henri; grandfather of Inez and Henry.

Louis Cerinus Doyon (1877–1930): Father of Leona; grandfather of Inez and Henry.

Lynda (née Scheidt) Gray Buresh: Retired emergency medicine physician. Ted and Inez's oldest daughter.

Marcel David (1897–1930): Henri's youngest brother and the best man in Henri's wedding; died of TB in Arizona. He never married and had no children.

Marthe Blanche David (1902–1972): Henri David's youngest sister. Inez met Marthe and her youngest son, Warren Pingery, at Tujunga Hills, CA in 1944

Mrs. Conrady: Landlady of rooming house, 1944.

Mrs. Grafton: Director of the Klamath Falls Commando Center, 1944.

Otto Mansker: A Marine from the Rehabilitation Center / Marine Barracks, 1944.

Regis Barthelon (1861–1938): Listed as an uncle to the David siblings; his wife was named Rosalie, and son, Regis, Jr.

Rose Aimee (née Turcotte) Doyon Schwartz (1884–1982): Married Louis Doyon in 1902. Rose was Inez's grandmother and Leona's mother. Custom designed and hand-sewed Barbie clothes for a local Montana toy store in 1960s.

Sainte-Anne-de-Beaupré Shrine: The oldest francophone Catholic shrine in North America. Outside of Quebec City, it is where prayers were offered when Rose Turcotte Doyon was sick with smallpox.

Sainte-Rose-de-Watford: County Dorchester, Province of Québec, Canada. Home of Evangeliste and Délima Turcotte, the parents of Rose Aimee and grandparents of Leona.

Saint John, New Brunswick: Leona's home in 1912 at time of the sinking of the SS *Titanic.*

Sedonia (Sid) Doyon: AKA Sister Providence of the Sisters of Charity order. Aunt of Inez and younger sister of Leona. Sid was a registered nurse, a nursing educator, and director of Gonzaga University's Health Center.

"Swede" Howard King: 24-year-old hired hand who helped at the farm after Henri died in 1930.

Teresa Scheidt MacAlpine: Retired Neonatal ICU, BSN. Ted and Inez's second daughter. Author of *The I in Inez.* Spouse of Steven MacAlpine and mother of Christine and Paul MacAlpine

Varacieux: A small village located in the southeast of France, in the department of Isère of the French region Rhône-Alpes. The town of Varacieux is in the township of Vinay part of the district of Grenoble. The birthplace of Henri Auguste David.

Wolf Point: The county seat of Roosevelt County, Montana, and the largest city in the county. Location of the Wild Horse Stampede rodeo where Henri and Leona fell in love.

Glossary

auto-camp: A place that accommodated automobile travelers. Forerunner to motels or trailer parks.

blacksnake whip: Known also as shot whip because a lead pellet was embedded into the end of the lash.

barrage balloon: A large, unmanned tethered kite balloon used to defend ground targets against aircraft attack. Used in the Seattle-Bremerton area

buffalo plaid: A plaid with large squares of two different colors, frequently red and black.

Castilian Spaniard: A person from the province of Castile in central Spain.

Chinese pagoda: A tiered Asian temple, often housing a Buddhist temple

coulee: A deep ravine or gulch, usually dry, originally formed by running water.

dryland farming: A technique for growing grain crops without irrigation in a region with minimal moisture. Also known as dry farming.

douche bag: Rubber device used to introduce a stream of water into the body for medical or hygienic reasons, usually for vaginal irrigation.

elephantiasis: A condition in which a limb or other part of the body becomes grossly enlarged due to obstruction of the lymphatic vessels, typically by the nematode parasites which cause filariasis.

eminent domain: The power of a government to take private property for public use without the owner's consent, provided just compensation is given.

Fixed-base Operator: an organization granted the right by an airport to operate at the airport and provide aeronautical services such as fueling, aircraft rental, aircraft maintenance, flight instruction, etc.

je t'aime, au revoir **(French):** I love you, good-bye.

joie de vivre **(French):** A cheerful enjoyment of life; an exultation of spirit, literally "joy of life."

junior clerk-typist: A position involving a variety of clerical tasks, including answering telephones, typing documents, and filing records.

Mantoux skin test: Also known as a PPD test, a skin test used as tool in screening for tuberculosis (TB).

marten: any of several weasel-like carnivores of the genus *Martes* (family *Mustelidae*), valued for its fur.

Multnomah trunk: A steamer trunk made by the Multnomah Baggageman Company of Portland, Oregon.

pessary: a vaginal suppository used to kill sperm and/or block their passage through the cervix.

pit sawyer: Someone who sawed planks of wood from a tree log by using a pitsaw which is a large double handsaw operated by two men, one standing on top of the log and the other in a pit underneath it.

redcap (porter): A porter who helps passengers with their baggage at a railroad station.

red point tokens: The red, dime-sized compressed wood-fiber tokens used in the WWII rationing system for meats and dairy items. Still in use after the war.

Selective Service Act: The act authorized by Congress on May 18, 1917, establishing the draft for all US men 21–30 years old.

Seabee: A member of the United States Naval Mobile Construction Battalion (CB). The word "Seabee" comes from initials "CB." The Seabees have a history of building bases, roadways, airstrips, and other construction projects.

***seigneuries* (French):** Established along the St. Lawrence Riverbanks, these thin, long pieces of land extended inland arranged in long, narrow strips.

souped-up: Describes a car that has been tuned or modified to produce additional horsepower.

steerage passage: The cheapest accommodation on a passenger ship, originally the compartments containing the steering apparatus.

threat display: Anything that an animal does to scare away other animals.

***vous avez sauvé sa vie* (French):** You have saved her life.

war bonds: Debt securities issued by the government to finance military operations in time of war.

WPA: The Works Progress Administration (1935–1939) later renamed the Work Projects Administration, was an American New Deal agency that carried out public works projects, including the construction of public buildings and roads.

1918 Influenza Pandemic (January 1918–December 1920) Known as the Spanish flu, this was an unusually deadly influenza pandemic caused by the H1N1 influenza virus.

~

Acknowledgments

This book would not be possible without the help and encouragement of Janice Stevens and fellow writers from her Memoirs classes and later her classes of Writing for Publication (*Central Valley Writers and Artists*). A special thanks to Pauline Smoke for her long distant attention to this project. With every constructive suggestion, each week my stories read "better and better." A heartfelt appreciation to all.

A loving thank you goes to Steve, my favorite computer and printer guy—and husband. He rescued me from my darkest technical terrors and kept me supplied with computer paper and ink. And he cooks! But most of all, he believed in me and my story of Inez and her family.

Made in the USA
Columbia, SC
08 June 2022